Fidelity Rebates in Competition Law

International Competition Law Series

VOLUME 76

Editor

In its series editor, Alastair Sutton, Kluwer is fortunate to engage and benefit from the experience and expertise of one of the world's outstanding authorities on European Union and international economic law.

Introduction

In their efforts to regulate competition in an increasingly complex business environment, competition authorities face a daunting task. The European Commission and Courts, as well as national courts and legislatures, policymakers, and regulators, are constantly proposing, enacting, reviewing, and enforcing new legal measures, often addressing novel situations. Every industry and service is affected.

Contents/Subjects

With many titles currently available and new ones appearing regularly, the series' coverage includes detailed analyses of relevant legislation and case law in major global trading jurisdictions, defences used in cases involving the digital network economy, state aid cases, enforcement methodologies and a great deal more.

Objective & Readership

The purpose of Kluwer's International Competition Law Series is to follow the ever-changing contours of this dynamic area of the law, keeping the practice in sharp focus so that practising lawyers (including in-house counsel) and academics can be assured of the most up-to-date guidance and sources, in the widest possible range of applications.

The titles published in this series are listed at the end of this volume.

Fidelity Rebates in Competition Law

Application of the 'As Efficient Competitor' Test

Miroslava Marinova

Wolters Kluwer

Published by:
Kluwer Law International B.V.
PO Box 316
2400 AH Alphen aan den Rijn
The Netherlands
E-mail: international-sales@wolterskluwer.com
Website: lrus.wolterskluwer.com

Sold and distributed in North, Central and South America by:
Wolters Kluwer Legal & Regulatory U.S.
7201 McKinney Circle
Frederick, MD 21704
United States of America
Email: customer.service@wolterskluwer.com

Sold and distributed in all other countries by:
Air Business Subscriptions
Rockwood House
Haywards Heath
West Sussex
RH16 3DH
United Kingdom
Email: international-customerservice@wolterskluwer.com

Printed on acid-free paper.

ISBN 978-94-035-0570-1

e-Book: ISBN 978-94-035-0571-8
web-PDF: ISBN 978-94-035-0572-5

Printed in the United Kingdom.

Table of Contents

Acknowledgements

This book was developed during my time as a doctoral student at the University of Reading, UK, supervised by Dr Pedro Caro de Sousa (OECD) and Professor Ioannis Kokkoris (Queen Mary, University of London). First and foremost, I want to thank my supervisors for their patience, support and for the critical and helpful comments.

The thesis was submitted on 22 March 2018 and defended on 4 May 2018. It was examined by Professor Stavroula Karapapa at the University of Reading, UK and Professor Philip Marsden at College of Europe, University in Bruges, Belgium. I would like to thank my examiners for their positive comments about my PhD project, which according to them makes a distinct contribution to the academic literature on competition law by offering an original perspective and also policy recommendations on how the abusive character of fidelity rebates should be assessed.

I am grateful to Professor Morten Hviid who accepted me as a visiting researcher at the Centre of Competition Policy at the University of East Anglia, Norwich, where I developed and enhanced my research. I am particularly grateful for the assistance given by Professor Kai-Uwe Kühn and his time to discuss my research.

I wish to thank various people I have met at different conferences that have helped me to develop my ideas during interesting and thoughtful discussions. Special thanks should be given to Robert O'Donoghue, Professor Peter Behrens, Professor Ariel Ezrachi, Professor Paul Nihoul, Professor Richard Whish and Professor Joshua Wright.

I would like to express my very great appreciation to my colleagues at the law firm SPASOV & BRATANOV in Bulgaria, where I was working as a legal and economic consultant during my PhD. I am particularly grateful for the encouragement and support given by Georgi Spasov and the assistance given by Kremena Yaneva-Ivanova, Associate at SPASOV & BRATANOV.

Last, but definitely not least, I would like to thank my family and friends. Special thanks to my brilliant friend, Paul Smith. His assistance, support and willingness to give his time so generously have been very much appreciated.

Miroslava Marinova
2 July 2018, London

CHAPTER 1

Introduction

§1.01 THE AIM OF THE BOOK

This book examines the treatment of fidelity rebates as one of the most controversial topics in EU competition law. The controversy arose from the lack of clarity as to how to distinguish between rebates that constitute a legitimate business practice and those that might have anticompetitive effects, as the same type of rebates could be pro-competitive or anticompetitive depending on their effects on competition. Regardless of their ambiguous effect, the EU Courts deemed fidelity rebates as an unlawful abuse of a dominant position. Many have questioned the strict approach adopted by the EU Court over the years. As a reaction, the European Commission undertook a modernisation of the EU competition law regime, pressing for the adoption of an 'effects-based' approach based on careful examination of a company's behaviour and an application of an 'As Efficient Competitor' (AEC) test in order to distinguish between anticompetitive conduct and legitimate competition. In recent years, the application of the AEC test in relation to the anticompetitive effects of fidelity rebates has been raised as a central issue in the *Intel* and the *Post Danmark II* judgments. Both judgments failed to clarify whether the test should be a part of the legal standard and highlighted the uncertain doctrine in this area, leading to a renewed debate on the appropriate legal standard to distinguish lawful from exclusionary fidelity rebates.

The aim of this book is to evaluate the principles underpinning the current case law and the economic theory on fidelity rebates in order to provide an interpretation of the law and to clarify the appropriate treatment of fidelity rebates. The critical discussion of the case law is centred on the idea as to whether the standard needs to reflect economic analysis and particularly, to understand whether the AEC test is an important part of the assessment of fidelity rebates and in which circumstances it could be used as one tool amongst others and to elucidate whether the treatment of fidelity rebates could be effects-based, without necessarily carrying out an AEC test. The recent

US case law regarding fidelity rebates is also studied in order to provide clarity on this question.

§1.02 BACKGROUND AND SIGNIFICANCE

Fidelity rebates are discounts granted, depending on conditions that have to be fulfilled, in order for a customer to obtain a lower price. The conditions may vary between the nature of the threshold that a customer must satisfy in order to obtain the rebates, for example it can be based on the amount of the purchased volume, or the increase of the amount of the purchased volume compared to a preceding period or the percentage of the total requirements of the purchaser. Rebates can be applicable only to those units that exceed the threshold once the particular threshold has been reached (incremental rebates) or to all of the purchased units when the threshold is reached, not only for the incremental purchases above the threshold (retroactive rebates). Rebates could apply depending on the number of products that are included, for example for one product (single-product rebates) or more than one (bundled rebate). Providing rebates is a common practice used to stimulate sales and intensify competition. Whereas providing the different types of rebates by non-dominant companies is accepted as a form of effective competition, the application of single-product retroactive rebates by dominant companies have been considered by the EU Courts[1] as an abuse of dominant position contrary to Article 102 TFEU[2] regardless of whether the questionable course of conduct generates actual or probable anticompetitive effects on the relevant market.[3]

This so-called form-based approach used in the case law, although in line with the principle of legal certainty with its simple and predictable rules, was broadly criticised by academics and practitioners for lack of accuracy because the same types of fidelity rebates could be either pro-competitive (creating efficiencies, stimulating sales, etc.) or anticompetitive (exclusion of competitors) depending on the circumstances and as such, their effect cannot be presumed prima facie without proper assessment.[4] It has also been argued that this strict approach is prone to over

1. Refers collectively to the Court of Justice (CJEU) and the General Court (GC) throughout this book.
2. Article 102 TFEU states: 'Any abuse by one or more undertakings of a dominant position within the common market or in a substantial part of it shall be prohibited as incompatible with the common market in so far as it may affect trade between Member States.'
3. Case C-62/86; Cases 40–48, 50, 54–56, 11, 113 and 114–173 *Coöperatieve Vereniging 'Suiker Unie' UA v. Commission*, joined [1975] ECR I-1663 (hereinafter *Suiker Unie*); Case 85/76 *Hoffmann-La Roche & Co AG v. Commission* [1979] ECR I-461 (hereinafter *Hoffmann-La Roche*); Case 322/81 *Michelin v. Commission* [1983] ECR I-3461 (hereinafter *Michelin I*); Case C-310/93 P *BPB Industries plc and British Gypsum Ltd v. Commission* [1995] ECR I-865 (hereinafter *British Gypsum*); Case C-497/99 P *Irish Sugar plc v. Commission* [2001] ECR I-5333 (hereinafter *Irish Sugar*); Case T-203/01 *Michelin v. Commission* [2003] ECR II-4071 (hereinafter *Michelin II*); Case T-219/99 *British Airways plc v. Commission* [2007] ECR I-2331 (hereinafter *British Airways*); Case C-549/10 P *Tomra Systems ASA v. Commission* [2012] ECR I-221 (hereinafter *Tomra*); Case T-286/09 *Intel v. Commission* [2014] ECR II-547 (hereinafter GC judgment).
4. John Temple Lang and Robert O'Donoghue, 'Defining Legitimate Competition: How to Clarify Pricing Abuses under Article 82 EC' (2002) 26 Fordham International Law Journal 83; Derek

enforcement because, some practices may be prohibited as abusive when they are pro-competitive – these are the so-called false positives or type I errors.[5] It is usually accepted that the cost of type I errors in competition law is greater than type II errors – when a practice is considered legal despite being anticompetitive – because it might lead to discouraging a dominant company's incentive to innovate and to provide better services – an outcome typically described as a 'chilling effect', which may harm consumer welfare.[6]

In contrast to a formed-based approach, an effects-based approach is based on an economic analysis that requires an assessment of the impact on business practices on competition. The effects-based approach has been implemented in Europe for the assessment of vertical restraint, horizontal agreements[7] and mergers by the revision of

---

Ridyard, 'Exclusionary Pricing and Price Discrimination Abuses under Article 82 – An Economic Analysis' (2002) 23(6) European Competition Law Review 286; John Kallaugher and Brian Sher, 'Rebates Revisited: Anti-Competitive Effects and Exclusionary Abuse under Article 82' (2004) 25(5) European Competition Law Review 263; Denis Waelbroeck, 'Michelin II: A Per Se Rule Against Rebates by Dominant Companies?' (2005) 1(1) Journal of Competition Law and Economics 149; John Vickers, 'Abuse of Market Power' (2005) 115 The European Journal 244; Simon Bishop, 'Delivering Benefits to Consumers or Per Se Illegal?: Assessing the Competitive Effects of Loyalty Rebates' (2005) The Pros and Cons of Price Discrimination, Konkurrensverket Swedish Competition Authority 65; Giulio Federico, 'When are Rebates Exclusionary?' (2005) 26(9) European Competition Law Review 477; David Spector, 'Loyalty Rebates: An Assessment of Competition Concerns and a Proposed Rule of Reason' (2005) (0514) CEPREMAP; Gianluka Faella, 'The Antitrust Assessment of Loyalty Discounts and Rebates' (2008) 4(2) Journal of Competition Law and Economics 375; Damian Geradin, 'A Proposed Test for Separating Pro-competitive Loyalty Rebates from Anti-competitive Ones' (2009) 32 World Competition 41; Giulio Federico, 'The Antitrust Treatment of Loyalty Discounts in Europe: Towards a More Proactive Economic Approach' (2011) 2(3) Journal of European Competition Law and Practice 277; Hans Zenger, 'Loyalty Rebates and the Competitive Process' (2012) 8(4) Journal of Competition Law and Economics 717.

5. The symmetrical situation occurs when a practice is considered legal despite being anticompetitive – this is known as a Type II error. Some scholars identified a type III errors, which occurs when giving the right answer asking the wrong question and type IV errors, which occurs when in a correct reasoning are provided wrong solutions – presentation delivered by Lars Henriksson (Bergen Competition Policy Conference, Bergen, Norway, April 2017).
6. Christian Ahlborn and Jorge Padilla, 'From Fairness to Welfare: Implications for the Assessment of Unilateral Conduct under EC Competition Law' in Claus-Dieter Ehlermann and Mel Marquis (eds) *European Competition Law Annual, A Reformed Approach to Art. 82 EC*, 2007 (Hard publishing 2008); *see also* John Temple Lang, 'The Requirements for a Commission Notice on the Concept of Abuse under Article 82 EC' CEPS Special Reports (2008) 32, who claims that: 'the economic costs if innovation is restricted by exclusionary conduct are likely to be much greater than the economic costs of monopoly pricing'); Frank Easterbrook, 'The Limits of Antitrust' (1984) 63 Texas Law Review 1, 3, who claims that 'judicial errors that tolerate baleful practices are self-correcting, while erroneous condemnations are not'.
7. Commission Regulation (EC) No. 2790/1999 of 22 December 1999 on the application of Art. 81(3) of the Treaty to categories of vertical agreements and concerted practices [1999] OJ L 336/21, since replaced by Commission Regulation (EU) No. 330/2010 of 20 April 2010 on the application of Art. 101(3) of the Treaty on the Functioning of the European Union to categories of vertical agreements and concerted practices [2010] OJ L 102/1 (hereinafter Block Exemption Regulation (BER); Guidelines on Vertical Restraints [2000] OJ C 292/1, since replaced by Guidelines on Vertical Restraints [2010] OJ C 130/01 (hereinafter Guidelines on Vertical Restraints); Commission Regulation (EC) No. 2659/2000 of 29 November 2000 on the application of Art. 81(3) of the Treaty to categories of research and development agreements [2000] OJ L 304/7; Commission Regulation (EC) No. 2658/2000 of 29 November 2000 on the application of Art. 81(3) of the Treaty to categories of specialisation agreements [2000] OJ L 304/ 3; Commission Notice – Guidelines on

Council Regulations and soft law instruments.[8] The key aspect of this reform was to guarantee effective competition policy by evaluating the impact of horizontal and vertical agreements and of mergers on competition and consumer welfare. In terms of consistency with the Commission's enforcement policy in the other areas of the EU competition regime – vertical restraint, horizontal agreements and mergers – and as a reaction to the criticism of the prevailing case law, the European Commission initiated a modernization of Article 102 TFEU.[9] The reform started in 2005 with the issuance of: 'The report by the Economic Advisory Group for Competition Policy',[10] 'DG Competition Discussion Paper on the application of Article 82 of the Treaty (now 102 TFEU) to exclusionary abuses'[11] and, at the end of 2008, the Commission published a Guidance Paper on the topic, named Guidance on the Commission's enforcement priorities in applying Article 82 of the EC Treaty [now Article 102 TFEU] to abusive exclusionary conduct by dominant undertakings.[12] The aim of the reform was to provide a general framework for the analysis of exclusionary conduct by adopting an effects-based approach.[13] In introducing the AEC test, as a foundation of the effects-based approach, the European Commission sought to distinguish between pro-competitive and anti-competitive practices, to depart from the presumptions of illegality 'per se' for certain types of behaviour and to create coherence with the reform of vertical restraint, horizontal agreements and mergers.

---

the applicability of Art. 81 to horizontal co-operation agreements [2001] OJ C 3/2, since replaced by Communication from the Commission – Guidelines on the applicability of Art. 101 of the Treaty on the Functioning of the European Union to horizontal co-operation agreements [2011] OJ C 11/1; Commission Regulation (EC) 772/2004 of 27 April 2004 on the application of Art. 81(3) of the Treaty to categories of technology transfer agreements [2004] OJ L 123/11; Commission Notice – Guidelines on the application of Art. 81 of the EC Treaty to technology transfer agreements [2004] OJ C 101/02.

8. Council Regulation (EC) No. 139/2004 of 20 January 2004 on the Control of Concentrations between Undertakings [2004] OJ L 24/1 (ECMR); Guidelines on the Assessment of Horizontal Mergers under the Council Regulation on the Control of Concentrations Between Undertakings [2004] OJ C 31/5; Guidelines on the Assessment of Non-horizontal Mergers under the Council Regulation on the Control of Concentrations between Undertakings [2008] OJ C 265/6; *see also* Wolter Wils, 'Community Report' in Dermot Cahill and John Cooke (eds) *The Modernization of EU Competition Law in the EU – FIDE 2004 National Reports* (CUP 2004) 661.
9. The beginning was in 2003 when the Commission announced that it would undertake a review of policy under Art. 102 TFEU. *See* e.g., Philippe Lowe's speech at the 30th Annual Conference on International Antitrust Law and Policy (23 October 2003) Fordham Corporate Law Institute and Nellie Kroes, 'Preliminary Thoughts on Policy Review of Article 82', Fordham Corporate Law Institute, New York, 23 September 2005 (speech/05/537).
10. Gual and others, 'An Economic Approach to Article 82' Report to the European Commission by the European Advisory Group on Competition Policy (2005) (hereinafter the EAGCP Report).
11. DG Competition, 'DG Competition Discussion Paper on the Application of Article 82 of the Treaty to Exclusionary Abuses' COM [2005] (hereinafter the Discussion Paper).
12. OJ C 45/7 (hereinafter the Guidance Paper).
13. There are three kinds of abuses: exploitative abuses (e.g., excessive pricing), exclusionary abuses and reprisal abuses, first mentioned in Bellamy and Child, *European Community Law of Competition* (2th edn, Sweet and Maxwell 1978); *see also* Robert O'Donoghue and Jorge Padilla, *The Law and Economics of Article 102 TFEU* (2th edn, Hart Publishing 2013) Ch. 5; John Temple Lang, 'Abuse of Dominant Position in European Community Law, Present and Future: Some Aspects' in Hawk (ed.) *Fifth Fordham Corporate Law Institute* (Law and Business 1979) 52.

A considerable amount of literature discussing the reform of Article 102 have been published since the introduction of the reform.[14] These studies supported the new effects-based approach as a long-awaited shift from the traditional form-based approach while at the same time criticising some of the Guidance's provisions and the AEC test in particular, as being difficult to implement in practice, leading to measurement errors, and creating more legal uncertainty.[15]

The treatment of fidelity rebates became even more controversial compared to their treatment before the reform, after the European Commission's decision in Intel,[16] the following judgment by the GC[17] and its review by the CJEU[18] and the *Post Danmark*

14. Damian Geradin and others, 'DG Comp's Discussion Paper on Article 82: Implications of the Proposed Framework and Antitrust Rules for Dynamically Competitive Industries' (2006) https://papers.ssrn.com/sol3/papers.cfm?abstract_id=894466 accessed 20 October 2016; Lang, CEPS Report (n. 6); John Temple Lang, 'How can Problems of Exclusionary Abuses under Article 102 TFEU be Resolved? (2012) 2 European Law Review 136; Andrea Renda and John Temple Lang, 'Treatment of Exclusionary Abuses Under Article 82 of the EC Treaty: Comments on the European Commission's Guidance Paper' (2009) Centre for European Policy Studies; Aude de Crayencour and John Temple Lang, 'Tomra: The Assessment of Retroactive Rebates by the Court of Justice after the Guidance Paper (2012) 4(1) Journal of European Competition Law and Practice 51; John Temple Lang and Robert O'Donoghue, 'The Concept of an Exclusionary Abuse under Article 82 EC' (2005) GCLC Research Papers on Article 82 EC; *see also* the Public contributions http://ec.europa.eu/competition/antitrust/art82/contributions.html accessed 14 December 2015.
15. Simon Bishop and Philip Marsden, 'The Article 82 Discussion Paper: A Missed Opportunity' (2006) 2(1) European Competition Journal 1; James Killick and Assimakis Komninos, 'Schizophrenia in the Commission's Article 82 Guidance Paper: Formalism Alongside Increased Recourse to Economic Analysis' Antitrust Chronicle (2009) 2 Global Competition Policy; Brian Sher and LLP Nabarro, 'Non-Contestability: Exclusive Dealing and Rebates under the Commission's Article 82 Guidance' (2009) 2(1) Antitrust Chronicle; Manuel Kellerbauer, 'The Commission's New Enforcement Priorities in Applying Article 82 EC to Dominant Companies' Exclusionary Conduct: A Shift Towards a More Economic Approach?' (2010) 31 European Competition Law Review 175, 184; David Spector, 'From Harm to Competitors to Harm to Competition: One More Effort Please' (2006) 2(1) European Competition Journal 145; For more critical comments *see also* Philip Marsden, 'Some Outstanding Issues from the European Commission's Guidance on Article 102: Not-so-Faint Echoes of Ordoliberalism' in Federico Etro and Ioannis Kokkoris (eds) *Competition Law and the Enforcement of Article 102* (OUP 2010) 53; Pinar Akman, 'The EC Discussion Paper on the Application of Article 82' (2006) Norwich Law School, Centre for Competition Policy; Ariel Ezrachi, 'The European Commission Guidance on Article 82 EC-The Way in Which Institutional Realities Limit the Potential for Reform' (2009) https://papers.ssrn.com/sol3/papers.cfm?abstract_id=1463854 accessed 1 February 2016; Martin Gravengaard and Niels Kjærsgaard, 'The EU Commission Guidance on Exclusionary Abuse of Dominance and its Consequences in Practice' (2010) 31(7) European Competition Law Review 285; Nicolas Petit, 'From Formalism to Effects?–The Commission's Communication on Enforcement Priorities in Applying Article 82 EC' (2009) 32 World Competition 485, 489; Philip Marsden and Liza Lovdahl Gormsen, 'Guidance on Abuse in Europe: The Continued Concern for Rivalry and a Competitive Structure' (2010) 55(4) The Antitrust Bulletin 875, 892; Viktor Vanberg, 'Consumer Welfare, Total Welfare and Economic Freedom: On the Normative Foundations of Competition Policy' in Josef Drexl and Others (eds) *Competition Policy and the Economic Approach* (Cheltenham Elgar 2011) 44; Victoria Mertikopoulou, 'DG Competition's Discussion Paper on the Application of Article 82 EC to Exclusionary Abuses: The Proposed Economic Reform from a Legal Point of View' (2007) 24(8) European Competition Law Review 241.
16. *Intel* (Case COMP/37.990) Commission Decision [2009] OJ C227/13 (hereinafter Commission Decision).
17. GC judgment.
18. Case C-413/14 P *Intel v. Commission* [2017] ECR I-632 (hereinafter CJEU judgment).

II judgment.[19] In both cases, the applicability of the effects-based approach and, in particular, the application of the AEC test in relation to the anticompetitive effects of fidelity rebates has been raised as a central issue.

In *Intel*, the Commission for the first time followed the Guidance's provisions and conducted an AEC test to assess the effect of fidelity rebates. On appeal, the GC upheld the Commission's decision but, instead of approving the Commission's approach and the implementation of the AEC test, it reasserted prior case law under Article 102 TFEU and rejected the implementation of the AEC test as unnecessary. It further clarified that economic analysis and the AEC test, in particular, were not required for an infringement of Article 102 to be found.

In its reasoning, the GC distinguished between three categories of rebates – quantity rebates, exclusivity rebates and 'other' rebates.[20] The GC made clear that the first category of rebates is generally considered lawful. For the second category, the GC stated that 'exclusivity rebates granted by an undertaking in a dominant position are by their very nature capable of foreclosing competitors',[21] and also that 'it is unnecessary to undertake an analysis of the actual effects of the rebates on competition',[22] which means that they are generally considered unlawful. For the third category, the GC considered the so-called all the circumstances test.[23,24] This means that only in the third category of rebates is a detailed analysis of their effects required. As regards an AEC test, the Court held that: 'even in the case of rebates falling within the third category, for which an examination of the circumstances of the case is necessary, it is not essential to carry out an AEC test'.[25]

Although the AEC test had been implemented and endorsed by the EU Courts as regards abuse of dominance cases concerning margin squeeze practices (*TeliaSonera*[26] and *Deutsche Telekom*[27]) and low price practices (*Post Danmark I),*[28] the GC made clear that, unlike with exclusivity rebates, in price-cost abuses there is an obligation for a price-cost test to be carried out because '*it is* impossible to assess whether a price is abusive without comparing it with other prices and costs'.[29]

Intel appealed the GC judgment. In its review by the CJEU, the case was sent back to the GC, requiring it to examine Intel's arguments in relation to the assessment of the anticompetitive effects of fidelity rebates and the applicability of the AEC test. While the GC's judgment in Intel has followed the settled case law of fidelity rebates and rejected the implementation of the AEC test as irrelevant, the CJEU clearly stated that

---

19. Case C-23/14, *Post Danmark A/S v. Konkurrencerådet* [2015] (hereinafter *Post Danmark II*).
20. GC judgment, paras 74–77.
21. *Ibid.*, para. 87.
22. *Ibid.*, para. 103.
23. *Ibid.*, para. 78.
24. The assessment of 'all the circumstances' was drawn from *Michelin I.*
25. GC judgment, para. 144.
26. Case C 52/09 *Konkurrensverket v. TeliaSonera Sverige AB* [2011] ECR I-527 (hereinafter *TeliaSonera*).
27. Case C 280/08 P *Deutsche Telekom v. Commission* [2010] ECR I-9555 (hereinafter *Deutsche Telekom*).
28. Case C-209/10 *Post Danmark A/S v. Konkurrencerådet* [2012] ECR I-172 (hereinafter *Post Danmark I*).
29. GC judgment, para. 152.

because the European Commission chose to conduct the AEC test, the GC must examine all the defendant's arguments 'seeking to call into question the validity of the Commission's findings concerning the foreclosure capability of the rebate concerned' including the correctness of the AEC test conducted by the European Commission. However, instead of clarifying whether the AEC test is a part of the legal assessment of fidelity rebates, the CJEU only clarified that if the defendant is able to provide evidence that its conduct is not capable of foreclosing competitors, it can rebut the presumption of illegality of its practice.

The second key ruling on fidelity rebates where the relevance of the AEC test has been raised is the *Post Danmark II* judgment. The CJEU was asked to clarify what framework had to be applied in order to establish whether a rebate scheme is liable to have an exclusionary effect on the market contrary to Article 102 TFEU, and to clarify the relevance of the AEC test in assessing a rebate scheme in this framework.[30]

Having in mind that the rebate schemes operated by Post Danmark in 2007 and 2008 were 'standardised',[31] 'conditional'[32] and 'retroactive',[33] the Court stated that the observed scheme was neither simple quantity rebate (because the rebates are not granted in respect of each individual order), nor exclusivity rebates (because there was no obligation for purchasers to obtain all or a given proportion of their supplies from Post Danmark). Thus, the Court classified the rebate schemes as falling in a category for which 'all the circumstances of the case should be examined, including the rules for granting the rebates, the extent of the dominant position, and the conditions of competition on the relevant market'.[34] Having evaluated 'all the circumstances', the Court concluded that the observed rebate scheme produced an anticompetitive exclusionary effect.

As regards the application of the AEC test, the CJEU stated that:

> [T]he application of the AEC test does not constitute a necessary condition for a finding of abuse. The AEC test, i.e. whether the conduct complained of could foreclose the market to a competitor at least as efficient as the dominant undertaking, is merely one tool amongst others to assess whether there is an abuse.[35]

The CJEU thus confirmed the GC's position in *Intel* that the AEC test is not necessary for rebates that fall into the third category, for which an examination of 'all the circumstances' of the case is necessary. The CJEU rejected the implementation of the AEC test as irrelevant in practice for this particular case because the market structure in Denmark was unlikely to accommodate the existence of an as efficient competitor.[36] In addition to this statement, the CJEU in *Post Danmark II* suggested that

30. The case was referred to the CJEU under Art. 267 TFEU from the Sø-og Handelsretten (Denmark) in proceedings between Post Danmark A/S and the Konkurrencerådet.
31. Rebates are standardised where the threshold is the same for all or a group of customers.
32. Conditional rebates are rebates granted to customers to reward them for a particular form of purchasing behaviour.
33. Retroactive rebates are granted to all purchase once the purchases over a defined reference period exceed a certain threshold.
34. *Post Danmark II*, para. 50.
35. *Ibid.*, para. 2.
36. *Ibid.*, para. 60.

the AEC test could be used as one tool amongst others, which means that the application of the test is not rejected in general.[37] At the same time, the CJEU left the question open as to in which circumstances the test could be usefully applied, or how it should be applied. If the AEC test is one of the factors in the assessment of abusive rebates, how can the added value of the test be weighed against the other relevant circumstances? Furthermore, does the cost of administering in practice such a test justify the cost of its implementation? This question is of great importance because the appropriate treatment of fidelity rebates needs not only to be accurate and to minimise enforcement errors but also easy to administer in terms of the limited resources of the National Competition Authorities and courts. On this point, the AG Kokott in her opinion argues that 'the added value of expensive economic analyses is not always apparent and can lead to the disproportionate use of the resources of the competition authorities and the courts'.[38] This statement puts into question whether the AEC test is appropriate given its cost of administering in practice and whether it justifies the resources for its implementation?[39]

The controversy surrounding the treatment of fidelity rebates ultimately arises from the different signals sent by the European Commission and the EU Courts. The Commission, on the one hand, is proclaiming the adoption of the effects-based approach in its Guidance Paper and policy statements and the application of the AEC test for the evaluation of the anticompetitive effect of fidelity rebates, which was tested in the *Intel* decision. On the other hand, the rejection of the test by the GC in *Intel* and the CJEU in *Post Danmark II* and the unclear position of the CJEU in *Intel* raise questions about whether the test should be part of the legal standard. From the above, it can be concluded that the recent case law of fidelity rebates fails to provide clarity as to the appropriate legal standard for the assessment of fidelity rebates, and that this controversy is largely related to the application of the AEC test.

A similar controversy can be found in the academic literature. The proponents of the effects-based approach argue that the application of Article 102 can be in line with this approach only if the AEC test is a part of the legal standard.[40] The opposite view holds that the Courts' rejection of the AEC test is justified because 'exclusivity rebates are not price-based abuse[41] and the problem is the exclusivity, not the price'.[42]

Similar conclusions were reached by a prominent US antitrust analyst who claims that there are two antitrust legal paradigms for exclusionary conduct – predatory pricing (where the price-cost test is appropriate) and raising rivals cost (where

37. *Ibid.*
38. Case C-23/14 *Post Danmark A/S v. Konkurrencerådet*, Opinion of AG Kokott, para. 66 (hereinafter Opinion of AG Kokott).
39. In Intel decision, the Commission applies the AEC test on 150 pages!
40. James Venit, 'Case T-286/09 Intel v Commission – The Judgment of the General Court: All Steps Backward and No Steps Forward' (2014) 10(2) European Competition Journal 203.
41. Exclusionary abuses may be both price based (predatory pricing, fidelity rebates, margin squeeze) and non-price based (contractual tying, single branding contracts and 'naked' refusals to supply). High rebates given on condition of single branding may have the same effect as contractual exclusive dealing. *See* the Discussion Paper, paras 61–62.
42. Richard Whish, 'Intel v Commission: Keep Calm and Carry on!' (2014) 6(1) Journal of European Competition Law and Practice 1.

foreclosure should be analysed under exclusive dealing law) – and concludes that a price-cost test is not relevant for evaluating fidelity rebates.[43] The recent US cases regarding fidelity rebates *ZF Meritor*[44] and *Eisai*[45] reflect the academic debate. In both cases, the Third Circuit declined to adopt the price-cost test holding that rebates were more similar to exclusive dealing while clarifying that the test might be applied as an element of the rule of reason only when the price is the predominant mechanism of exclusion. Under this position, the AEC test is irrelevant for evaluating fidelity rebates and they have to be treated under the rule of reason approach in a similar way to that applied under Article 101 TFEU.[46] Thus, the inapplicability of the AEC test does not mean that fidelity rebates should be treated as illegal 'per se'.

Ultimately, the practical and academic controversy is about whether the AEC test is accurate in terms of its relevance to distinguish pro-competitive from anticompetitive rebates, which indicates that that the appropriate treatment of fidelity rebates is unclear. This lack of clarity undermines legitimate expectations and thus, creates legal uncertainty.[47] This uncertainty revealed the need for clear administrable rules that enable both the enforcement agencies and the companies to reach sensible solutions. The lack of clear rules is problematic because, it creates legal uncertainty, making the dominant firms unable to engage in self-assessment and unable to evaluate in advance whether a rebate scheme is likely to be found abusive.[48] As a consequence, the dominant companies might not engage in pro-competitive and efficiency oriented activities for the benefit of consumers, 'for fear of becoming embroiled in costly, lengthy litigation'.[49]

---

43. Steven Salop, 'Exclusionary Conduct, Effect on Consumers and the Flawed Profit-Sacrifice Standard' (2006) 73 Antitrust Law Journal 311; Joshua D. Wright, *Simple but Wrong or Complex but More Accurate? The case for an Exclusive Dealing Based Approach to Evaluating Loyalty Discounts* (2013) US FTC, Speech delivered at the Bates White 10th Annual Antitrust Conference, Washington DC, 3 June 2013; Patrick DeGraba and John Simpson, 'Loyalty Discounts and Theories of Harm in the Intel Investigations' (2013) 2(1) Journal of Antitrust Enforcement 170.
44. *ZF Meritor LLC v. Eaton Corp*, 696 F3d 254 (3d Cir. 2012) (hereinafter *Meritor*).
45. *Eisai Inc v. Sanofi Aventis U.S., LLC*, 821 F.3d 394 (3d Cir. 2016) (hereinafter *Eisai*).
46. The rule of reason approach denotes balancing the pro-competitive and anticompetitive effect of the alleged anticompetitive conduct. Article 101(3) TFEU grants an efficiency exemption from the prohibition only if there is no substantial elimination of competition. Thus, an agreement must satisfy four cumulative conditions: It must contribute to improving the production or distribution of goods or contribute to promoting technical or economic progress, Consumers must receive a fair share of the resulting benefits, The restrictions must be indispensable to the attainment of these objectives, and The agreement must not afford the parties the possibility of eliminating competition in respect of a substantial part of the products in question.
47. Legal certainty is 'one of the most important general principles recognised by the European Court', *See* Trevor Hartley, *The Foundations of European Community Law: An Introduction to the Constitutional and Administrative Law of the European Community* (OUP USA 2010) 142.
48. *See* panel discussion in pricing abuses (other than excessive pricing) in Claus-Dieter Ehlermann and Isabela Atanasiu (eds), *European Competition Law Annual 2003: What is an Abuse of a Dominant Position?* (Bloomsbury Publishing 2006) where it is stated that 'it is contrary to the rule of law to argue that in this area the enforcement approach can only be determined on a case-by-case basis, and that we always have to determine retroactively whether what the dominant company did was legal or not', 184; On self-assessment, *see* Wolter Wils, *Principles of European Antitrust Enforcement* (Bloomsbury Publishing 2005).
49. Hewitt Pate, 'Exclusionary Conduct: Refusals to Deal and Bundling and Loyalty Discounts' Testimony before the Antitrust Modernization Commission (September 29, 2005) 1, 20.

Given the importance of the issue and the lack of a clear and coherent standard to evaluate the legality of fidelity rebates, which creates legal uncertainty, this book will contribute significantly to improving the understanding of the legal treatment of fidelity rebates and its practical implication by all stakeholders (enforcement agencies, courts, private entities and their advisors). Moreover, the legal treatment of fidelity rebates has been the centre of intense academic debate in legal and economic scholarship for decades. Therefore, the conclusions of this book will contribute not only to clarify the legal standard for the evaluation of the legality of fidelity rebates and its practical implications but also it will have a significant theoretical contribution.

The book offers original insights on the way in which abusive rebates should be identified. It offers an appropriate legal test for the assessment of the legality of fidelity rebates, which is administrable, creates predictability and legal certainty in accordance with the principles of EU law,[50] and at the same time minimises the risk of errors and the cost of those mistakes.

§1.03 METHODOLOGY

This section outlines the research methodology of the book. The appropriate research design is of great importance for its successful completion. Achieving the aim of this research requires an application of a combination of research methods.

[A] Legal Approach

This book evaluates and discusses case law; thus most of the chapters adopt a traditional legal approach which involves analyses of the EU Court's case law – including judgments of the CJEU and of the GC (in cases when the case is pending, not appealed, or when the CJEU has not discussed all of the aspects of the GC judgment) – and of the Commission's decisional practice as a primary source of law. It involves also analyses of secondary sources, i.e., secondary legislation, soft law, policy documents and scholarly sources collected mostly via EUR-lex databases, Westlaw, HeinOnline, Jstor, Google Scholar and SSRN.

The focus of this book is on the EU level. Nonetheless, this book will review recent US case law on fidelity rebates in order to clarify some of the issues not addressed by the Commission and the EU Courts rather than to conduct a comparative study between the EU and US antitrust law regimes.

While some of the chapters apply positive law theory in order to understand the rationale behind the EU Courts approach, others look into how the law should be.

---

50. Consistency, legal certainty, legitimate expectations and right of defence, *see* Herwig Hofmann, 'General Principles of EU law and EU administrative law' in Catherine Barnard and Steve Peers (eds) *European Union Law* (OUP 2014).

[B] Law and Economics

The combination of legal and economic analyses in EU competition law is an integral part of the assessment of a companies' behaviour. Economic analyses can provide empirical support in explaining how legal rules work, but also, play a normative role in showing how the law can be improved in order to benefit society.[51] The normative aspect of the economic approach to law seemed to make its way into the introduction of the so-called more economic approach in applying EU competition law by the European Commission – a clear message to develop its enforcement policy in line with modern economic theory. Consequently, economic analyses were recognised as an essential part of the legal assessment of illegal agreements, mergers and abuses by the EU Courts.

The central question this book deals with is whether the treatment of fidelity rebates should in all respects reflect modern economic thinking and to what extent, and in particular whether a price-cost test should be adapted as a part of the legal test. Therefore, the law and economics approach forms an important part of the research, aiming to clarify whether and under which circumstances an assessment of the legality of fidelity rebates requires economic analysis. The positive aspect of the theory will be applied to the interpretation of the law as it stands, whereas the normative aspect will be adopted to provide supporting evidence and arguments to clarify how the anticompetitive effect of fidelity rebates can be identified in the most efficient way.

§1.04 DELIMITATION

The scope of this book is limited to the treatment of fidelity rebates as an abuse of dominant position under Article 102 TFEU. This book does not examine other types of abuse with the exception of the exclusionary abuses where the AEC test had been endorsed by the EU Courts (margin squeeze practices such as in *TeliaSonera* and *Deutsche Telekom* and low price practices such as in *Post Danmark I*).

Dominant position is a prerequisite for the establishment of abuse of dominant position under Article 102 TFEU. For the purpose of this book, the dominant position will be presumed as established, and it will not be discussed.

So far as the earlier EU Courts decisions regarding fidelity rebates are still cited (the first fidelity rebates case *Hoffmann-La Roche* is from 1979), the scope of the book does not need to be limited to the recent case law.

The analysis in Chapter 6 is limited to the recent US cases *ZF Meritor* and *Essai* because those cases are more illustrative of the debate about the implementation of a price-cost test for the evaluation of the legality of fidelity rebates. The book does not discuss the older US fidelity rebates cases in order to keep the focus on the analysis of the current EU debate. A full discussion comparing the legislative history of the Sherman Act and the TFEU lies beyond the scope of this book.

51. Richard Posner, *Economic Analysis of Law* (3rd edn, Wolters Kluwer Law & Business 2014) Ch. 2.

§1.05 OUTLINE AND STRUCTURE OF THE BOOK

The book comprises eight chapters, including this introductory chapter.

Chapter 2 of the book provides an overview of the most significant judgments on fidelity rebates, prior to the adoption of the Guidance Paper. This line of case law is still cited by the EU Courts, and it is necessary to understand what motivated the European Commission and EU Courts to develop a legal test that led to a very strict approach, akin to per se prohibition for certain types of fidelity rebates regardless of whether they generated actual or probable anticompetitive effects on the market. The description of the facts pattern in each of the judgments is necessary to understand under which circumstances rebates were condemn abusive. This clarification is necessary for the analysis in Chapter 3, which aims to evaluate the economic theories identifying under which circumstances rebates might be anticompetitive and whether the strict approach by the EU Court can be supported from economic standpoint. This chapter also seeks to explain why this case law has provoked so much criticism from academics and other commentators.

Chapter 3 of the book reviews the economic theory of fidelity rebates. The goal is to clarify under which circumstance fidelity rebates can have an anticompetitive effect and when they can be justified by efficiencies. This is necessary to understand if there is an economic rationale behind EU Courts' approach in the case law discussed in Chapter 2. By presenting the different forms of rebates, their characteristics and effects on the market, this chapter also seeks to clarify if there is an economic logic behind the EU Courts' position to separate rebates into different categories depending on their form. Lastly, in reviewing the relevant economic literature, the chapter aims to clarify under which circumstances a price-cost test can be used as a tool for the evaluation of possible anticompetitive effects of fidelity rebates. This clarification is necessary for the analysis in Chapter 4, which aims to evaluate whether the reformed approach to Article 102, and the proposed framework for the assessment of fidelity rebates in particular is in line with the economic theory.

Chapter 4 of the book aims to evaluate whether the modernisation of Article 102 TFEU by the European Commission satisfied those who criticised the treatment of fidelity rebates as outlined in Chapter 2 and whether the analytical framework proposed in its Guidance Paper is in line with the economic theories analysed in Chapter 3. It seeks first to clarify the meaning of the effects-based approach, in order to understand what the appropriate treatment of fidelity rebates should be. It then compares the modernisation of Article 101 and of EU Merger Control with the introduction of the effects-based approach to Article 102, in order to determine whether a coherent approach across competition law was achieved. It also aims to clarify whether the effects-based approach adopted in the European Commission's Guidance Paper provides clarity on how to distinguish between pro-competitive and anticompetitive fidelity rebates. Lastly, it seeks to understand whether the proposed analytical framework offers a clear standard to distinguish the circumstances in which a price-cost test is crucial for the proper assessment of the possible anticompetitive effect of fidelity rebates.

Chapter 5 of this book evaluates the recent EU case law on fidelity rebates, where the applicability of the AEC test (in terms of price-cost test) in relation to the anticompetitive effects of fidelity rebates has been raised as a central issue. This chapter analyses the Commission's decision in Intel, where the price-cost test was applied, and the judgment of the GC that rejected the test as not relevant, in order to understand the main points in which the Commission and the GC could be said to disagree. It then contrasts the GC's judgment with that of the CJEU, and particularly with the opinion of AG Wahl. Lastly, the chapter discusses the *Post Danmark II* judgment. The analysis focuses on clarifying the Courts' position on the application of the AEC test.

The relevance of the price-cost test was raised as a central issue in recent US case law of fidelity rebates and associated scholarly debate. A particular topic of contention concerned under which circumstances the price-cost test should be used as a tool to determine an anticompetitive effect of fidelity rebates, an issue which has not been addressed by the European Commission and the EU Courts in the *Intel* and *Post Danmark II* judgments. Thus, Chapter 6 of this book focuses on the development of the recent case law in the US and on the academic disputes regarding the relevance of the price-cost test in the assessment of the legality of fidelity rebates. Ultimately, this chapter aims to understand whether the assessment of fidelity rebates could be effects-based even if it does not involve the carrying out of a price-cost test. Subsequently, it aims to review the academic debate in US scholarship comparing the two paradigms for exclusionary conduct – predatory pricing and exclusive dealing – in order to understand whether the economic theory of raising rivals cost (RRC) may underlie the Courts' reasoning in rejecting the relevance of the price-cost test as a reliable tool to determine an anticompetitive effect of fidelity rebates.

Chapter 7 aims to combine all the findings of the previous chapters, and attempts to identify the appropriate legal standard for the assessment of fidelity rebates. This chapter evaluates several different potential approaches, including the naked abuse test, the profit sacrifice test, the no economic sense test, the AEC test and the consumer welfare test. It seeks to understand why, among all these tests, the European Commission chose the AEC test as a single unifying test for all types of exclusionary abuses. Consequently, it aims to clarify whether the test could be considered as a necessary or sufficient condition for establishing an exclusionary abuse. Finally, this chapter seeks to identify which standard is best suited to distinguish between pro-competitive and anticompetitive fidelity rebates, in line with the EU competition law objectives protecting competition for the benefits of consumers while simultaneously creating predictability and legal certainty and minimising the risk of errors and administrative costs.

By this point, the main arguments for and against a more economics-based approach to fidelity rebates, regardless of whether they are found in official documents or academic writings and also the main developments in EU and US law on this topic will be reviewed. By this stage the controversy over the application of the AEC test will be clarified and therefore potentially, policy recommendations with regard to the appropriate treatment of fidelity rebates under EU law will be provided. This forms the final chapter of the book.

The state of law reflected in the book is that of September 2017.

CHAPTER 2

The Case Law on Fidelity Rebates Prior to the Adoption of the Guidance Paper

§2.01 INTRODUCTION

Fidelity rebates granted by a dominant company were treated by the European Commission and the EU Courts as a 'by object' restriction of competition under EU competition law since the oldest case on the topic – *Hoffmann-La Roche*.[52] Under 'by object' approach, particular forms of market behaviour by dominant companies are presumed to be abusive without further investigation of the possible competitive effect of these practices.

Since it focuses on the form of the conduct instead of on its effects, this approach is also called 'form-based' approach. The underlying rationale of this approach is that certain practices have a high risk of producing anticompetitive effects, and they are unlikely to generate efficiencies. In those cases, it might be logical to suggest 'that the benefit/harm resulting from a practice is so clear and unambiguous that there is no point in wasting court or regulatory resources in investigating its effects'.[53] For that reason it is reasonable to condemn such practices without further assessment of their effects.[54]

However, an approach based on the form of a practice might fail to distinguish anticompetitive behaviour from legitimate competition in cases when the effect of a practice is context-dependent, or when the practice is justified by efficiency-related

52. In para. 89 the CJEU held that rebates at issue were abusive within the meaning of Art. 102 TFEU without evaluation of their effect without explicitly mentioning the term *'by object'*. Reference to abusive object of a practice can be found explicitly in *Michelin II*, para. 241. The term *'by object'* restriction is used for practices that by their very nature have the potential to restrict competition and it will be used interchangeably with the term 'per se' restriction, which is used to similar effect in US antitrust law. The distinction is that 'per se' prohibition is incapable to be justified.
53. O'Donoghue and Padilla (n. 13) 225.
54. Eirik Østerud, *Identifying Exclusionary Abuses by Dominant Undertakings under EU Competition Law: The Spectrum of Tests* (Vol. 45, Kluwer Law International 2010) Ch. 4.

objectives, such as avoiding double marginalization[55] or free riding.[56] For that reason, a large number of commentators have criticised the form-based approach as regards fidelity rebates on the grounds that such rebates could have either pro-competitive or anticompetitive effects depending on the circumstances of each case.[57] From this point of view, the adoption of fidelity rebates can reflect intense competition, which explains why they are a common practice in economic life. Further, consumers can 'benefit from the existence of loyalty rebates not only through the creation of better products, but also through lower prices'.[58] In this sense, a strong presumption of illegality of fidelity rebates is unjustified because it fails to take into consideration their possible pro-competitive effects.[59]

The aim of this chapter is to provide a review of the courts' decisions, prior to the reform of Article 102 TFEU regarding fidelity rebates in order to understand what motivated them to treat such rebates as illegal 'by object'.[60] Section 2.02 will review the main cases supporting an understanding that fidelity rebates are unlawful by object including *Hoffmann-La Roche, British Gypsum, Michelin I, Irish Sugar, British Airways, Michelin II* and *Tomra*.[61] By describing the factual background and the legal assessment by the EU Courts in each case, this section aims to outline the specific facts pattern under which fidelity rebates were condemned as abusive. Section 2.03 aims to outline what motivated the EU Courts to apply this strict presumption of illegality. This clarification is necessary for the analysis in Chapter 3, which evaluates the economic theories identifying under which circumstances rebates might be anticompetitive and whether the strict approach by the EU Court can be supported by the economic theories. Finally, the chapter seeks to review the relevant literature criticising the case law in order to explain why this case law has drawn so much criticism from academics and other commentators.

---

55. Bishop (n. 4); David Spector, 'Loyalty Rebates and Related Pricing Practices: When Should Competition Authorities Worry?' (2004) Global Competition Policy: Economic Issues and Impacts 317.
56. O'Donoghue and Padilla (n. 13); *see also* Howard Marvel, 'Exclusive Dealing' (1982) 25(1) Journal of Law and Economics 1; Benjamin Klein and Andres Lerner, 'The Expanded Economics of Free-Riding: How Exclusive Dealing Prevents Free-Riding and Creates Undivided Loyalty' (2007) 74(2) Antitrust Law Journal 473. The pro-competitive justifications of granting rebates are discussed in Chapter 3.
57. *See* n. 4.
58. Zenger (n. 4).
59. O'Donoghue and Padilla (n. 13) 463.
60. The term '*by object*' restriction' is used for practices that by their very nature have the potential to restrict competition (presumption of illegality) and it will be used interchangeably with the term 'per se' restriction, which is used to similar effect in US antitrust law. The distinction is that 'per se' prohibitions can never be justified, whereas for the 'by object' prohibition, the presumption of illegality is rebuttable.
61. *See* n. 3.

§2.02 EU CASE LAW[62]

[A] *Hoffmann-La Roche*

[1] Background

Hoffmann-La Roche was the world's largest vitamin producer. It produced a wide range of vitamins and sold them to clients for further use in the food industry, the animal feed industry and the pharmaceutical industry. The Court established that Hoffmann-La Roche was dominant on the basis of its market share, the market shares of its competitors, product differentiation, its technological advantage over its competitors, its developed sales network and the lack of potential competition.[63]

Hoffmann-La Roche entered into agreements with its purchasers under which they undertook to obtain exclusively from it most or all of their requirements, or a percentage of their total requirements of vitamins. The duration of most of the contracts was for an indefinite period and as such, they were designed to establish long-term trading relations between Hoffmann-La Roche and its clients.[64] These agreements provided grant of discounts or rebates, calculated on the basis of the total purchases of all groups of vitamins at the end of a certain reference period.[65] For some of the clients the percentage of the rebates was not fixed, but would increase by 1%–3% depending on the amounts purchased each year.[66] The European Commission deemed this discounting scheme to amount to a fidelity rebate.[67]

[2] Assessment

In its reasoning, the CJEU held that when a company 'holds very large market share, it is by virtue of that share in a position of strength which makes it an unavoidable trading partner' for its customers.[68] If a company possessing a dominant position grants rebates to its customers on the condition that they obtain all or most of their requirements exclusively from it, such a rebate scheme constitutes a fidelity rebate and an abuse of its dominant position within the meaning of Article 102, regardless of 'whether the obligation in question is stipulated without further qualification or whether it is undertaken in consideration of the grant of a rebate'.[69] Further, the Court observed that if the rebate scheme is 'not based on an economic transaction', which may justify the agreement in the context of Article 101(3), the rebate schemes must be assumed to have been 'designed to deprive the purchaser of or restrict his possible

62. This is not a complete list of all cases dealing with fidelity rebates but the judgments to which the GC in Intel refer.
63. *Hoffmann-La Roche*, paras 36 et seq.
64. *Ibid.*, para. 86.
65. *Ibid.*, para. 87.
66. *Ibid.*, para. 87.
67. *Ibid.*, para. 80.
68. *Ibid.*, para. 41.
69. *Ibid.*, para. 89.

choices of sources of supply and to deny other producers access to the market'.[70] The Court also pursued a distinction between fidelity rebates and quantity rebates, concluding that the latter are exclusively linked to the purchased volume whereas fidelity rebates 'are designed through the grant of a financial advantage to prevent customers from obtaining their supplies from competing producers'.[71]

The Court clarified its understanding of what constitutes an abuse of dominant position stating that:

> [t]he concept of abuse is an objective concept relating to the behaviour of an undertaking in a dominant position which is such as to influence the structure of a market where, as a result of the very presence of the undertaking in question, the degree of competition is weakened and which, through recourse to methods different from those which condition normal competition in products or services on the basis of the transactions of commercial operators, has the effect of hindering the maintenance of the degree of competition still existing in the market or the growth of that competition.[72]

In concluding that the rebate schemes under consideration were fidelity rebates, contrary to Hoffmann-La Roche's argument that the rebates were mere quantity rebates, the Court analysed the agreements between Hoffmann-La Roche and its main customers.[73] It found that none of the contracts at issue contained discounts related to fixed or estimated volume of purchases, but that instead 'they all refer to requirements or proportion of the said requirements'.[74] Further, the Court observed that 'the estimate of requirements differ from contract to contract and from year to year, obviously to allow for the customer's capacity of absorption'.[75] In other words, the rebates were tailored for each specific customer, and as such 'they are in fact a specially worked out form of fidelity rebate'.[76] The Court further considered that although the contracts contained elements that left Hoffmann-La Roche's customers with considerable freedom of action, this effect was 'offset by an estimate of annual requirements and by the granting of a rebate increasing in accordance with the percentage of the requirements which are met'.[77]

The progressive rate of rebates at issue was accepted by the Court as a powerful incentive for purchasers to obtain the maximum percentage of said requirements from Hoffmann-La Roche.[78] According to the Court, this method of calculating the rebates at issue was, first, designed to obtain not the maximum quantity but the maximum of the customers' requirements and second, they were applicable 'on estimates made, from case to case, for each customer'. These two features distinguish the rebate scheme *sub*

70. *Ibid.*, para. 90.
71. *Ibid.*, para. 90.
72. *Ibid.*, para. 91.
73. *Ibid.*, para. 92.
74. *Ibid.*, para. 95.
75. *Ibid.*, para. 97.
76. *Ibid.*, para. 98.
77. *Ibid.*, para. 99.
78. *Michelin I*, para. 99.

judice from quantity rebates, the calculation of which is linked solely to the purchased volume.[79]

From the description of the facts, it can be summarized that the rebates were condemned as abusive under the following circumstances: the unavoidable partner status of the dominant company, the retroactivity of rebates linked to exclusivity, barriers to entry, economies of scale and lack of objective justifications.

[B] *Michelin I*

[1] Background

NV Nederlandsche Banden-Industrie Michelin (hereinafter 'Michelin NV') was a subsidiary of the Michelin group responsible for the manufacture and sale of Michelin tyres in the Netherlands, where it had a factory for the production of new tyres for vans and lorries. Michelin NV held a dominant position in the retail market for new replacement tyres for lorries, buses and similar vehicles in the Dutch market.

The dominant position of Michelin NV was established on the basis of its market share (which rose from 57%–65% between 1975 and 1980), the market shares of its competitors, (its main competitors had market shares between 4% and 8%), its substantial commercial and technical service, and its investment and research advantages over its competitors.[80] It was also established that the users of heavy-vehicle tyres had a strong preference for Michelin's tyres and as such, 'a dealer established in the Netherlands normally cannot afford not to sell Michelin tyres', which made the company an unavoidable trading partner.[81]

Michelin NV granted two types of discounts to its dealers. The first type of agreement took the form of a fixed invoice and cash discount for payment before the due dates. These discounts were the same for all dealers, and were not at issue in this case. The second type of discount took the form of an annual variable discount, a proportion of which was 'paid initially every month and then every four months in the form of an advance on the annual discount'.[82] The actual discount rate depended on the individual dealer's turnover in the previous year, and was applied on a progressive scale. The annual discount was not granted to dealers until they achieved their yearly target.[83] Michelin NV discussed with the dealers the target level at the beginning of each year, but the criteria on the basis of which the sales targets were fixed or agreed and the scale of discounts were not known in advance.[84]

79. *Ibid.*, para. 100.
80. *Ibid.*, paras 29 et seq.
81. *Ibid.*, para. 56.
82. *Ibid.*, para. 66.
83. *Ibid.*, para. 67.
84. *Ibid.*, para. 69.

[2] Assessment

The Court began by distinguishing between quantity discounts – which were linked solely to the volume of purchases – and loyalty rebates – which offered customers financial advantages that tended to prevent them from obtaining their supplies from competing manufacturers.[85] The Court observed that the rebates under consideration were not mere quantity discounts because of the application of a progressive scale based on the previous year's turnover. However, they were also not fidelity rebates as described in *Hoffmann-La Roche,* because there was no requirement for the dealers to enter into an exclusive dealing agreement to obtain most or all of their requirements from the dominant company.[86]

For that reason, the Court held that, when deciding whether the discount scheme applied by Michelin NV amounted to an abuse it was 'necessary to consider all the circumstances, particularly the criteria and rules for the grant of the discount'; and also whether 'the discount tends to remove or restrict the buyer's freedom to choose his sources of supply, [and] to bar competitors from access to the market' in the absence of 'any economic service justifying it'.[87]

After evaluating all the circumstances, the Court found that the rebates at issue were based on an annual reference period, a time period deemed long enough to have an effect that would 'increase the pressure on the buyer to reach the purchase target which is needed to obtain the discount or to avoid suffering the expected loss for the entire period';[88] an effect later called 'fidelity-enhancing' effect.[89] In addition, the Court observed that this increasing pressure on customers was further accentuated by the difference between the dominant company's market share and those of its main competitors, which made it very difficult for those smaller competitors to offer competitive proposals, especially taking into account Michelin NV's annual target discount.[90]

The lack of transparency and written communication about the scale of discounts and sales targets created uncertainty to the dealers as to how to predict the overall effect of the discounts scheme.[91] According to the Court, this uncertainty intended to prevent dealers from choosing freely at any time the offers of Michelin NV's competitors and to prevent them from changing supplier without suffering any appreciable economic disadvantage.

In short, this conduct would 'limit the dealers choice of supplier and makes access to the market more difficult for competitors',[92] and as such, constitutes an abuse of a dominant position. The Court clarified that dominance as such is not unlawful or

85. *Ibid.*, para. 71.
86. *Ibid.*, para. 72.
87. *Ibid.*, para. 73.
88. *Ibid.*, para 81.
89. *Michelin II*, para. 81.
90. *Ibid.*, para. 82.
91. *Ibid.*, para. 83.
92. *Ibid.*, para. 85.

censurable; however, a dominant company 'has a special responsibility not to allow its conduct to impair genuine undistorted competition on the common market'.[93]

The facts pattern under which fidelity rebates were condemned as abusive are as follow: the unavoidable trading partner status of the dominant company, economies of scale, progressive retroactive rebates linked to increase of marker share of each customer' total requirements (without buyers commitment to purchase all or almost all of their requirements), a long reference period, uncertainty about the level of rebates, the inability of the competitor to offer similar offers due to their limited scope of sales, the economic disadvantages for the customers if they switch to alternative suppliers and lack of objective justification. All of these circumstances made competitors' access to the market more difficult.

[C] British Gypsum

[1] Background

BPB Industries, through its subsidiary British Gypsum, was the main producer of plasterboard in the UK. The company was found to be dominant based on its very high market share of all plasterboard sold in the UK (about 96%). Before 1982, there were no regular imports of plasterboard into the UK and the market was supplied mainly by British Gypsum. Between 1982 and 1984 two companies entered the market, namely Lafarge and Iberian Trading, who started importing plasterboard produced in France and Spain respectively.

Between July 1985 and August 1986, British Gypsum entered into trade agreements with individually selected customers located in the UK, Ireland and Northern Ireland on condition that these customers would obtain all their requirements from British Gypsum rather than from the recent market entrants.[94] The agreements between British Gypsum and the merchants also set up a system that provided regular contributions to the advertising and promotional expenses of those merchants who were prepared to obtain their supplies exclusively from British Gypsum.[95]

[2] Assessment

In its reasoning, the GC[96] observed that offering promotional payments to buyers could be a standard commercial practice between a supplier and its distributors in competitive markets.[97] However, in markets where a dominant company operates, such a

93. *Ibid.*, para. 57.
94. *Case T-65/89 BPB Industries and British Gypsum v. Commission* [1993] ECR II-389, para. 40.
95. *Ibid.*, para. 39.
96. At the time of the delivery of the judgment (before the Lisbon Treaty came into force on 1 December 2009) the GC was known as the Court of First Instance. For consistency, the court is called GC throughout the book.
97. *Ibid.*, para. 65.

scheme could raise competition issues because competition is already restricted.[98] The argument that the promotional payments were granted as a response to the growing buying power of the merchants was dismissed.[99]

Regarding the supply agreements, the Court relied on the observation in *Hoffmann-La Roche* that, when a dominant company ties purchasers by an obligation or promise on their part to obtain all or most of their requirements exclusively from that dominant company – even if it does so at the purchasers request, and regardless of the form such exclusivity takes – the conduct constitutes an abuse of dominant position.[100] The Court further clarified that exclusive contracts in respect of a substantial proportion of purchases such as those at issue can create unacceptable obstacles to a new competitor entering the market.[101]

As regards the quantity rebates granted to the merchants, the Court found that the dominant company decided to withdraw a 4% rebate from those merchants which intended to import plasterboard from Spain, while granting a rebate of 5% to those who agreed to obtain their supplies exclusively from it. This conduct 'clearly intended to penalize those merchants who intended to import plasterboard' and had the intention to prevent the merchants from obtaining plasterboard from the dominant company's competitors.[102]

The assessment of the GC was endorsed by Advocate General Léger and confirmed by the CJEU on appeal.[103] In particular, the AG suggested that an exclusive dealing arrangement between companies without market power might be contrary to Article 101 only if it is shown that access to the market has become difficult or impossible for competitors. When a dominant company is involved in such an agreement, however, a strict prohibition is required because in this markets the degree of competition is already restricted and 'the exclusive supply agreement causes "additional interference" with the structure of competition on that market'.[104]

From the description of the facts, it can be summarised that the rebates were condemned as abusive under the following circumstances: the unavoidable partner status of the dominant company, the retroactivity of rebates linked to exclusivity, a long reference period, uncertainty about the level of rebates, economies of scale and lack of objective justifications. All of these circumstances made it difficult or impossible for a competitor to enter the market.

98. *Ibid.*, para. 67.
99. *Ibid.*, para. 68.
100. *Ibid.*, para. 68.
101. *Ibid.*, para. 68.
102. *Ibid.*, paras 119–120.
103. Case C-310/93 P *BPB Industries plc and British Gypsum Ltd v. Commission* [1995] ECR I-865, Opinion of AG Léger.
104. *British Gypsum*, paras 43–46.

[D] Irish Sugar

[1] Background

Irish Sugar held a market share of industrial sugar in Ireland of about 90% throughout the period from 1985 to 1995. During that period, Irish Sugar and its distribution company SDL were engaged in two different types of conduct.

The first conduct concerned its pricing policy towards customers in the industrial sugar markets in Ireland. Irish sugar provided fidelity rebates to the potential customers of its competitor ASI International Foods (ASI), the importer of French sugar to the Irish market. The rebates were granted on condition that the customers would purchase all or a large proportion of its sugar requirement from Irish Sugar.[105]

The second conduct concerned the granting of border rebates, target rebates and selective prices to Irish Sugar's customers in the retail sugar market. Border rebates were available for certain customers operating in the border area between Ireland and Northern Ireland including the grant of special allowances to selected customers.[106] Target rebates were conditional on customers purchasing an increased quantity by reference to a previous six months period. The rules for the granting of those rebates were not determined by reference either to the volume of the purchases or to the distance between the customer and the applicant, which made their calculation by the clients unknown in advance, i.e., the rebates system lacked transparency.[107] Selective rebates were granted to certain customers of competing sugar packers, which were conditional on the purchase of increased quantities from Irish Sugar over a period of twelve months. In addition, Irish Sugar bought some quantities (from the industrial market) which had already been supplied from its competitor ASI to its client Allied Distribution Merchants (ADM) and swapped these products with its own on the retail sugar market.[108]

[2] Assessment

Regarding the fidelity rebates granted to ADM, the GC remarked that they were only granted if ADM met a given target purchase level, which distinguished them from a normal quantity discount.[109] When assessing these rebates, the GC referred to *Michelin I* and *British Gypsum* and held that these rebates were designed 'by granting financial advantages, to prevent customers from obtaining their supplies from competing producers'. These rebates had the effect of tying a customer to the dominant supplier and, as such, were an abuse of dominant position.[110]

105. *Case T-228/97 Irish Sugar plc v. Commission* [1999] ECR II-2969, para. 194. The analysis is focused on the GC judgment because the CJEU has not discussed all of the aspects of the GC judgment.
106. *Ibid.*, para. 173.
107. *Ibid.*, para. 150.
108. *Ibid.*, para. 226 et seq.
109. *Ibid.*, para. 194.
110. *Ibid.*, paras 197–198.

Importantly, the GC observed that, in the assessment of this type of rebates, it is necessary to consider:

> [a]ll the circumstances, and in particular the criteria and detailed rules for granting rebates, and determine whether there is a tendency, through an advantage not justified by any economic service, to remove or restrict the buyer's choice as to his sources of supply, to block competitors' access to the market, to apply dissimilar conditions to equivalent transactions with other trading parties, or to reinforce the dominant position by distorting competition.[111]

According to the rebates in the retail market, the GC found that the border rebates were granted to customers in order to reduce the imports of cheaper retail packets from Northern Ireland into Ireland. These rebates were not related to the sales volume purchased by customers, to marketing and transport costs, or to any promotional, warehousing, servicing or other functions. As such, these border rebates could not be objectively justified.[112] The GC stressed that, in order to be lawful, a rebate scheme should be 'based on criteria of economic efficiency and consistent with the interest of consumers'.[113] The GC further considered that these rebates were intended to deter the import of sugar from Northern Ireland, and led to the exclusion of competitors to the detriment of customers.[114] The GC held that the 'border rebates were aimed at securing the loyalty of purchasers exposed to offers from competitors'.[115]

Concerning target rebates, they were granted conditional on the increases in the amount of retail sugar by Irish Sugar customers' over a six months' period (between April and September 1993), and had the effect of tying these customers to Irish Sugar to the detriment of competitors.[116] The selective rebates were granted only to certain customers on the condition that those customers increase their purchases from Irish Sugar over a period of twelve months and they were intended to restrict competition with other competing sugar packers.[117] Lastly, product-swapping by a dominant company was considered by the GC as abusive, 'whenever it has as its object or effect the restriction or elimination of competition from a new entrant in the market'.[118] The assessment of the GC was confirmed by the CJEU on appeal.

In summary, the rebates were condemned as abusive under the following circumstances: the unavoidable partner status of the dominant company, the retroactivity of rebates linked to increase of marker share of each customer' total requirements (without buyers commitment to purchase all or almost all of their requirements), additional anticompetitive conditions (product-swapping), barriers to entry, economies of scale and lack of objective justifications.

111. *Ibid.*, para. 197.
112. *Ibid.*, para. 173.
113. *Ibid.*, para. 189.
114. *Ibid.*, para. 173.
115. *Ibid.*, para. 191.
116. *Ibid.*, para. 203.
117. *Ibid.*
118. *Ibid.*, para. 226.

[E] British Airways

[1] Background

British Airways (BA) is the largest UK airline company, and was held to have a dominant position based on its market share, the size of the company, the range of its air transport services and its network.

BA agreed to pay travel agents established in the UK commissions amounting to 9% on sales of international flight tickets and 7.5% on sales of domestic flight tickets between 1976 and 1997. In 1998, the company introduced three distinct systems of financial incentives for sales of tickets through travel agents in addition to its basic commission system (which was reduced to 7%) – 'marketing agreements', 'global agreements', and subsequently, a 'performance reward scheme':

- 'Marketing agreements' enabled certain travel agents to receive payments – including cash sums for business development and staff training – if they met certain individualised one-year volume targets calculated on a sliding scale.
- 'Global agreements' were entered into with three travel agents, and allowed the agents to receive additional commissions calculated by reference to the growth of BA's share of their worldwide sales on a six months basis.
- Under 'performance rewards', travel agents received an additional commission of up to 3% for international tickets and up to 1% for domestic tickets in addition to their basic commission rate of 7%. The additional commission depended on the agents' selling performance, measured through a comparison of total revenues in a particular calendar month with revenues achieved during the corresponding month in the previous year.

Payments under the schemes were calculated on the basis of all the tickets sold during the reference period, rather than on incremental sales (i.e., the tickets sold once the sales target had been met).

[2] Assessment

In its assessment of rebates granted by BA to travel agents, the Court deemed the *Michelin I* judgment to be relevant, since that case concerned rebates conditional on individual sales targets. Such conditional rebates are neither pure quantity discounts linked to the volume of purchases, nor fidelity rebates linked to an obligation that all or most of the requirement of a customer be obtained from the dominant company as discussed in *Hoffmann-La Roche*.[119]

Given this, the Court observed that in this case it was necessary to consider all the circumstances and particularly the criteria and rules governing the grant of the discount.[120] In order to determine whether a rebate scheme constitutes an abuse, it is

119. *British Airways*, para. 65.
120. *Ibid.*, para. 67.

necessary first to determine whether it can produce an exclusionary effect and, second whether there are pro-competitive efficiencies and/or objective justifications for the rebate.[121]

According to the Court, exclusionary effect can be determined first, by evaluating whether the rebates are capable of either making market entry very difficult or impossible for competitors of a dominant company or, second, whether the rebate scheme 'makes it more difficult or impossible for its co-contractors to choose between various sources of supply or commercial partners'.[122] In conducting its assessment, the Court classified BA as an unavoidable business partner in the market, because its market share was significantly higher compared to its competitors.[123] The Court further observed that a dominant company granting discounts or bonuses does not necessary amount to an abuse, particularly if they can be justified by economic efficiencies and rejected BA's arguments about the high level of fixed costs in air transport and the importance of aircraft occupancy rates amount to an objective economic justification.[124]

BA argued that its discounts and bonus schemes had no material effect because the market share of their competitors grew during the period of the alleged infringement, whereas BA's market share fell from 47.7% to 39.7%, alongside its share of travel agents' sales. The Court dismissed BA's arguments and held that the growth in the market shares of some of BA's airline competitors, which was modest in absolute terms having regard to the small size of their original market shares, did not mean that BA's practices had no effect, since, in the absence of those practices, 'it may legitimately be considered that the market shares of those competitors would have been able to grow more significantly'.[125] In that respect, the Court clarified that 'for the purposes of establishing an infringement of Article 102, it was not necessary to demonstrate that the abuse in question had a concrete effect on the markets concerned', because it is sufficient to demonstrate that the conduct tends to restrict competition.[126] In that respect, the Court clarified that when a dominant company is engaged in a conduct that has the effect of ousting its competitors, failure to achieve that is not sufficient to prevent a finding of abuse.[127]

The Court found that BA's performance reward schemes had an exclusionary effect which arose from their 'fidelity-building' nature. First, the progressive nature of the scheme made it possible for the commission rates to increase exponentially from one period to the next. Second, the Court found that a 'disproportionate reduction in those rates [could occur] in the event of even a slight decrease in sales of BA tickets in comparison with the previous period'.[128] Moreover, because the BA's market share was significantly higher than that of its main competitors, they were not in a position

121. *Ibid.*, paras 68–69.
122. *Ibid.*, para. 68.
123. *Ibid.*, para. 75.
124. *Ibid.*, paras 84 and 88.
125. *Ibid.*, para. 33.
126. *Ibid.*, para. 30.
127. *Ibid.*, para. 32.
128. *Ibid.*, para. 97.

to obtain sufficient sales in order to be capable to offer a similar rebate schemes.[129] The court also took the opportunity to clarify that, Article 102 'is aimed not only at practices which may cause prejudice to consumers directly, but also at those which are detrimental to them through their impact on an effective competition structure, such as is mentioned in Article 3(1)(g) EC'.[130]

From the description of the facts, it can be summarised that the rebates were condemned as abusive under the following circumstances: the unavoidable partner status of the dominant company, progressive retroactive rebates linked to increase of marker share of each customer' total requirements (without buyers commitment to purchase all or almost all of their requirements), inability of the competitors to obtain sufficient sales in order to be capable to offer a similar rebate schemes, barriers to entry and lack of objective justifications.

[F] *Michelin II*

[1] Background

The second Michelin case was concerned with rebate schemes adopted by Manufacture française des pneumatiques Michelin (Michelin France), a manufacturer of tyres for various vehicles. Its activity in France includes the manufacture and sale of new and retreaded tyres for heavy trucks. The market of new tyres was divided between original equipment (i.e., tyres purchased by vehicle producers) and replacements (i.e., tyres purchased by final consumers through commercial outlets, operated by professional dealers). Michelin France occupied a dominant position in each of those product markets.

Michelin France introduced a special commercial policy in France for replacement and retreaded tyres for heavy trucks, consisting of three components: general price conditions for France for professional dealers, an agreement for optimal use of Michelin truck tyres (the PRO agreement) and an agreement on business cooperation and assistance service (known as the 'Michelin Friends Club').

The general price conditions consisted of a 'list' price and a set of rebates, divided into three categories: 'quantity rebates', rebates for the quality of the dealer's service to users ('service bonus') and rebates conditional on increases in new tyre sales ('progress bonus'). Quantity rebates were calculated according to the volumes (of all tyres combined) actually purchased in the previous year on a sliding scale, increasing, according to the turnover achieved. The service bonus was paid to improve dealer's facilities and services if the dealers achieve a minimum annual turnover. The progress bonus was paid to those dealers who agreed to exceed a minimum purchased base, depending on past performance.

The PRO agreement was introduced only for dealers that purchased new truck tyres from Michelin France. This agreement enabled them to receive additional rebates,

129. *Ibid.*, para. 76.
130. *Ibid.*, para. 106.

such as a truck progress bonus limited by the number of new truck tyres bought by the dealers in the previous year, paid in the form of a credit towards the dealer's purchases of new truck tyres in the following year.

Lastly, the 'Michelin Friends Club' benefited from a contribution towards investment and training and a financial contribution amounting to 0.75% of Michelin's annual service turnover. In return, the dealer had to promote the Michelin brand and its new products, to carry a sufficient stock of Michelin products to meet any customer demand immediately, and to provide statistical information regarding its turnover, services provided and information of its statistics and sales forecasts.

[2] Assessment

Regarding the so-called quantity rebates, the GC began by pointing out that the fact that Michelin's discount schemes were described as 'quantity rebates' did not mean that they were compatible with Article 102. Instead, it was necessary to consider all the circumstances, particularly the criteria and rules governing the grant of the discounts, as established in settled case law.[131] In this regard, the GC noted that there was a scale of quantity rebates[132] and that the quantity discount rate increased according to the total turnover of the dealer.[133] The GC noted that the discount applied to the overall turnover of the dealer, and not only to the additional quantities above the threshold achieved during a certain reference period.[134] This was held to increase the dealer's incentive to purchase from the dominant company creating loyalty-inducing effect.[135] In this regard, the GC clarified that rebates has no loyalty-inducing effect if a discount applies only to the quantities exceeding a certain threshold during the reference period.[136] Moreover, the GC considered that the longer the reference period, the more apparent the loyalty-inducing element of the quantity rebates system would become.[137] Regarding the considerable variation in discount rates between the lower and higher steps and the reference period of one year, it was held that this system put the dealers under appreciable pressure and had the characteristics of a loyalty-inducing discount system.[138]

While agreeing with Michelin's arguments that the aim of any competition on price – and of discount systems in particular – is to encourage customers to purchase more from the same supplier, the Court nonetheless noted that under settled case law 'an undertaking in a dominant position has a special responsibility not to allow its conduct to impair genuine undistorted competition on the common market'. Having concluded that the quantity rebates had a loyalty-enhancing effect, the Court rejected

131. *Michelin II*, para. 62.
132. *Ibid.*, para. 68.
133. *Ibid.*, para. 71.
134. *Ibid.*, para. 79.
135. *Ibid.*, para. 81.
136. *Ibid.*, para. 85.
137. *Ibid.*, para. 88.
138. *Ibid.*, para. 95.

Michelin's arguments that the quantity rebates were justified by objective considerations. In particular, the Court held that the arguments presented about economies of scale in production costs and distribution were too generic, insufficient, and unable to explain the discount rates chosen for the various steps in the rebate system.[139]

As regards so-called service bonus rebates, the Court observed that the bonus rate was fixed annually according to the quality of service which the dealer was able to provide in the form of remuneration for services rendered, rather than in the form of a discount.[140] The Court found that the service bonus was unfair because of the subjectivity of the assessment of the criteria, and that it must be regarded as an abuse within the meaning of Article 102. The Court further found that the service bonus had a fidelity-inducing nature because, by granting financial advantages to the dealers, Michelin France 'sought to prevent dealers from obtaining their supplies from rival manufacturers'.[141] In addition, the Court found that the service bonus had a tied sales effect and blocked access of other retreaders to the market -because a dealer could earn an extra point if he systematically returned used tyres to Michelin for retreading, which was considered a lever to ensure that Michelin France would be chosen as a retreader by the dealers.[142]

As regards the 'Michelin Friends Club' scheme, the Court found that Michelin imposed an obligation to obtain a certain market share in Michelin products (Michelin 'temperature' obligation) on the dealers who wanted to join the Club.[143] In addition, the Court found that, in order to become members of the Club, the dealers had to increase their 'temperature' significantly and to diminish the products from other brands that they sold in order to be able to join the Club.[144] Furthermore, membership of this club came with a requirement for the dealer to carry a sufficient stock of Michelin's products to meet any customer demand immediately, which was seen by the Court as a means of consolidating Michelin's dominant position and as an attempt to block access to the market for other tyre manufacturers.[145]

Michelin argued that 'its market shares and its prices are steadily falling, that its competitors have significantly reinforced their position on the market and that new foreign manufacturers have entered the market'.[146] The Court dismissed this by referring to settled case law, according to which an anticompetitive object or potential restrictive effects are sufficient to prove an abuse. It was thus not necessary for the practice at issue to have the actual effect of hindering competition.[147] In the Court's words, 'if it is shown that the object pursued by the conduct of an undertaking in a dominant position is to limit competition, that conduct will also be liable to have such

139. *Ibid.*, paras 108–109.
140. *Ibid.*, para. 136.
141. *Ibid.*, para. 160.
142. *Ibid.*, paras 162–164.
143. *Ibid.*, para. 183.
144. *Ibid.*, para. 204.
145. *Ibid.*, para. 208.
146. *Ibid.*, para. 236.
147. *Ibid.*, para. 239.

an effect' and as such, 'establishing the anticompetitive object and the anticompetitive effect are one and the same thing'.[148]

Ultimately, the Court held that the rebates at issue formed part of a complex system of discounts, which were applied simultaneously. The system included quantity rebates, service bonus, progress bonus, and bonuses linked to the PRO Agreement and the Michelin Friends Club. The system 'made it impossible for the dealer to calculate the exact purchase price of Michelin tyres at the time of purchase', and consequently put the dealers in a position of uncertainty and dependence on the dominant company.[149]

The rebates were condemned as abusive under the following circumstances: the unavoidable partner status of the dominant company, progressive retroactive rebates linked to increase of marker share of each customer' total requirements (without buyers commitment to purchase all or almost all of their requirements), a long reference period, additional anticompetitive condition (diminishing the products from other brands), lack of transparency about the exact level of rebates, barriers to entry and lack of objective justifications.

[G] *Tomra*

[1] Background

Tomra is a Norwegian manufacturer of reverse vending machines (RVM) with distribution subsidiaries around the world. These machines are used to collect empty beverage containers and calculate the amount of the deposit that must to be reimbursed to customers. The machines were used by supermarket chains and independent outlets.

Tomra was found to be dominant, on the basis of its high market share in Europe – which exceeded 70% before 1997 and 95% after that – the (lack of) market position of its competitors and the absence of countervailing buyer power.

Tomra's corporate group – through its parent company Tomra Systems ASA, and through Tomra Europe AS, which coordinated the European distribution subsidiaries – implemented agreements with its customers in Germany, the Netherlands, Austria, Sweden and Norway. The agreements involved exclusivity agreements, individualised quantity commitments, and individualised retroactive rebate schemes:

- The exclusivity agreements were entered into between 1998 and 2002. Under these agreements, Tomra's customers agreed to purchase RVMs exclusively from it. In return, the customers would receive discounts or free machines (or free upgrades for those machines). Under the agreements, if competing RVMs were purchased the discounts were to be paid back.

148. *Ibid.*, para. 241.
149. *Ibid.*, para. 111.

- The quantity agreements imposed individual obligations on each of Tomra's customers to purchase target quantities of RVMs. The target quantities corresponded to the customers total (or almost total) requirements.
- Individualised retroactive rebate schemes were granted if a customer reached specific quantities of RVM's at the end of a certain reference period. The rebate could also take the form of other rewards, such as free machines.

[2] Assessment

Regarding exclusivity agreements, the GC observed that it was necessary to pursue an assessment of all the circumstances of the case, including the context in which the agreements were carried out.[150] In that regard, the Court noted that the Commission's decision examined: (i) the structure of the relevant markets; (ii) the positions of Tomra and its competitors in the market; (iii) each of Tomra's practices individually; (iv) the buyer power of the customers; (v) the development of demand in the relevant market; (vi) the agreed terms; and (vii) what percentage of demand was tied as a result of these agreements. As such, the Commission's decision took into account all of the relevant circumstances before concluding that Tomra's 'practices were capable of impairing the emergence or growth of competition' and 'tended to foreclose a significant part of demand'.[151] Further, the Court observed that even though the case law does not require an actual effect of the practices at issue to be shown, the Commission did demonstrate the effect of the practice in the market[152] – in this case, the Commission showed that Tomra's practices foreclosed a considerable proportion (two-fifths) of total demand.[153] In this regard, the GC observed that 'competitors should be able to compete on the merits for the entire market and not just for a part of it'.[154] In addition, the Court observed that the practices at issue tied the end-customer and not the distributor, which meant that Tomra's competitors were unable to use alternative distribution methods to mitigate the effect of Tomra's practices.[155] Further, the Court pointed out that Tomra failed to provide evidence that its conduct gave rise to efficiency gains, which might have resulted in lower prices or any other benefits for consumers.[156]

Interestingly – for the purposes of this book – Tomra argued that its prices were above cost and 'that in all cases competitors would have been able to earn positive revenues from their sales'. This is ultimately a variant *avant la letter* of the argument that an as efficient competitor would still be able to compete, and would not be excluded from the market, that some would come to see as underpinning the

150. Case T-155/06 *Tomra Systems ASA v. Commission* [2010] ECR II-4361, para. 215. The analysis is focused on the GC judgment because the CJEU has not discussed all of the aspects of the GC judgment.
151. *Ibid.*, para. 218.
152. *Ibid.*, para. 219.
153. *Ibid.*, para. 243.
154. *Ibid.*, para. 241.
155. *Ibid.*, para. 245.
156. *Ibid.*, para. 224.

Commission's more economic approach. However, the Court held that the fact that the retroactive rebate schemes oblige competitors to ask negative prices from the applicants' customers cannot be regarded as one of the fundamental bases in showing that retroactive rebate schemes are capable of having anticompetitive effects.[157] Instead, the GC held that there were 'a whole series of other considerations relating to the retroactive rebates' operated by Tomra that demonstrated that its practices were capable of excluding competitors contrary to Article 102.[158] In this regard, the Court pointed out that the incentive of a customer to obtain exclusively, or almost exclusively its supplies from Tomra was strong, because once the relevant threshold was reached the discounts applied to all the purchases made by the customer during the reference period, and not only to those purchases exceeding the threshold.[159] Moreover, the thresholds were established individually for each customer on the basis of its estimated requirements or past purchases.[160] For that reason, the Court held that, by imposing a retroactive rebate scheme which contained thresholds corresponding to the total or to a large proportion of the customers' requirements, Tomra created a strong incentive for its customer to buy exclusively and 'artificially raised the cost of switching to a different supplier, even for a small number of units'.[161] In that regard, the exclusionary mechanism (called loyalty-building effect)[162] associated with fidelity rebates does not require a dominant undertaking to sacrifice profits, because 'the cost of rebates is spread across a large number of units' which means that 'the average price obtained by the dominant undertaking may well be far above cost and ensure a high average profit margin'.[163] The reason for that conclusion was based on the consideration that the effective price for the last unit was very low because of the 'suction effect' of retroactive rebates.[164]

Concerning individualised quantity commitments, the Court found that the Commission took into account the specific economic context in which the agreements operated when considering that they were capable of excluding competitors.[165] In this regard, the Court noted that the individualised quantity commitments at issue tied and/or induced the purchaser 'to obtain all or most of its requirements from the dominant undertaking' while not being 'based on an economic transaction which justifies this burden or benefit'.[166] Thus, according to the Court, these commitments are 'designed to remove or restrict the purchaser's freedom to choose his sources of supply and to deny producers access to the market, even if it is accepted that they do not bind the purchaser by a formal obligation'.[167] In addition, the Court observed that these agreements were similar to retroactive rebates because first, the discount was

157. *Ibid.*, para. 258.
158. *Ibid.*, para. 259.
159. *Ibid.*, para. 260.
160. *Ibid.*, para. 261.
161. *Ibid.*, para. 262.
162. *Ibid.*, para. 15.
163. *Ibid.*, para. 267.
164. *Ibid.*, para. 267.
165. *Ibid.*, para. 297.
166. *Ibid.*, para. 298.
167. *Ibid.*, para. 298.

conditional upon achievement of a target of certain volume and, second, the risk of losing the discount retroactively was considered a 'strong incentive to the customer to reach the target'.[168] Finally, the GC held that although the Commission evaluated the actual effects of Tomra's conduct, for the purposes of establishing an infringement of Article 102, it is not necessary an actual effect to be demonstrated; it sufficient that the conduct is capable of having that effect.[169] The assessment of the GC was confirmed by the CJEU on appeal.[170]

From the description of the facts, it can be outlined that the rebates were condemned as abusive under an extensive set of circumstances: the unavoidable partner status of the dominant company, progressive retroactive rebates linked to increase of marker share of each customer' total requirements (without buyers commitment to purchase all or almost all of their requirements), a long reference period, inability of the competitors to compete for the entire market and not just for a part of it (contestable share of demand), thresholds corresponding to the total or to a large proportion of the customers' requirements, which artificially raised the costs that a customer had to incur of switching to a different supplier and lack of objective justifications. Lastly, the dominant undertaking was not required to sacrifice profits, because the cost of rebates is spread across a large number of units and for that reason the average price was above cost.

§2.03 OUTLINING THE EU COURTS' APPROACH

The review of the major cases involving fidelity rebates prior to the reform of Article 102 pursued above suggests that the EU Courts distinguished between two types of fidelity rebates, which have been condemned as abusive, namely fidelity rebates linked to exclusivity obligations (*Hoffmann-La Roche, British Gypsum, Tomra* (in part)) and fidelity-enhancing rebates, that have a similar effect to those in the first category (*Michelin I, Irish Sugar, Virgin/British Airways, Michelin II* and *Tomra*).

The first type of rebate is linked to exclusivity obligations, which means that in practice the rebates require customers to obtain all or most of their requirements exclusively from the dominant company. If a dominant company is engaged in such a practice, the conduct is abusive because there is a high degree of probability that the practice will have an anticompetitive effect.[171] In this regard, the EU Courts consistently considered that a conduct is abusive if its *purpose* is to strengthen the dominant position of a company engaged with such a conduct. For example, the GC in *British Gypsum* held that when a dominant company holds a strong dominant position and is engaged in exclusivity supply agreements for a substantial portion of the market, this conduct constitutes an unacceptable obstacle to entry to that market.[172] Similarly, in *Hoffmann-La Roche* the Court equated rebates linked to exclusivity with exclusive

168. *Ibid.*, para. 300.
169. *Ibid.*, para. 288.
170. Case C-549/10 P *Tomra Systems ASA v. Commission* [2012] ECR I-221.
171. *Hoffmann-La Roche*, para. 91.
172. *British Gypsum*, para. 68.

dealing agreement because the grant of a financial advantage was designed to prevent customers from obtaining their supplies from competing producers.[173] Another possible reading of the cases is that a conduct is abusive if its object is a distortion of competition.[174]

The EU Courts developed a strict approach towards this type of rebates because they are designed to restrict the customer's freedom and its ability to choose other suppliers of a product or service.[175] This seems to be based on an assumption that, in a market where the competition is already restricted because of the presence of a dominant company, conduct that restricts customers' freedom and ability to choose other suppliers will inevitably hinder competitors and competition. Such a conduct by a dominant company will prevent competitors from entering the market or foreclose them from the market, which is incompatible with the objective of undistorted competition unless the conduct is based on efficiency justifications.[176]

The EU Courts can thus be said to have created an abbreviated test for this type of fidelity rebates that could be viewed as abusive by object 'in the same way that Article 101(1) TFEU distinguishes between agreements that restrict competition "by object" and "by effect".[177] The test consists of two elements, namely: (i) the existence of a dominant position and unavoidable trading partner status of the dominant company; and (ii) a practice, such as an exclusive purchasing agreement or fidelity rebates linked to an exclusivity obligation, that leads customers to purchase all or a significant proportion of its requirements from the dominant company in the absence of efficiency considerations. According to the Courts' approach, once a company is found dominant, engaging in such practices amounts to an abuse of dominant position, which means that the decisive factor to trigger the application of Article 102 is the finding of dominance. In all of the discussed cases, the Courts found that the dominant companies were dominant not only because of their high market share, barrier to entry, etc. but because they were 'unavoidable trading partners' for their customers, which means that (1) the customers were dependent upon the dominant company and they have strong preference to purchase from them;[178] (2) competitors were not able to compete for the whole customers' demand.[179] In all such cases, rebates were retroactive.

In short, the EU Courts established a strict presumption of illegality for this category of rebates, assuming that their object is to restrict competition.[180] This

173. *Ibid.*, para. 90.
174. *Ibid.*, para. 70.
175. *Ibid.*, para. 120.
176. *Hoffmann-La Roche*, para. 90.
177. Pablo Ibáñez Colomo, 'Beyond the "More Economics-Based Approach": A Legal Perspective on Article 102 TFEU Case Law' (2016) 53 Common Market Law Review 709.
178. *Hoffmann-La Roche*, para. 41; *Michelin I*, para. 56; *British Airways*, para. 75; *Tomra*, para. 269.
179. *Hoffmann-La Roche*, para. 51; *Michelin I*, para. 56.
180. Liza Lovdahl Gormsen, 'Are Anti-Competitive Effects Necessary for an Analysis under Article 102 TFEU?' (2013) 36(2) World Competition 223, 227.

approach seems to resemble the prohibition of naked restraints under Article 101:[181] if an agreement is found to restrict competition by object, it is not necessary that the effect of the agreement be shown.[182]

However, *Tomra* can be regarded as a halfway departure from the strict approach adopted for the assessment of exclusivity obligations because the EU Courts considered that Tomra's exclusivity agreements have to be evaluated in the light of all the circumstances, instead of considering them abusive per se like in *Hoffmann-La Roche* and *British Gypsum*.

The second category of fidelity rebates concerns rebates schemes that are neither linked to exclusivity nor solely to the volume of purchases made from a dominant company, but which may have an exclusionary effect, called 'fidelity-inducing (building/enhancing)' effect.[183] The concept of 'fidelity-enhancing' rebates was developed by the Courts to distinguish this type of rebates from quantity rebates, (which are presumptively lawful under Article 102) on the one hand and from rebates that are directly conditional on exclusivity on the other.

For the assessment of this category of rebates, the EU Courts developed an approach that evaluates their possible anticompetitive effect in the light of the 'all the circumstances' test. Thus, the anticompetitive effect of this type of rebates is not presumed in the abstract or related to their form. Instead, evaluating all the circumstances means assessing the ultimate impact or a fidelity-inducing effect of a rebate scheme. However, the EU Court did not set a particular threshold for the establishment of a fidelity-enhancing effect of rebates. In *Michelin I*, the Court considered that the rebates under consideration were anticompetitive because Michelin 'bound tyre dealers to itself'[184] because of the retroactivity of rebates and a relatively long reference period but also because the rate of rebates was unknown till the end of the reference period when it becomes clear whether the sales target is attained or not.[185] This condition of uncertainty put strong pressure on the customers, aiming to induce them to purchase additional units from the dominant company instead of its competitors so as to reach the target and obtain rebates not only for the purchases above the threshold, but also for all previous purchases during the reference period. In this case, the increase of purchases above the target would affect customers' margin of profit for the whole reference period, which is a strong inducement to switch purchases from the competing supplier – an effect later called 'suction effect'.[186]

In *Irish Sugar*, the Court set a very low threshold for the establishment of an anticompetitive effect of rebates, based on the grounds that rebates were granted to all

181. Thomas Eilmansberger, 'How to Distinguish Good From Bad Competition under Article 82 EC: In Search of Clearer and More Coherent Standards for Anti-Competitive Abuses' (2005) 42(1) Common Market Law Review 129, 148.
182. Gormsen, 'Are Anti-competitive Effects Necessary for an Analysis under Article 102 TFEU?' (n. 180) 227.
183. The term 'fidelity-inducing' effect was used for the first time by the GC in the *Michelin II* judgment, para. 81. In *British Airways*, para. 240, the GC used the term 'fidelity-building' effect.
184. *Michelin I*, para. 75.
185. *Michelin I*, para. 78.
186. *Michelin I*, para. 81. The term 'suction effect' was used for the first time in the Commission's Discussion Paper and in *Tomra*.

purchases once the purchases exceeded a certain threshold, i.e., when the rebates were retroactive. The GC considered that the granting of financial advantages, had the effect of tying a customer to the dominant supplier, which aimed to prevent customers from obtaining their supplies from competing producers'.[187] Thus, the rebates were aimed at securing the loyalty of purchasers, which was enough for the establishment of abusive conduct without consideration of the length of the reference period (which were in some of the agreements linked to weekly dealer performances).[188] Respectively, in *British Airways*, the GC concluded that the rebates at issue had a 'fidelity-building' effect because of the progressive nature of performance reward schemes and the increased commission rates from one reference period to another, leading to a penalty in the form of a disproportionate reduction of rebates even in the case of a slight decrease in sales of BA tickets in comparison with the previous period.[189] The fidelity-building effect was also established due to the fact that competitors were not able to achieve the same scope of sales so as to be able to grant similar reward schemes.[190] However, the reference period, which was one month, was not relevant for the conclusion that rebates had a fidelity-enhancing effect.[191] In contrast, in *Michelin II*, the GC considered that the retroactivity of rebates combined with a reference period of one year was long enough to create a fidelity-enhancing effect.[192] Next, similarly to *Michelin I*, the GC considered that the uncertainty of the level of rebates 'made it impossible for the dealer to calculate the exact purchase price of Michelin tyres at the time of purchase', and consequently put the dealers in a position of uncertainty and dependence on the dominant company.[193]

In Tomra, the GC developed the concept of fidelity-enhancing effects of rebates and explained why the suction effect of rebates created an exclusionary mechanism/fidelity-enhancing effect and why it would be not possible for a competitor to offer a price for the incremental units (above the threshold) in order to compensate the customer for the loss of rebates for the units below the threshold. All these grounds need to be restated here.

First, the Court established that Tomra had a position of unavoidable trading partner because there were not proper substitutes for a significant part of demand,

187. *Irish Sugar*, paras 197–198.
188. Luc Gyselen, 'Rebates: Competition on the Merits or Exclusionary Practice?' in Claus-Dieter Ehlermann and Isabela Atanasiu (eds), *European Competition Law Annual 2003: What Is an Abuse of a Dominant Position?* (Bloomsbury Publishing 2006) 287, 310, who suggests that the fact that the reference period was not considered means that 'the Court shares the Commission's view according to which the length of the reference period does not matter.'
189. *British Airways*, paras 272–273.
190. *Ibid.*, para. 276.
191. In contrast, the same programs were challenged under the US antitrust law where the plaintiff alleged that as a result of fidelity rebates the incremental sale were below cost and as such anticompetitive. The proposed price cost test was based on comparing additional/incremental revenues to the average variable cost of serving additional passengers, which suggest that they considered this practices as incremental rebates rather that retroactive. The Court held that the evidence are not enough for this conclusion and granted summary judgment to BA. *See Virgin Atl. Airways LTD v. British Airways PLC*, 257 F.3d 256 (2d Cir. 2001).
192. *Michelin II*, para. 75.
193. *Ibid.*, para. 111.

naming this part of demand a 'non-contestable' part of the market.[194] This part of demand was secured for the dominant company, which means that customers would purchase these quantities at the list price anyway. Hence, customers would purchase only a limited portion of their purchases from a competing supplier; this part of demand was called a 'contestable part' of the market.[195] Therefore, the unavoidable trading partner status of the dominant company leads to the establishment of a non-contestable and contestable part of demand, making competitors unable to compete for the whole demand. In this regard, the GC observed that 'competitors should be able to compete on the merits for the entire market and not just for a part of it'.[196]

Tomra was able to establish the non-contestable part of demand on the basis of the customer's estimated requirements and/or past purchasing volumes and to set thresholds for obtaining rebates above this level, i.e., to attract additional purchases from the contestable part of demand.[197] Because rebates were retroactive, they were applicable to all of the purchased units when the threshold is reached, not only for the incremental purchases above the threshold. This means, that Tomra was able to use that portion of demand of each customer, that would be purchased anyway from the dominant undertaking (non-contestable part) as leverage to decrease the price of the other portion of demand for which the customer may prefer and be able to find another source of supply. For the customers, this technically means that the price for the additional units is very low, while at the same time the dominant company was not required to sacrifice profit, because the lower price for the additional units can be recouped, since the cost of the rebates is spread across the whole range of sales.[198] For that reason, a competitor would not be able to offset the lower prices for the units above the threshold in order to compensate the customer for the loss of rebates for the units below threshold by selling additional units to the same customer due to fact that customers' remaining demand is limited.[199] Accordingly, whether or not the price for the incremental units was very low or even negative was not considered as a prerequisite to finding rebate schemes abusive.[200]

Thus, customers were incentivised to buy additional units from Tomra instead of another supplier so as to reach the rebate threshold and to obtain a lower price not only for the additional units but for all purchases made during the reference period (including for those that would be purchased anyway at the list price); alternatively if a customer does not reach the threshold, it will lose the rebate on all purchases over the reference period.

194. Customers may prefer dominant company's product because it is a 'must-stock' product (i.e., the company is dominant because the product has strong brand or because of the inelastic demand) or because a competitor is capacity constrained to serve the total demand, the dominant company is an essential trading partner and customers normally buy certain amounts of their requirements from the dominant company.
195. *Tomra*, para. 269. The EU Courts refer to unavoidable trading partner status of the dominant company also in *Hoffmann-La Roche*, para. 41; *Michelin I*, para. 56; *British Airways*, para. 75.
196. *Ibid.*, para. 241.
197. *Ibid.*, para. 261.
198. *Ibid.*, para. 267.
199. *Ibid.*, para. 270.
200. *Ibid.*, para. 266.

When customers are close to the threshold, only a small increase in purchases will trigger rebates applicable to all purchased units in the past. This condition creates a stronger inducement for the customers to commit purchases preferably from the dominant supplier, thus, enhancing loyalty. Thus, the dominant undertaking may hamper their competitors ability to compete for that portion of the market (which is open to competition), as customers tempted by the discount when reaching the threshold will not transfer the sensitive part of the demand to an alternative supplier because they will lose the discount. Hence, placing a high threshold as a requirement for discounts combined with a high percentage discount will make it unprofitable for the customers to purchase part of their demand from a competitive supplier as they will lose the high discount and will pay a higher price if buying from another supplier. This means that the rebates artificially raised the cost of switching that the customer has to incur in order to purchase from a competitor.[201]

Thus, the position of the dominant company as an unavoidable trading partner is the condition that makes possible the creation of a system that incentivises customers to transfer the purchases of all or almost all of their requirements from the dominant company. Alternatively, if the dominant company's product is not essential, there is no non-contestable part of sales.

Lastly, the fact that Tomra's conduct foreclosed a considerable proportion (two-fifths) of total demand, which was regarded as a very high proportion of 'tied' demand,[202] was considered as a complementary but not necessary for the finding of infringement of Article 102 TFEU.[203]

From the above, it can be concluded that, a fidelity-enhancing effect of rebates was established on the grounds of the retroactive nature of rebates and the unavoidable trading partner status of the dominant company for a substantial part of demand. Consequently, 'all the circumstances' test developed by the Courts is limited to the assessment of the criteria and rules for granting rebates, but fails to take into account the extent of coverage and the percentage of the tied market, which is inconsistent with the evaluation of an anticompetitive effect in similar practices under Article 101 as will be discussed in Chapter 4 of this book. In short, the Courts set a very low threshold for the establishment of a fidelity-enhancing effect, above which every form of fidelity rebates were condemned as abusive with no further evaluation of their effect. Since, once a rebates' fidelity-inducing effect was established, the rebates were equated to an exclusive purchasing commitment and condemned as abusive with no further requirement to evaluate their effect, it could be said that fidelity-enhancing rebates by dominant companies amounted to an 'by object' restriction of competition.[204] While this might be contradicted by the CJEU's clarification that a conduct is condemned as

201. *Ibid.*, para. 262.
202. *Ibid.*, paras 243–244.
203. *Ibid.*, para. 289.
204. Gyselen, 'Rebates: Competition on the Merits or Exclusionary Practice?' (n. 188) 287; James Venit, 'Article 82: The Last Frontier-Fighting Fire with Fire' (2004) 28 Fordham International Law Journal 1157, 1166; *see also* Brian Sher, 'Keep Calm – Yes; Carry on – No! A Response to Whish on Intel' (2015) 6(4) Journal of European Competition Law and Practice 219, who argues that the strict approach to the third category of rebates is closer to object restriction.

abusive only if it might cause prejudice to consumers through their impact on an effective competition structure,[205] the EU Courts position nonetheless seems to be that it is not necessary to demonstrate the concrete effect of such a conduct because it is sufficient to establish that it is capable of restricting competition.[206] Thus, if a conduct tends to restrict competition, that conduct is capable of having that effect, i.e., the anticompetitive object and effect are one and the same thing.[207] This statement was considered by some as an explanation as to why Article 102 prohibits 'any abuse by one or more undertaking of a dominant position' without reference to the by object or effect of the abusive conduct, whereas Article 101 outlines the difference between object and effect of the agreements.[208]

The EU Courts emphasized that the degree of dominance is important to trigger the presumption that fidelity rebates are abusive. This implies not only that the company has a significant market share but also often means that the company is an unavoidable trading partner, which creates a strong preference for customers to purchase from them.[209] As a result of this market structure, customers can choose an alternative supplier only for a small proportion of their requirements, and these suppliers can compete only for those limited proportions. If a dominant supplier concludes agreements with its customers that ultimately amount to exclusivity arrangements, the dominant company's competitors access to even those limited proportions of the market is restricted, thereby leading to market foreclosure.

This strict approach of the EU Courts, akin to a 'per se' prohibition of certain discounting practices, has been considered by some as an approach that provides legal certainty for companies and reduces the administrative cost of the competition enforcers.[210] In this respect, a strict presumption of illegality provides clear rules, which make it possible for the companies to assess their conduct in advance, whereas the need for an evaluation of the effects in each particular case 'would be a nightmare if everything became an *ex post* review on the bases of effects'.[211] It has also been suggested that evaluating the effect of fidelity rebates on a case-by-case basis creates legal uncertainty and thus, discourages legitimate competition.[212] Other proponents of this strict approach argue that if there is evidence of distortion of the effective

205. *Hoffmann La-Roshe*, paras 89 et seq. and 125; *British Airways*, para. 244, *Suiker Unie*, para. 518 and *Michelin I*, para. 70; *British Airways*, para. 106. This position was made by the CJEU yet in Case C- 6/72 *Europemballage and Continental Can v. Commission* [1973] ECR I-215 judgment where it is stated that consumers could be harmed – either directly, when prices are raised above the competitive level (exploitative abuse), or indirectly, when the competitive structure of the market is damaged (exclusionary/anticompetitive abuse, which reduces competition).
206. *Irish Sugar*, para. 170; *British Airways*, para. 30; *Michelin I*, para. 70; *Michelin II*, para. 241; *British Airways*, para. 241; *Tomra*, para. 17.
207. *Michelin II*, para. 241; *see also Tomra*, para. 42.
208. Arjen Meij and Tristan Baumé, 'Object and Effects-Based Approaches in Identifying Abuses of a Dominant Position under Article 82 EC' in Heikki Kanninen, Nina Korjus and Allan Rosas (eds) *EU Competition Law in Context Essays in Honour of Virpi Tiili* (Hart Publishing 2009).
209. *Hoffmann-La Roche*, para. 41; *Michelin I*, para. 56; *British Airways*, para. 75; *Tomra*, para. 269.
210. Eilmansberger (n. 180) 146.
211. *See* n. 48.
212. *Ibid.*, 184.

competitive structure, 'the likelihood is sufficiently high to infer harm to consumers without the need to show that they are actually harmed'.[213]

§2.04 CRITICISM OF THE CASE LAW

Despite the academic support just mentioned above, the treatment of exclusivity rebates has been criticized by many authors as being too interventionist, and for condemning allegedly abusive behaviour by dominant firms based on the form of the conduct rather than on the actual or expected effect of that conduct on the market.[214] These criticisms also apply for the treatment of rebates that have a fidelity-enhancing effect. According to some, the CJEU 'incorrectly assumes that any rebate scheme that has a "fidelity-enhancing" effect will lead to competitive harm' and thus 'this approach fails to recognise the welfare benefits of rebate schemes that go beyond transaction-specific cost savings'.[215]

The rationale behind this criticism arises from an economic consensus that fidelity rebates could be either pro-competitive or anticompetitive depending on their effect on the competition on the market. For example, the OECD in its report on fidelity discounts and rebates states that because of their ambiguous effect, which is 'highly dependent on specific features of the discounts and the markets, a case by case approach to fidelity discounts seems warranted'.[216]

Arguably, when a dominant firm employs fidelity rebates, it does so in order to make its offers more attractive for its customers. As a result, making life harder for competitors of a dominant company does not necessarily mean that competition would be harmed.[217] For example, it has been argued that the incentive of a dominant company to engage in rebate schemes is to create an incentive for its purchaser to increase their sales efforts, which may lead to an increase in the total sales in the relevant market. This effect could explain the popularity of rebate schemes for both dominant and non-dominant firms,[218] which would mean that rebates 'represent a form of healthy price competition between firms'.[219] According to this view, 'the potential of rebate schemes to increase total output while lowering overall prices is simply ignored in the traditional assessment'.[220] For that reason it has been suggested that 'there is no obvious reason why antitrust law should view such practices with any particular suspicion, since they typically lead to lower prices, which should in nearly all

213. Gormsen, 'Are Anti-competitive Effects Necessary for an Analysis under Article 102 TFEU?' (n. 180) 231.
214. *See* n. 4.
215. John Kallaugher, 'Rebates Revisited (Again) – The Continuing Article 82 Debate' http://www.scribd.com/doc/54155483/Rebates-revisited-again-2013-the-continuing-debate-on-rebates-under accessed 14 October 2015.
216. OECD Report, Loyalty and Fidelity Discounts and Rebates DAFFE/COMP(2002)20. Same position was expressed in OECD Report, Fidelity and Bundled Rebates and Discounts DAF/COMP(2008)29 and recently in OECD Report, Fidelity Rebates DAF/COMP(2016)5.
217. Bishop (n. 4) 70.
218. Kallaugher (n. 215).
219. Federico, 'When are Rebates Exclusionary?' (n. 4) 478.
220. Kallaugher (n. 215) 3.

cases benefit from strong presumptions of legality'.[221] Other pro-competitive rationales that may underpin fidelity rebates will be discussed in detail in the next chapter.

Another criticism directed at the EU Courts is that their position amounts to a prohibition of certain practices once a firm is deemed to be dominant – which confuses analytical categories by using dominance as a short cut to conclude that conduct is abusive.[222] According to this view, the dominance is a necessary but not sufficient condition for liability and the evaluation of the legality of fidelity rebates should be established by reference to their coverage and duration.[223] Some suggested that the assessment should look at the possibility for competitors to match the rebate offered by the dominant company, without providing much clarity as to how this assessment should be done.[224]

A corollary of these criticisms is that a prohibition of fidelity rebates without consideration of their actual effects could lead to type I errors (i.e., a false positive, in this case finding pro-competitive conducts to be abusive). As a result, regulatory intervention risks discouraging legitimate competition and the dominant companies' incentives to innovate and to provide better products/services to consumers.[225] Such a strict approach 'can have the effect of chilling price competition, protecting possibly inefficient competitors and raising prices to consumers'.[226] In other words, given the possible pro-competitive effects of fidelity rebates, a strict prohibition of these practices could discourage potential efficient behaviour.

As shall be seen in Chapter 4, these criticisms were instrumental in the Commission rethinking its approach to abuses of a dominant position, and therefore proposing to adopt a more economic approach. This development was, to an extent, perceived as being supported by judicial developments as well. In *Tomra*, the anticompetitive effect of fidelity rebates was analysed not only in the light of previous case law; the rebates' likely and actual effects were demonstrated by economic analyses.[227] For that reason, it was at the time submitted that the case was in line with the envisaged reform of Article 102.[228] Others, however, criticised the judgment because it confirmed that the Commission was not required to demonstrate the actual effect of fidelity rebates.[229] In

221. Lang and O'Donoghue, 'Defining Legitimate Competition' (n. 4) 83.
222. James Kavanagh and Others, 'Reform of Article 82 EC- Can Law and Economics be Reconciled?' in Ariel Ezrachi (ed.) *Article 82 EC: Reflections on its Recent Evolution* (Bloomsbury Publishing 2009).
223. *Ibid.*, (n. 222).
224. Alberto Heimler, 'Pricing Below Cost and Loyalty Discounts: Are They Restrictive and If So When?' (2004) https://papers.ssrn.com/sol3/papers.cfm?abstract_id=634723 accessed 26 January 2016; *see also* Faella (n. 4) 390; Waelbroeck (n. 4) 162.
225. *See* n. 6.
226. Waelbroeck (n. 4) 150.
227. Luc Peeperkorn and Ekaterina Rousseva, 'Article 102 TFEU: Exclusive Dealing and Rebates' (2011) 2(1) Journal of European Competition Law and Practice 36; Frank Maier-Rigaud and Dovile Vaigauskaite, 'Prokent/Tomra, A Textbook Case? Abuse of Dominance under Perfect Information' (2011) Competition Policy Newsletter.
228. Maier-Rigaud and Vaigauskaite (n. 227) clarify that the Commission's decision was taken in 2006, one year after the adoption of the Discussion Paper, but before the Guidance Paper, i.e., the midst of the reform of Art. 102.
229. Derek Ridyard, 'The Tomra Decision: A Disappointing Start to the Effects-based Era of Article 82 Enforcement' (2007) Competition Law Insight; Giulio Federico, 'Tomra v Commission of the

essence, it was argued, the Court's approach in *Tomra* reaffirmed its previous case law according to which it is not necessary for actual or likely effect to be demonstrated; instead, it is sufficient for the conduct to tend to or be able to restrict competition.[230] This was contrasted with AG Mazák's opinion, who argued that the effects should be assessed and demonstrated, rather than presumed.[231]

§2.05 CONCLUSION

The aim of this chapter was to understand what motivated EU Courts to identify a legal test that led to treating fidelity rebates as illegal 'by object' without evaluating their effect on competition. For that reason, a thorough description of the background and the legal analysis of each of the cases were necessary.

In all of the discussed cases, the EU Courts found that the dominant companies held a strong dominant position and was an unavoidable trading partner, which meant that customers were dependent upon the dominant company's product and competitors were not able to compete for the customers' whole demand.[232] The Commission and the EU Courts considered that, in a market where competition is already restricted because of the presence of a dominant company, only part of the market is open to competition due to the unavoidable trading partner status of the dominant company. Additionally, in such markets the dominant company has a special responsibility not to allow its conduct to impair undistorted competition.[233] Consequently, any further agreements between the dominant company and its customers that induce customers through financial advantages to purchase additional volumes from it were designed to prevent customers from obtaining their supplies from competing producers,[234] and as such, the purpose of such agreements was to strengthen a company's dominant position through anticompetitive means.[235]

The EU Courts identified two main categories of anticompetitive rebates. The first category consists of rebates that are linked to exclusivity obligations, and that lead to customers being required to obtain all or most of their requirements exclusively from the dominant company. The EU Courts consistently applied a strict legal test condemning this type of rebates as abusive 'by object'. A second category of abusive discounts consisted of rebates that do not contain exclusivity obligations, but instead are conditional on an achievement on specific threshold (target/growth rebates) or a certain share of customers' requirements, which have a fidelity-enhancing effect. For

European Communities: Reversing Progress on Rebates?' (2011) 32(3) European Competition Law Review 139; Crayencour and Lang (n. 14) 52; Ariel Ezrachi, *EU Competition Law: An Analytical Guide to the Leading Cases* (Bloomsbury Publishing 2016).

230. Some argued that, despite this, *Tomra* and an effects-based approach were not incompatible. In particular, it was held that an effect-based analysis 'does not always require proof of actual negative effect on the market', because it is the time of the implementation of the conduct that should be relevant for the competitive assessment. *See* Peeperkorn and Rousseva (n. 227) 37.
231. Case C 549/10 P *Tomra Systems ASA v. Commission* [2012] ECL I-55, Opinion of AG Mazák.
232. *Hoffmann-La Roche*, para. 41; *Michelin I*, para. 56; *British Airways*, para. 75; *Tomra*, para. 269.
233. *Michelin I*, para. 57.
234. *Hoffmann-La Roche*, para. 89; *Michelin I*, para. 71; *British Gypsum*, para. 90; *Tomra*, para. 70.
235. *Tomra*, para. 13.

this type of rebates, the EU Courts developed and consistently applied a legal standard that requires an evaluation of all the circumstances in which the rebate was granted. The legal standard aims to identify whether they have a fidelity-enhancing effect – a feature that makes them anticompetitive in similarity to fidelity rebates linked to exclusivity. The EU Courts ultimately seemed to hold all rebates that have a fidelity-enhancing effect are abusive in general unless justified by any efficiency considerations. However, the EU Courts set a very low threshold above which every form of fidelity rebates were equated to exclusive dealing and condemned as abusive with no further evaluation of their effect. Because the threshold for a practice to be considered as fidelity-enhancing was so low, some considered that fidelity-enhancing rebates should be categorized as 'by object' restriction of competition.[236]

Finally, the case law had never considered the use of a price-cost test for the evaluation of fidelity rebates. In this regard, the GC rejected Tomra's arguments that the Commission failed to establish whether the prices for the additional units were negative in order to establish the level below which prices would be exclusionary or predatory. The GC held that the fact that the retroactive rebate schemes oblige competitors to ask negative prices from the customers cannot be regarded as one of the fundamental bases in showing that retroactive rebate schemes are capable of having anticompetitive effects.[237]

In short, the EU Courts were perceived as applying a very strict rule akin to a per se prohibition against all forms of rebates, that were linked to exclusivity or had fidelity-enhancing effects (due to the fact that rebates were retroactive, granted by a dominant company with an unavoidable trading partner status, for the long reference period). This case law was criticized by many as being too strict, and as ignoring the possible pro-competitive justifications for implementing fidelity rebates. The predominant conclusion of the literature critical to this case law was that a strict presumption of illegality of fidelity rebates and discounts was not justified.[238] For example, similar practices (even when applied by dominant companies) are treated as an infringement 'by effect' under Article 101 TFEU, as discussed in more detail in Chapter 4 of this book.[239] For that reason, some argued that the analysis of these rebates required detailed economic analysis. This was not only to ensure that the law was in line with economic theory, but also in order to align Article 102 with Article 101, which at the time was perceived as being implemented in accordance with modern economic

236. Gyselen, 'Rebates: Competition on the Merits or Exclusionary Practice?' (n. 188).
237. *Tomra*, para. 258.
238. O'Donoghue and Padilla (n. 13) 463; Spector, 'Loyalty Rebates: an Assessment of Competition Concerns and a Proposed Rule of Reason' (n. 4).
239. On this point *see* Massimiliano Kadar, 'The Meaning of "Anticompetitive Effects" under Article 102 TFEU' (2016) CPI Antitrust Chronicle https://www.competitionpolicyinternational.com/wp-content/uploads/2016/03/The-Meaning-of-Anticompetitive-Effects.pdf accessed 30 September 2017.

thinking.[240] This literature was an important part of the calls for reform of Article 102 which will be discussed in Chapter 4 of this book.[241]

However, before discussing the reform of Article 102 and whether the analytical framework proposed by the Commission satisfied those who criticised the Commission and the Courts for their formalistic approach with regard to fidelity rebates, as outlined in section 2.03 of this chapter, it is necessary first to look at the economic theory of rebates. This is necessary in order first, to clarify under which circumstances fidelity rebates might have an anticompetitive effect in order to understand whether the rationale behind the strict approach by the EU Courts can be defended from an economic standpoint, and second, whether a price-cost test is suitable to identify anticompetitive fidelity rebates. This will then allow to evaluate whether the reformed approach to Article 102, and the proposed assessment framework of fidelity rebates, which will be discussed in Chapter 4, is in line with the economic theory.

240. Brian Sher, 'The Last of the Steam-Powered Trains: Modernising Article 82' (2004) 25(5) European Competition Law Review 245.

241. Ioannis Lianos, 'Categorical Thinking in Competition Law and the "Effects-Based" Approach in Article 82 EC' in Ariel Ezrachi (ed.) *Article 82 EC: Reflections on Its Recent Evolution* (Bloomsbury Publishing 2009) 19, 20.

CHAPTER 3
The Economics of Fidelity Rebates

§3.01 INTRODUCTION

Granting rebates is a common and widespread practice in economic life, as discounts are often used to stimulate sales. Implementation of schemes of rebates is a standard marketing nostrum, which serves as an instrument to intensify competition and to increase sales via lowering prices.

Whereas the implementation of various types of rebates by non-dominant firms is accepted as a form of effective competition (known as competition on the merits), their implementation by dominant firms has been considered by the EU Courts to be abusive conduct contrary to Article 102 TFEU on some occasions – in particular, when they amount to fidelity rebates.[242] The implementation of fidelity rebates by a dominant company linked to exclusivity was deemed to amount to a 'by object' restriction of competition, whereas a very low threshold set for the fidelity-enhancing rebates above which every form of rebates were condemned as abusive with no further evaluation of their effect was established. As noted in Chapter 2, this case law was criticized by many as being too strict, and as ignoring the possible welfare benefit of granting rebates. These criticisms claimed support on a significant number of economic studies, which reported that fidelity rebates could have pro-competitive or anticompetitive effects (or a mixture of the two) depending on the circumstances.[243]

The ultimate aim of this chapter is to review the modern economic literature dealing with the possible effects of fidelity rebates in order to determine whether the

242. *See* Chapter 2 of this book.
243. Bogdan Genchev and Julie Holland Mortimer, Empirical Evidence on Conditional Pricing Practices' (2016) No. w22313, National Bureau of Economic Research. They summarised all empirical evidence and reach to the conclusion that: 'results demonstrate that the pro- and anticompetitive effects of conditional pricing practices exist simultaneously and must be carefully analysed in different contexts'.

strict approach of the Courts can be supported by the economic theories and to understand the motivation of those who criticised the case law.

This chapter will begin by describing the various types of rebates in order to clarify whether there is an economic rationale for separating rebates into different categories, which are subject to different assessment in line with the case law reviewed in the previous chapter. Second, it discusses economic theories analysing the anticompetitive effects of fidelity rebates, including the circumstances under which these effects might arise. The intention is to identify whether the economic theories provide support, which can be used to understand the rationale behind the courts' position as to why fidelity rebates can have a fidelity-enhancing effect, which makes them anticompetitive. Particular attention will be devoted to whether the economic theories provide support for the implementation of a price-cost test to identify anticompetitive rebates. This will allow us to identify the circumstances under which a price-cost test can be a useful tool in the assessment of the effect of fidelity rebates. This analysis is necessary to evaluate whether the reformed approach to Article 102 and the proposed framework for the assessment of fidelity rebates in particular are in line with the economic theory, which will be the subject of Chapter 4.

Finally, the chapter will review pro-competitive justifications for fidelity rebates and the empirical evidence concerning such justification, in order to clarify the circumstances under which fidelity rebates may create efficiencies. This will allow us to understand the main argument of those who criticised the case law in supporting the view that all types of fidelity rebates require thorough economic assessment.

§3.02 THE CONCEPT OF REBATES AND THEIR IMPLICATIONS

There is a considerable diversity in the types of rebates and discounts companies engage in. Some forms of discounts are granted to some customers or segmented group of customers, depending only on the basis of these customers characteristics (excluding their pricing behaviour).[244] This form of discounting occurs 'when consumers are charged different prices but each consumer faces a constant price for all units of output purchased'.[245] Bishop and Walker argue that this form of discounting occurs when 'firms use information about their customers such as age or location' and are able to group their customers according to these parameters in order to price discriminate between the different groups of customers.[246] This type of discounting is called 'third-degree price discrimination'.[247] It is accepted that these types of rebates are

244. The Discussion Paper, para. 137.
245. Hal Varian, 'Price Discrimination' in Richard Schmalensee and Robert D Willig (eds) *Handbook of Industrial Organization* (Vol. 1, Elsevier 1989) 617.
246. Simon Bishop and Mike Walker, *The Economics of EC Competition Law* (2nd edn, Sweet & Maxwell 2010) 251.
247. Varian, 'Price Discrimination' (n. 245) 617.

welfare enhancing when they lead to an increase of the total sales,[248] and they are generally pro-competitive and can intensify competition.[249]

Other forms of discounts are granted depending on the number of units that the customer buys, in which case a rebate is granted if a customer increases it purchases – that pricing scheme is called quantity/volume discount.[250] When the discount applies only to those units that exceed a particular threshold once the particular threshold has been reached, the pricing scheme is called incremental rebates, i.e., rebates applicable only for the incremental purchases above the threshold. When the lower price applies to all sales when the customer's purchases equal or exceed some quantity threshold, the pricing scheme is called all-units discount,[251] retroactive rebates or 'fidelity/loyalty rebates'.[252] All of these discounting practices are also referred to collectively as 'conditional discounting'.[253]

While the definition of volume rebates applies to both incremental and retroactive rebates, there are some characteristics that make them completely different practices. This shall now be looked at step-by-step.

[A] Characteristics of Incremental Rebates

In general, incremental rebates are granted to a customer, depending on the purchased volume and are applicable only to those units that exceed the threshold once the particular threshold has been reached.

Incremental rebates could be applied either when the threshold is set as a standardised volume target applicable to all customers (*standardised incremental rebates*) or as an individualized volume target, specific to each particular customer (*individualised incremental rebates*). The difference is that in the former case, rebates are granted across the board, whereas, in the latter, rebates are offered taking into account the specificities of individual clients.

In the first case, discounts are offered to all customers regardless of their size and applied only for additional units once the threshold has been reached. In this format, the rebates are designed to expand manufacturer's production by selling more units. The higher sales will bring incremental cost savings and, thus, a realisation of economies of scale (because the unit costs of production fall with the increase of total production) and faster recovery of fixed costs.[254] On the other hand, customers have to increase their sales efforts to be able to purchase additional units and to obtain the

248. Richard Schmalensee, 'Output and Welfare Implications of Monopolistic Third-Degree Price Discrimination' (1981) 71(1) The American Economic Review 242; Hal Varian, 'Price Discrimination and Social Welfare' (1985) 75(4) The American Economic Review 870.
249. Mark Armstrong, *Price Discrimination* (MIT Press 2008).
250. Bishop and Walker (n. 246) 251.
251. Sreya Kolay, Greg Shaffer and Janusz Ordover, 'All-unit Discounts in Retail Contracts' (2004) 13(3) Journal of Economics and Management Strategy 429.
252. OECD Report (2002) 21.
253. OECD Report (2008) 29.
254. Ridyard, 'Exclusionary Pricing and Price Discrimination Abuses under Article 82' (n. 4).

discount.[255] As a result, total sales in the market will be increased. In this sense, volume rebate schemes serve as a tool that increases sales, total output and consumer welfare. In this sense, it is safe to assume that this form of rebate is beneficial to consumers because they reflect cost savings in distribution. Consequently, they have been considered by the EU Courts as legal.[256]

In the second case, discounts are offered and negotiated with each customer individually. They are linked to volume targets and applied only for the purchased additional units once the threshold has been reached. If the threshold is set as an individualised volume target depending on the customer's total demand, a loyalty effect is likely to occur. If the dominant company offers a very high percentage discount, and the threshold is set at a level that would anyhow be purchased by the client (i.e., individually), the customer will be induced to buy additional units at a lower price from the dominant company instead of another supplier. In this sense, the lower price for the additional units is the feature that urges the customers to purchase more units from the discounter, which means that the price is the feature that is driving customer's behaviour.[257]

[B] Characteristics of Retroactive Rebates

As already mentioned, retroactive rebates are applicable for all purchases not only on those that exceed the threshold, which means that a customer will be more incentivised to buy additional units from the dominant company instead of another supplier so as to reach the rebate threshold and to obtain a lower price for all purchases. Thus, the retroactive rebates might have the effect of inducing loyalty. However, this loyalty depends only on certain circumstances. First, if the customers prefer a dominant company's product because it is a 'must-stock' product (i.e., the company is dominant because the product has a strong brand or because of the inelastic demand) or because a competitor is capacity constrained to serve the total demand, the dominant company is an essential trading partner and customers normally buy certain amounts of their requirements from the dominant company.[258] This is the so-called assured (non-contestable) base of sales, which is secured for the dominant company – i.e., customers will purchase these quantities at the list price anyway. This position of the discounter leads to the establishment of a non-contestable part of demand for which the competitors are not able to compete. Thus, the real competition is for that part of sales for which the customer may prefer another supplier ('non-assured' part of sales/contestable part of demand). The situation might be completely different if the

255. Kallaugher (n. 215).
256. In *Hoffmann-La Roche* the CJEU held that quantity discounts linked to customers' purchasing volume are legal. In *Irish Sugar*, para. 153 the Court held that quantity discounts are normally unobjectionable. *See also Michelin I*, para. 71; *Michelin II*, para. 58 and *British Airways*, para. 101.
257. Anders Jessen, *Exclusionary Abuse after the Post Denmark I Case: The Role of the Effects-Based Approach under Article 102 TFEU* (Wolters Kluwer 2017) 101.
258. Derek Ridyard, 'Exclusive Contracts and Article 82 Enforcement: An Effects-Based Perspective' (2008) 4(2) European Competition Journal 585.

dominant company is dominant but not necessarily an unavoidable trading partner due to characteristics of the market and the product.[259] If the dominant company's product is not essential, i.e., there is no assured part of sales, the dominant company and its competitors compete for the whole demand (not only for the non-assured base of sales), which means that an establishment of a non-contestable part of demand is not possible and as such, a fidelity-enhancing effect described above cannot occur.[260]

When the dominant company is an unavoidable trading partner, it has information about the assured base of its customer's demand; it might set the threshold above this level in order to attract additional purchases.[261] Thus, the position of as an unavoidable trading partner is the condition that makes it possible for the dominant company to use the non-contestable part of demand as leverage to decrease the price of the contestable part of demand, which leads to the creation of loyalty that incentivises customers to transfer the purchases of all or almost all of their requirements from the dominant company.[262]

[C] Forms of Fidelity Rebates

Fidelity rebates may take many different forms, depending on the conditions that have to be fulfilled in order for a customer to obtain the discount. The conditions can be based on purchased volume, on an increase of the amount of the purchased volume compared to a preceding period or of the share of purchase requirements (categorised by the EU Courts as target/growth rebates),[263] or a commitment of a customer to supply all or almost all of its requirement from the dominant company (categorised by the EU Courts as exclusivity rebates),[264] or depending on the supply of a certain service by the customer.[265]

Rebates could also apply depending on the number of products that are included. Rebate schemes could be for one product (single rebates) or more than one (multi-product rebate). The main difference between single-product and multi-product rebates is that in the former, the granting of rebates applies for a single product and depends on the conditions mentioned above, whereas in the latter, the rebate applies when two (or more) products are sold in a bundle, which means that the bundled price is lower than the sum of the prices when the products are sold separately.[266]

Like incremental rebates, retroactive rebates could be applied when the threshold is set as a standardised volume target applicable to all customers (standardised

259. Jessen (n. 257) 114.
260. O'Donoghue and Padilla (n. 13) 469. On this point *see also* the Discussion Paper, para. 146.
261. Janusz Ordover and Greg Shaffer, 'Exclusionary Discounts' (2013) 31(5) International Journal of Industrial Organization 569, 578.
262. Ridyard, 'Exclusive Contracts and Article 82 Enforcement' (n. 258) 579.
263. *See* Chapter 2 and the discussion of *Michelin I and II, British Airways, Tomra.*
264. *See* Chapter 2 and the discussion of *Hoffmann-La Roche, British Gypsum.*
265. The Discussion Paper, para. 170.
266. OECD Report (2008) defined a 'bundled' discount as a combination of products offered at a lower price than the sum of the prices of the components of the bundle.

retroactive rebates) or as an individualized volume target, specific to each particular customer (individualised retroactive rebates).

In the first scenario, the threshold is set at the same level for all buyers. It could be too high for smaller buyers and/or too low for large buyers, which means that it is not related to the total customer's requirement. This means that a loyalty-enhancing effect is less likely to occur.[267] However, if the customers are limited in number and have similar demand patterns, the threshold may be standardised for all customers but still reflect their individual demands, in which case the rebate could still have a loyalty-inducing effect. This shows how, under certain circumstances, standardised retroactive rebates might create loyalty, leading to anticompetitive foreclosure.[268]

In the second scenario, the discounts are negotiated individually with each customer and applied for all units during a certain period once the threshold has been reached (retroactively). Because the threshold for obtaining rebates is negotiated individually depending on each customer's requirements, the dominant company may be able to set the threshold at levels above its customers assured base of sales, ensuring the rebate's loyalty-enhancing effect. The loyalty-enhancing effect will be stronger when the level of the threshold is close to or reflects the total requirements of customers, and when the rebate percentage is higher.[269] Other factors that may contribute to the strength of the loyalty-inducing effect is whether the discounter has a large assured base of sales and whether the market is characterised with significant economies of scale.[270]

The next section will review the economic theories analysing the anticompetitive effects of fidelity rebates in order to clarify whether there is an economic rationale for separating rebates into different categories, which are subject to different assessment and to understand under which circumstance they may have anticompetitive effects and whether these circumstances fit into the facts pattern of the case law discussed in Chapter 2. A more specific question in this regard is whether a price-cost test is well suited to identify when rebate schemes are anticompetitive.

§3.03 ECONOMIC THEORIES ANALYSING ANTICOMPETITIVE EFFECTS OF FIDELITY REBATES AND THE RELEVANCE OF A PRICE-COST TEST IN ITS ASSESSMENT

[A] Early Economic Theories of Anticompetitive Exclusionary Practices

The earliest economic theories analysing the effect of vertical contracts between a dominant company and its customers can be traced to the Chicago School scholars' contributions.[271] They argued that firms could not successfully employ these practices

267. The Discussion Paper, para. 159.
268. *See* Chapter 2 and the discussion of the *Michelin II* judgment.
269. The Discussion Paper, para. 153.
270. O'Donoghue and Padilla (n. 13) 479.
271. Robert Bork, *The Antitrust Paradox: A Policy at War with Itself* (The Tree Press 1993); Richard Posner, *Antitrust Law: An Economic Perspective* (2nd edn, University of Chicago Press 2009).

to maintain or extend its market power. Their explanation is based on the 'single monopoly profit theorem', according to which there is only one monopoly profit and there is nothing to be monopolised in the vertical market, i.e., vertical restraints should be per se legal.[272] The economic logic behind this explanation is that if a dominant company (which already is charging prices that maximises its profits) wants to sign exclusivity contracts with its customers, it has to compensate them for the loss of an alternative source of supply and to offer a price discount (Chicagoans assumed that they are final consumers) in order to convince them to accept the offer. According to this school of thought, these contracts would not be profitable for both sides because first, the monopoly profit would not be enough to compensate customers, and second, the price discount will lead to similar discounts offered by competing suppliers.[273] Thus, these practices will enhance competition and the dominant company will not be able to enhance its power and to obtain supra profits from imposing exclusive dealing as a method of excluding a competitor.[274] Consequently, these practices are pro-competitive and should be treated per se legal.

The Chicago School theorists' considerations had been criticised by the Post-Chicago's economists on the ground that 'certain market structure and certain type of collaborative activity are much more likely to have anticompetitive consequences than Chicago School antitrust writers imagine'.[275] These assumptions lead to the development of the so-called naked exclusion literature.

[B] Economic Theories of Exclusive Dealing: Naked Exclusion Literature

The economic literature developed a series of models that refuted the Chicagoans single monopoly profit theorem.[276] A series of studies developed models that provide a theoretical foundation for the concern that certain discounting practices can exclude a rival cheaply.[277] These conclusions are based on a number of models, which demonstrate empirically that a dominant company can offer slight discounts in the form of a

---

272. Richard Posner, 'The Next Step in the Antitrust Treatment of Restricted Distribution: Per Se Legality' (1981) 48(1) University of Chicago Law Review 6.
273. Bork, *The Antitrust Paradox* (n. 271) 304–307; Richard Posner, 'Exclusionary Practices and the Antitrust Laws' (1974) 41(3) The University of Chicago Law Review 506, 529.
274. Posner, 'Exclusionary Practices and the Antitrust Laws' (n. 273) 530.
275. Herbert Hovenkamp, 'The Reckoning of Post-Chicago Antitrust' in Cucinotta and Others (eds) *Post-Chicago Developments in Antitrust Law* (Edward Elgar Publishing 2002) 1, 5; Joseph Farrell, 'Deconstructing Chicago on Exclusive Dealing' (2005) 50(3) The Antitrust Bulletin 465.
276. Einer Elhauge, 'Tying, Bundled Discounts, and the Death of the Single Monopoly Profit Theory' (2009) 123 Harvard Law Review 397; Nicolas Economides, 'Tying, Bundling and Loyalty/Requirement Rebates' in Einer Elhauge (ed.) *Research Handbook on the Economics of Antitrust Law* (Edward Elgar Publishing 2012) 130.
277. Philippe Aghion and Patrick Bolton 'Contracts as a Barrier to Entry' (1987) 77 American Economic Review 388; Eric Rasmussen, Mark Ramseyer and John Wiley, 'Naked Exclusion' (1991) 81 American Economic Review 1137; Ilya Segal and Michael Whinston, 'Naked Exclusion: Comment' (2000) 90 American Economic Review 296; Einer Elhauge, 'How Loyalty Discounts Can Perversely Discourage Discounting' (2009) 5(2) Journal of Competition Law and Economics 189; Einer Elhauge and Abraham Wickelgren, 'Anticompetitive Market Division Through Loyalty Discount Without Buyer Commitment' (2012) Harvard discussion paper No. 723 http://papers.ssrn.com/sol3/papers.cfm?abstract_id=2125428 accessed 2 October 2015;

fixed fee or reduced wholesale price to its customers in order to induce them to accept exclusivity, which can lead to anticompetitive exclusion. The type of rebates in these models is not considered, but the grant of a fixed fee or reduced wholesale price for exclusivity suggests that the discount is applicable to all units, which correspond to the characteristics of retroactive rebates linked to exclusivity obligation, discussed above in section 3.02[C].

These studies could be separated into three groups depending on the market setting that the authors used in their models. The first group of models assume that the rival is not present in the market when the exclusive contracts are offered; there are economies of scale and the manufacturer has a first-mover advantage (in terms of pre-existing contract); the buyers are end users and they are not able to coordinate their behaviour; the entrant faces a significant fixed cost and the incumbent has to offer only a minimum number of buyers in order to prevent the entrant from reaching minimum viable scale to cover its cost.[278]

In one of the models, an additional commitment for a customer to pay the dominant company a penalty if he purchases from a competitor, was considered, in which case an entrant has to compensate the customer for the loss of rebates.[279] The model demonstrates that due to the limited scope of sales of the entrant, he would not be able to compensate the customer and will be excluded from the market. These models assume that the product of the supplier is essential for the customers and there are economies of scale.[280] This assumption fits neatly into the pattern of the case law discussed in Chapter 2, where the EU Court considered these circumstances as a fidelity-enhancing effect of rebates leading to the conclusion that they have potential anticompetitive effects.

The economic theory in these studies is mainly based on scale economies and the coordination failure theory. These economic theories are discussed in turn.

According to the coordination failure theory, a customer will be motivated to sign a contract not only because of the discount but also because he expects that if he refuses to sign, the other customers will sign and probably obtain a better discount.[281] Thus, the dominant company, by using the lack of coordination between customers can successfully deter entry by 'playing customers against each other', while customers may be better off in the long run if they all reject exclusivity, and entry occurs.[282] If enough customers sign exclusivity contracts, a competitor or an entrant will be

Einer Elhauge and Abraham Wickelgren, 'Robust Exclusion and Market Division through Loyalty Discounts with Buyer Commitment' (2014) Harvard discussion paper No. 722 http://papers.ssrn.com/sol3/papers.cfm?abstract_id=2125398 accessed 2 October 2015; Ordover and Shaffer (n. 261); David Spector, 'Exclusive Contracts and Demand Foreclosure (2011) 42(4) The RAND Journal of Economics 619; Timothy Brennan, 'Bundled Rebates as Exclusion Rather than Predation' (2008) 4 Journal of Competition Law and Economics 335.

278. Rasmusen, Ramseyer and Wiley (n. 277); Segal and Whinston, 'Naked Exclusion' (n. 277).
279. Aghion and Bolton (n. 277).
280. Derek Moore and Joshua Wright, 'Conditional Discounts and the Law of Exclusive Dealing' (2014) 22 George Mason Law Review 1205, 1215.
281. Segal and Whinston, 'Naked Exclusion' (n. 277).
282. Patrick Rey and Jean Tirole, 'A Primer on Foreclosure' in Mark Armstrong and Robert Porter (eds) Handbook of Industrial Organization (Vol. 3, Elsevier 2007) 2145.

prevented from achieving sufficient sales and would not be able to achieve minimum efficient scale (MES). Achieving MES means that a company needs to reach a certain level of output at which point the average costs are minimised (i.e., the average costs fall with the increase of output), and the company realises economies of scale and productive efficiency.

The second group of studies are based on models, which assume that the rivals are already present in the market when the dominant company offers exclusive contracts and the customers are competing downstream firms (instead of final consumers considered in the first set of models described above).[283] This assumption also fits into the facts of the case law discussed in Chapter 2, because in all of the cases, the dominant companies offered fidelity rebates to competing downstream customers.

The mechanism of exclusion in these models is based on the downstream competition theory. According to this theory, the dominant company can put its customers (which are competing downstream firms) in the position of the prisoner's dilemma, according to which the firm must choose whether to sign an exclusive contract and to get a discount or to refuse to sign the exclusive contract, losing profits.[284] Each customer will choose to sign the contract and to obtain a discount, expecting that if it refuses, its competitors (other downstream companies) would sign and obtain a lower price for the input, putting it at a cost disadvantage, even when in the longer term, they will get the input at a lower price if they all refuse to sign, hindering the possibility of the dominant company excluding its competitor.[285] On the other hand, if a customer decides not to sign exclusivity with the dominant company and accepts the lower price from the entrant, the dominant company will lower the price for the customers that remain exclusive. For that reason, all of the customers will accept signing for exclusivity even though 'it is not in the buyers' collective interest'.[286] Thus, only a small discount will be enough for the customer to accept the offer, which means that the dominant company would not be required to price below cost.[287] Some of the theoretical models demonstrate that an upstream monopolist that sells to competing downstream firms can profitably use exclusive contracts to deter entry even where scale economies are absent and the incumbent and the entrant have similar costs.[288]

283. John Simpson and Abraham Wickelgren, 'The Use of Exclusive Contracts to Deter Entry' (2001) https://papers.ssrn.com/sol3/papers.cfm?abstract_id=287059 accessed 17 October 2017; John Simpson and Abraham Wickelgren, 'Naked Exclusion, Efficient Breach, and Downstream Competition' (2007) 97 American Economic Review 1305; Jose Miguel Abito and Julian Wright, 'Exclusive Dealing with Imperfect Downstream Competition' (2008) 26(1) International Journal of Industrial Organization 227; DeGraba, 'Naked Exclusion' (n. 299).
284. Simpson and Wickelgren, 'The Use of Exclusive Contracts to Deter Entry' (n. 283).
285. *Ibid.*
286. Spector, 'Loyalty Rebates: An Assessment of Competition Concerns and a Proposed Structured Rule of Reason' (n. 4) 99.
287. Simpson and Wickelgren, 'Naked Exclusion, Efficient Breach, and Downstream Competition' (n. 283).
288. Simpson and Wickelgren, 'The Use of Exclusive Contracts to Deter Entry' (n. 283); Simpson and Wickelgren, 'Naked Exclusion, Efficient Breach, and Downstream Competition' (n. 283); Elhauge and Wickelgren, 'Anticompetitive Market Division through Loyalty Discount without Buyer Commitment' (n. 277).

Other studies revealed, that in some cases, rebates do not constitute a real price reduction because the grant of rebates is accompanied by an increase in the initial prices.[289] In this case, the dominant company does not lose any profits but, at the same time, the customers receive rebates. In this case, rebates are not technically a real discount because the dominant company increased the 'a la-carte prices above the but-for levels'; it serves as a punishment mechanism for disloyal customers.[290] A recent empirical study shows, that 'the prices in the counterfactual without rebate scheme may be lower than under the rebate scheme'.[291] Under this scenario, the discounter's prices will always remain above cost, which makes the application of a price-cost test unable to identify the anticompetitive effects that would occur.[292]

The third set of studies assumed that the product is differentiated. When a product offered by a rival is differentiated, from that of the dominant company, customers might be tempted to increase their purchases from the dominant company so as to obtain the rebates while simultaneously be willing to purchase a competitor's differentiated product. In this case, the customer may decide to buy a part of its requirement from an alternative supplier even if the price is above the dominant firm's prices.[293] In this situation, even if the dominant company's effective price for the incremental units is below cost, i.e., the dominant company fails the price-cost test; an anticompetitive effect is less likely to occur.[294] Under this scenario, a price-cost test cannot help to determine whether the rebates might lead to anticompetitive exclusion for the following reasons.[295] First, the customer might choose a competitor's product regardless of the price because the product is differentiated in terms of characteristics or quality. Second, because the product is different, it might require a higher cost of production, which means competitor's cost are higher than that of the dominant company, which does not mean that the competitor is less efficient. For some of the customers, the differentiated product might be superior and they might consider that the competitor is more efficient even if his costs are higher than the dominant

289. Faella (n. 4) 380.
290. Economides, 'Tying, Bundling and Loyalty/Requirement Rebates' (n. 276) 149; *see also* Elhauge, 'How Loyalty Discounts Can Perversely Discourage Discounting' (n. 277); Elhauge, 'Tying, Bundled Discounts, and the Death of the Single Monopoly Profit Theory' (n. 276) 397; Nicholas Economides and Ioannis Lianos, 'The Elusive Antitrust Standard on Bundling in Europe and in the United States in the Aftermath of the Microsoft cases' (2009) 76(2) Antitrust Law Journal 483.
291. Frank Maier-Rigaud and Ulrich Schwalbe, 'Do Retroactive Rebates Imply Lower Prices for Consumers?' (2013) https://papers.ssrn.com/sol3/papers.cfm?abstract_id=2276396 accessed 15 November 2017. The empirical model also demonstrates 'that consumers may not only be harmed by higher prices but also by what has been termed overbuying'.
292. Jonathan Jacobson, 'A Note on Loyalty Discounts' (2010) 9(5) The Antitrust Source-American Bar Association.
293. Economides, 'Tying, Bundling and Loyalty/Requirement Rebates' (n. 276) 130; Nicholas Economides, 'Quality Variations in the Circular Model of Variety-Differentiated Products' (1993) 23(2) Regional Science and Urban Economics 235.
294. Geradin, 'A Proposed Test for Separating Pro-Competitive Loyalty Rebates from Anti-competitive Ones' (n. 4) 62.
295. Economides, 'Tying, Bundling and Loyalty/Requirement Rebates (n. 276) 193.

company.[296] Thus, there is no economic sense to compare a dominant firm's costs with the price 'to evaluate the survival of the rival's products that differ in quality and variety from those of the dominant firm'.[297]

The same economic theories are relevant in the case of anticompetitive exclusion with partial exclusivity. Several researchers who study the effect of fidelity rebates have reported that rebates agreements could take the form of partial exclusivity while having the same effect as absolute exclusive dealing.[298] Where the contracts are near-exclusive (with threshold level below 100%, and a large dominant supplier competing with small rivals) DeGraba found that exclusivity agreements still lead to anticompetitive results even if the rival remains in the market (which suggests that there is no actual exit of a competitor).[299] Moreover, his model shows that exclusion is possible even if the effective price is above cost, because the loyalty payments still result in anticompetitive exclusion, which make the price-cost test invalid.[300] These conclusions provide support for the argument that the loyalty payments lead to a fidelity-enhancing effect of fidelity rebates. These models demonstrate that fidelity rebates that require 70% of the customers' demand, i.e., partial exclusivity, could have the same effect as in 100% requirement, i.e., similar to exclusive dealing.

In some of the studies, the models identify an anticompetitive effect of fidelity rebates without buyer commitment to purchase exclusively from the dominant company because of the switching costs that the customer has to incur in order to purchase from a competitor.[301] The switching costs arise from the retroactivity of rebates, i.e., the dominant company can use the non-contestable part of demand as leverage to decrease the price for the contestable part of demand, thereby creating artificially switching costs.[302] These switching costs combined with the inability of competitors to expand their scope and to compensate the customers for the loss of rebates can create

296. Steven Salop, 'The Raising Rivals' Cost Foreclosure Paradigm, Conditional Pricing Practices and the Flawed Incremental Price-cost Test' (2016) http://papers.ssrn.com/sol3/papers.cfm?abstract_id=2381016 accessed 3 May 2016.
297. Economides and Lianos (n. 290) 509; *see also* Spector, 'Loyalty Rebates: An Assessment of Competition Concerns and a Proposed Structured Rule of Reason' (n. 4) 104; Nicolas Economides, 'Loyalty/Requirement Rebates and the Antitrust Modernization Commission: What is the Appropriate Liability Standard' (2009) 54(2) The Antitrust Bulletin 259, 274.
298. Willard Tom, David Balto and Neil Averitt, 'Anticompetitive Aspects of Market-Share Discounts and Other Incentives to Exclusive Dealing' (2000) 67(3) Antitrust Law Journal 615; Spector, 'Loyalty Rebates: An Assessment of Competition Concerns and a Proposed Structured Rule of Reason (n. 4) 89; Einer Elhauge, 'Loyalty Discount and Naked Exclusion' (2008) http://lsr.nellco.org/harvard_olin/608/ accessed 12 October 2017; Andrew Gavil, 'Exclusionary Distribution Strategies for Dominant Firms: Striking a Better Balance' (2004) 72(1) Antitrust Law Journal 3.
299. Patrick DeGraba, 'Naked Exclusion by a Dominant Input Supplier: Exclusive Contracting and Loyalty Discounts' (2013) 31 International Journal of Industrial Organization 516; Tom, Balto and Averitt (n. 298); Gavil (n. 298).
300. DeGraba, 'Naked Exclusion' (n. 299) 538.
301. Ilya Segal, 'Contracting with externalities' (1999) 114(2) The Quarterly Journal of Economics 337; Kolay, Shaffer and Ordover (n. 251).
302. Frank Maier-Rigaud, 'Switching Costs in Retroactive Rebates-What's Time Got to Do with it?' (2005) https://papers.ssrn.com/sol3/papers.cfm?abstract_id=666722 accessed 17 April 2017.

anticompetitive effects even if conditions require less than 100% requirement.[303] This reasoning can be found in *British Airways* and *Tomra* where the GC held that competitors were not able to achieve the same scope of sales due to the limited customer's remaining demand so as to be able to grant similar rebates and to offset the lower price of the dominant company.[304]

In some of the theoretical models, an upstream monopolist that sells to competing downstream firms can profitably use exclusive contracts to deter entry even where scale economies are absent and the incumbent and the entrant have similar costs.

In one survey, Fumagalli and Motta have challenged the previous results, arguing that if the buyers are intermediate (not final consumers), and if there is an intense competition between the buyers, exclusive dealing does not deter entry.[305] Soon after these findings, other studies have analysed their results and take the opposite view claiming that even if the buyers compete effectively in the downstream market 'it would be wrong to conclude that it makes anticompetitive exclusive deals less likely'.[306]

All of the models covered by the naked exclusion literature, summarised above, demonstrate that the incumbent could exclude the rival without profit sacrifice, which suggests that a price-cost test cannot be a relevant tool for the assessment of a possible anticompetitive effect. The central economic logic is that a dominant company can foreclose a substantial part of the market through fidelity rebates agreements by preventing its competitors from achieving a MES, which ultimately will result in raising their cost – an economic concept known as 'Raising Rivals' Cost' (RRC).[307]

[C] Economic Theory of RRC

The RRC theory provides a theoretical foundation of how the conduct by a dominant company can deprive its rivals of access to crucial sales or inputs, causing them to raise their price or reduce their output and exit the market in the long run. This, in turn, allows the dominant company to price at an above competitive level to the detriment of consumers.[308]

To be profitable and remain successful (if they are already in the market) or to enter the market, the rivals need to achieve MES. The relevant level of MES is different

303. Elhauge, 'How Loyalty Discounts Can Perversely Discourage Discounting' (n. 277); Elhauge and Wickelgren, 'Anticompetitive Market Division Through Loyalty Discounts Without Buyer Commitment' (n. 277).
304. *British Airways*, para. 276; *Tomra*, para. 270.
305. Ciara Fumagalli and Massimo Motta, 'Exclusive Dealing And Entry When Buyers Compete' (2006) 96(3) The American Economic Review 785.
306. Simpson and Wickelgren, 'Naked Exclusion, Efficient Breach, and Downstream Competition' (n. 283); Jose Miguel Abito and Julian Wright, *Exclusive Dealing and Entry, when Buyers Compete: Comment* (mimeo, National University of Singapore 2005); Julian Wright, 'Exclusive Dealing and Entry, When Buyers Compete: Comment' (2009) 99(3) American Economic Review 1070.
307. Thomas Krattenmaker and Steven Salop, 'Anticompetitive Exclusion: Raising Rivals' Costs to Achieve Power over Price' (1986) 96 Yale Law Journal 209, 234.
308. Salop, 'The Raising Rivals' Cost Foreclosure Paradigm' (n. 296); Moore and Wright (n. 280).

for each industry.[309] In some markets, the MES could be very low and each competitor is able to easily obtain enough sales to reach MES and to compete successfully with the dominant undertaking. In others – e.g., innovative industries – the level of MES will likely be higher because the ratio between fixed and variable costs is high, which means that a competitor or entrant needs to significantly increase its level of output in order to minimise its average costs (since average costs fall with the increase of output), otherwise 'the likelihood of the firm surviving would presumably be lower'.[310] Admittedly, technology industries with high costs for development and research (which can be associated with sunk costs) can reach large economies of scale, which might create significant entry barriers.[311]

In markets characterised by high fixed costs and constant demand, it may be difficult for a competitor to achieve MES by serving only part of the market.[312] If the dominant company is engaging in practices that make it difficult for a competitor to achieve MES, its marginal cost would be higher than the dominant supplier and he will be inefficient, marginalised as a competitor even if not completely excluded from the market.[313] An even worse outcome occurs if fidelity rebates preclude a competitor from achieving minimum viable scale (MVS), which is the minimum scale of output that a company needs to achieve in order to cover its costs (average cost equals price). If a company cannot reach MVS, it will exit the market.

Two types of raising rivals' costs are conceivable in the context of rebates. If a rebate makes a rivals' access to crucial inputs more difficult or even impossible, this might result in raising rivals' input costs; if it forecloses rivals' access to customers instead, it might result in reducing rivals' revenues. In both cases, competitors might be foreclosed from the market, or become marginalised and less competitive. Thus, RRC could be achieved either through raising rivals' input costs (input foreclosure) or limiting rivals' output/reducing rivals' revenues (customer foreclosure).[314]

In an input foreclosure scenario, an agreement with the suppliers of a crucial input might substantially raise the input costs of the purchaser's competitors, as they

309. Roger Arnold, *Microeconomics* (Cengage Learning 2008) 190.
310. David Audretsch and Others, 'The Post-Entry Performance of New Firms' in Arjen van Witteloostuijn (ed.) *Market Evolution: Competition and Cooperation* (Vol. 20, Springer Science & Business Media 2013) 248.
311. David Harbord and Tom Hoehn, 'Barriers to Entry and Exit in European Competition Policy' (1994) 14(4) International Review of Law and Economics 411.
312. On this point *see* O'Donoghue and Padilla (n. 13) 470. They explain that if demand is constant, competitors are dependent on the existing customer base, whereas if demand is growing competitors have opportunities to achieve minimum efficient scale and to minimize the effect of fidelity rebates. On this point *see* O'Donoghue and Padilla (n 13) 470. They explain that if demand is constant, competitors are dependent on the existing customer base, whereas if demand is growing competitors have opportunities to achieve minimum efficient scale and to minimize the effect of fidelity rebates.
313. Salop, 'The Raising Rivals' Cost Foreclosure Paradigm' (n. 296) 16; Joshua Wright, 'Moving Beyond Naïve Foreclosure Analysis' (2012) 19(5) George Mason Law Review 1163, 1166.
314. Steven Salop, 'Conditional Pricing Practices and the Two Anticompetitive Exclusion Paradigms' Georgetown University Law Center, Presentation at the DOJ/FTC Workshop on Conditional Pricing Practices (23 June 2014); Salop, 'The Raising Rivals' Cost Foreclosure Paradigm' (n. 296).

have to 'shift to a higher cost supplier or less efficient inputs'.[315] In this case, the rivals might keep its output at the MES or even at the MVS, but their costs will be higher (because of the higher cost of the input) – with the result that they will become weaker and less efficient competitors.[316] Input foreclosure will also raise the prices charged to customers, which means that consumer harm will be simultaneous.[317] In effect, this means that input foreclosure can reduce competition in situations 'not limited to failure to achieve MES or MVS'.[318] For that reason, in evaluating input foreclosure the issue is not the degree of foreclosure but merely whether the foreclosure will raise rivals' costs.[319]

In a customer foreclosure scenario, a fidelity rebate might foreclose competitors' access to a significant customer base. This will prevent them from reaching MVS – which will force them to exit the market or from reaching MES – in which case they might remain in the market, but will become marginalised as competitors.[320] According to Salop, an anticompetitive effect can occur even if the rival can achieve MES or MVS because customer foreclosure might restrain the competitors' ability to expand profitably (i.e., it will limit the incentives to invest or innovate), and reduce the competitive constraints on the dominant company's pricing.[321]

Input and customer foreclosure can occur at the same time if the exclusive agreement is between a dominant company and its distributors, which would reinforce the impact of the conduct.[322] In that case, the distributors are both customers and input providers – since they are the direct customers of the relevant product, but they also provide distribution services that are an important input for making the product reach final consumers.[323] Exclusive agreements with distributors may 'cause rivals to incur greater costs in seeking out new avenues of distribution or in using higher cost distributors or methods of distribution'.[324] As a result, the dominant company may use an exclusive agreement with its distributors to exclude or hinder competitors by locking up a sufficient part of the distribution.[325] On the other hand, coordination failure/downstream competition theory discussed above, may prevent dealers resisting

315. Krattenmaker and Salop, 'Anticompetitive Exclusion: Raising Rivals' Costs to Achieve Power over Price' (n. 307) 234.
316. Salop, 'The Raising Rivals' Cost Foreclosure Paradigm' (n. 296) 18.
317. Steven Salop, https://truthonthemarket.com/2013/06/07/wright-is-right-and-price-cost-safe-harbors-are-wrong-the-raising-rivals-cost-paradigm-loyalty-discounts-and-exclusive-dealing/ 7 June 2013 accessed 13 February 2015.
318. Salop, 'The Raising Rivals' Cost Foreclosure Paradigm' (n. 296) 19.
319. Steven Salop, https://truthonthemarket.com/ accessed 15 February 2015.
320. Daniel Crane and Graciela Miralles, 'Toward a Unified Theory of Exclusionary Vertical Restraints' (2011) 84 Southern California Law Review 605, 639–640 (explaining how foreclosure limiting entrant's share to below minimum viable scale is sufficient to harm competition).
321. Salop, 'The Raising Rivals' Cost Foreclosure Paradigm' (n. 296) 21.
322. *Ibid.*, 23.
323. *Ibid.*
324. Jonathan Jacobson, 'Exclusive dealing, Foreclosure, and Consumer Harm' (2002) 70(2) Antitrust Law Journal 311, 352.
325. Sean Gates, 'Antitrust by Analogy: Developing Rules for Loyalty Rebates and Bundled Discounts' (2013) 79(1) Antitrust Law Journal 99.

the fidelity rebates offer, and as such, to prevent a competitor from entering or from bidding for sales/access.[326]

In both cases – input and customer foreclosure – competitor's cost are raised, i.e., he becomes less efficient and can be excluded or marginalised without the dominant company being required to set prices below cost. If a dominant company enters into agreements with its distributors, even small discounts might lead to de facto exclusivity.[327]

In markets where achieving MES is crucial, the discounter has to target only a part of the sales open to competition that is large enough to prevent the rivals achieving MES.[328] In this sense, the rebates scheme might be used to deprive a competitors' access to sufficient scale of sales, which might in turn make them less efficient and prevent them from imposing a competitive constraint on the dominant company or of hindering the entry of a potential competitor.[329] In those cases, whether the price for the contestable part of demand is above or below cost is not relevant, because even if a competitor can offer a price that can compensate the customer for the loss of rebates, the competitor might still not be in position to reach MES because he does not have enough scale of production. If a competitor is not able to achieve MES, its cost will rise, being higher than that of the dominant company. It makes no economic sense to compare a dominant firm's cost with the price in order to assess whether a competitor can offset the effect of rebates. Thus, with this strategy a dominant company might exclude a competitor by raising their costs without profit sacrifice.[330]

[D] The Relevance of the Price-Cost Test

Fidelity rebates are discounting practices in their nature. As noted above in section 3.02[A], when incremental volume rebates apply, the lower price for the additional units will nudge customers to commit purchases preferably from the dominant supplier, which they have to transfer from rival suppliers. Thus, the lower price for the additional units is the feature that urges the customers to purchase more units from the discounter, which means that the price is the feature that is driving customer's behaviour.[331] If the price for the incremental units could be lower than the average incremental cost per unit, it might lead to an anticompetitive exclusion of competitors.[332] Thus, this form of rebate is a pricing conduct and the assessment of incremental volume rebates should take the same form as the test for predation, where the

326. Alan Meese, 'Exclusive Dealing, the Theory of the Firm, and Raising Rivals' Costs: Toward a New Synbook' (2005) 50(3) The Antitrust Bulletin 371, 407.
327. Salop, https://truthonthemarket.com/ accessed 15 February 2015.
328. OECD Report (2002), UK contribution.
329. Spector, 'Loyalty Rebates: An Assessment of Competition Concerns and a Proposed Structured Rule of Reason' (n. 4) 110.
330. Krattenmaker and Salop (n. 307); Alden Abbott and Joshua Wright, 'Antitrust Analysis of Tying Arrangements and Exclusive Dealing' in Keith N Hylton (ed.) *Antitrust Law and Economics* (Ch. 8, Edward Elgar Publishing 2010) 183; Vickers, 'Abuse of Market Power' (n. 4).
331. Jessen (n. 257) 101.
332. DeGraba and Simpson (n. 43).

price-cost test is applicable.[333] In this case, rebates have to be treated under the law of predatory pricing.[334]

The same principle would seem to be relevant, when the dominant company is dominant but not necessarily an unavoidable trading partner.[335] In this case, the dominant company and its competitors compete for the whole demand (not only for the contestable sales), which means that competition will be based on prices. If a dominant company's pricing is predatory, anticompetitive exclusion of competitors is more likely, which makes the price-cost test in this particular case an important tool in the assessment of the legality of rebates.[336] In summary, only when all sales are contestable, the economically appropriate test that can distinguish pro-competitive from anticompetitive rebates is the traditional predatory pricing price-cost test.[337]

In contrast, when retroactive rebates apply, the lower price for the additional purchases above the threshold leads to a price reduction for the units purchased up to the threshold. This condition creates a stronger inducement (compared to incremental rebates) for the customers to commit purchases preferably from the dominant supplier thus, enhancing loyalty. As indicated above, this pricing strategy is relevant only if the dominant company is an essential/unavoidable trading partner and customers must buy certain amounts of their requirements from the dominant company. This leads to the establishment of a non-contestable part of demand for which the competitors are not able to compete. Thus, the real competition is for part of sales, i.e., contestable part of demand.

As can be recalled from Chapter 2, those who criticised the treatment of fidelity rebates by the EU courts suggested that if a competitor can match (without pricing below cost) and beat the dominant company's rebates, he would be able to compete. This leads to the conclusion that a price-cost test should be used. However, some economists were aware that due to the characteristics of the retroactive rebates when applied by a dominant company with unavoidable trading partner status, a traditional predatory pricing price-cost test is not relevant because the demand is separated into non-contestable and contestable parts and the real competition is only for the latter.[338] Therefore, it seems reasonable that the effects of a rebate scheme be analysed only on contestable share. For that reason a modified price-cost test, which aims to compare

333. O'Donoghue and Padilla (n. 13) 484; Bishop and Walker (n. 246) correction made by Walker for the second edition.

334. The European Commission has dealt with incremental rebates only in Case COMP/39.451 Velux (not published). The case was closed after evaluation of the rebates at issue and the conclusion that they were not below costs and as such unable to lead to anticompetitive foreclosure. For comments of the case *see* Svend Albaek and Adina Claici, 'The Velux Case – An in-depth Look at Rebates and More' (2009) 2 Competition Policy Newsletter 44; Bill Batchelor and Kayran Jebelli, 'Rebates in Stage of Velux: Filling in the Gaps in the Article 102 TFEU Enforcement Guidance' (2011) 11 European Competition Law Review 545.

335. Jessen (n. 257) 114.

336. Ordover and Shaffer (n. 261) 577.

337. Benjamin Klein and Andres Lerner, *Price-Cost Tests in Antitrust Analysis of Single Product Loyalty Contracts* (2016) 631, 640 https://papers.ssrn.com/sol3/papers.cfm?abstract_id=2775455 accessed 1 December 2017.

338. Jacobson, 'A Note of loyalty Discounts' (n. 292); Klein and Lerner, 'Price-Cost Tests in Antitrust Analysis of Single Product Loyalty Contracts' (n. 337) 633.

the price with the loyalty discount for the whole purchased units attributed only for the contestable sales with the costs of providing these incremental units, was proposed.[339]

This modified test mirrors the logic of the discount attribution test developed for the assessment of bundle rebates, according to which the discounts of all products in the bundle is attributed to the competitive product.[340] Then, the price-cost test is asking whether the price of the competitive product (with the attributed discount) is below an appropriate measure of cost; an affirmative answer shows that the dominant company is selling the competitive product below its cost, which might foreclose an as efficient competitor, leading to negative effect on competition.[341] It should be noted that the main difference between single-product and bundled rebates is that in the former case, the demand for one product is separated into non-contestable and contestable parts and the dominant company is trying to increase the sales in the contestable part, whereas in the latter, the dominant company aims to increase sales for the competitive product in the bundle.[342] Thus, in the bundling rebates context, it is only necessary to distinguish between competitive and non-competitive products in the bundle and to compare the attributed discounted price for the competitive product with the cost over the total units of the competitive product sold.[343]

Following the same logic, the modified test for fidelity rebates, asks whether the price for the contestable sales is predatory, in which case the rival may be forced to offer very low or even negative price in order to compete with the dominant company, which could force the competitor to exit the market or to become inefficient (or to deter entry).[344]

A simple hypothetical example can help in understanding the logic of this proposal. Assume that the dominant company's list price is EUR 10 per unit and a customer's assured base of sales is 100 units, and the customer is willing to buy 30 units from a competitor. The dominant company might set a threshold for obtaining rebates above the level of customers' assured base, i.e., at 130 units, and to offer a 10% rebate for all units, not only for the incremental purchases, once the threshold is reached. If a customer reaches the threshold, the price will be EUR 9 for all units. This means that the total price paid by a customer before the rebates is 100 x 10 = 1000 and 130 x 9 = 1170 with rebates, which means that the last 30 units were sold for EUR 170, which makes the price per unit EUR 5.67 (for the incremental 30 units). This

339. Initially, the modified price-cost test for fidelity rebates was recommended by Phillip Areeda and Herbert Hovenkamp, *Antitrust Law* (3th edn, Little Brown 2008) 341 and later on supported by Klein and Lerner, 'Price-Cost Tests in Antitrust Analysis of Single Product Loyalty Contracts' (n. 337) 633. *See also* Waelbroeck (n. 4); Federico, 'When are rebates exclusionary' (n. 4). The test was proposed by the US DoJ, Competition and Monopoly: Single-Firm Conduct Under Section 2 of the Sherman Act 101 (September, 2008) and withdrawn one year later.

340. Jacobson, 'A Note of loyalty Discounts' (n. 292) 7; Timothy Muris and Vernon Smith, 'Antitrust and Bundled Discounts: An Experimental Analysis' (2008) 75 Antitrust Law Journal 399, 425.

341. Antitrust Modernization Commission (AMC), Report and Recommendations (2007) 83. The Report recommended the attribution test as 'the most promising source of an economically sensible and administrable safe harbour for bundled rebates or discounts'.

342. Economides, 'Tying, Bundling and Loyalty/Requirement Rebates' (n. 276).

343. Geradin, 'A Proposed Test for Separating Pro-Competitive Loyalty Rebates from Anti-competitive Ones' (n. 4) 63. The same approach was adopted by the AMC, *see* n. 341.

344. O'Donoghue and Padilla (n. 13) 469.

technically means that the effective price for the last 30 units will be discounted with 43.3%; which makes the discount for the incremental units much higher than the rebate percentage.

Under this scenario, the price that the competitor has to offer for the incremental units to compensate the customer for the loss of rebates is EUR 5.67. This price is below the cost (EUR 6). With this strategy, it will be impossible for a competitor to compete with the dominant company for this part of demand because he cannot match the rebates of the dominant company without losses. On the other hand, the dominant supplier does not incur losses as far as it can recoup the rebate on its whole range of sales.[345] The rationale behind this argument is that if the attributed price is above the costs for the contestable part of sales, any as efficient as the discounter competitor will be able to compete for the contestable sales.[346]

However, although this logic seems reasonable, many have questioned the usefulness of this modified test, arguing that it is subject to significant implementation errors, for a number of reasons.[347] First, the accuracy of the test depends on the proper estimation of the contestable share of sales, which is a difficult, expensive and unpredictable task.[348] In the context of bundled rebates, the discount for the bundle should be attributed to the competitive product in the bundle (which is a distinct product), whereas in the context of single-product rebates, the discount should be attributed to the contestable share of demand for one product. From this perspective, although the economic logic of the test is similar for both single-product retroactive rebates and bundle rebates, its practical implementation differs significantly in terms of estimation of the contestable part of demand.

This raises the question as to how to identify the contestable share of demand. One may argue that contestable share is equal to the market share of the dominant company, i.e., if a dominant company has 70% market share, it means that contestable part is 30%, or as an alternative, contestable share may relate to the dominant company discount level, i.e., if the threshold for obtaining rebates is 80%, then the contestable part is 20%.[349] Others, may argue that contestable share is the difference between non-contestable units and the threshold for obtaining the discounts, i.e., if non-contestable share is 60% and the threshold for obtaining rebates is 80%, it means that contestable share is 20%.[350] Thus, the uncertainty of defining contestable share may lead to an unpredictable outcome, leading to disagreement between the two sides relying on different calculations.[351] For these reasons, the application of the test in practice is questionable. Second, the identification of the appropriate measure of cost

345. Geradin, 'A Proposed Test for Separating Pro-Competitive Loyalty Rebates from Anti-Competitive Ones' (n. 4) 58.
346. Benjamin Klein, 'The Economics of Alternative Legal Standards for Loyalty Discounts', presentation at FTC/DOJ Workshop On Conditional Pricing Practices 23 June 2014.
347. Salop, 'The Raising Rivals' Cost Foreclosure Paradigm' (n. 296).
348. Zenger (n. 4) 35; Moore and Wright (n. 280) 1242; Robert Lande, 'Should Predatory Pricing Rules Immunize Exclusionary Discounts?' (2006) Utah Law Review 863, 880.
349. Moore and Wright (n. 280) 1243.
350. Economides, 'Tying, Bundling and Loyalty/Requirement Rebates' (n. 276) 31.
351. Salop, 'The Raising Rivals' Cost Foreclosure Paradigm' (n. 296).

might be an issue in industries with high fixed costs and relatively low marginal costs and with corresponding difficulties in accounting sunk costs.[352]

However, even if one accepts that the test can be reliable, in the following scenarios drawn from the economic literature discussed above the test cannot rule whether the conduct would lead to anticompetitive exclusion:

(i) When the product is differentiated – there is no economic sense to compare an efficiency level of firms producing differentiated products.
(ii) When rebates are not real price reduction and serve as a punishment mechanism for disloyal customers – there is no economic sense to apply a price-cost test because the dominant company's cost will remain always above cost.
(iii) When rebates limit competitor's ability to reach MES – there is no economic sense to apply a price-cost test because if a competitor cannot reach MES he cannot operate profitably given their fixed cost and his costs will always be higher than the incumbent.

Having mapped the circumstances under which fidelity rebates can have anticompetitive effects and the relevance of the price-cost test in identifying these effects, the next part of this chapter analyses under which circumstances fidelity rebates can have pro-competitive effects, which might balance their anticompetitive effects.

§3.04 EFFICIENCY JUSTIFICATIONS FOR FIDELITY REBATES

There is a large volume of published studies describing that fidelity rebates could have anticompetitive or pro-competitive effects depending on the circumstances.[353] Some of the studies reporting that the main purpose of granting rebates may be that the dominant company is trying to increase sales and consequently their profits by achieving efficiencies and that volume discount and non-linear pricing exists in a variety of models where exclusionary motives are absent.[354] These efficiency considerations could be summarised into several categories, which are discussed in turn.

[A] Economies of Scale and Recovery of Fixed Cost

Since rebates allow sellers to charge their customers different prices for the same good or services, technically they are a form of price discrimination. In some industries characterised by high fixed costs and low marginal costs, firms cannot charge all their

352. Jacobson, 'A note of loyalty rebates' (n. 292).
353. *See* n. 4.
354. Patrick Greenlee and David Reitman, *Competing With Loyalty Discounts* (2005) http://papers.ssrn.com/sol3/papers.cfm?abstract_id=502303 accessed 4 April 2015; *see also* Benjamin Klein, 'Exclusive Dealing as Competition for Distribution on the Merits' (2003) 12 Global Market Law Review 119, 140–141; Patrick Greenlee and David Reitman, 'Distinguishing Competitive and Exclusionary Uses of Loyalty Discounts' (2005) 50(3) The Antitrust Bulletin 441.

customers with a uniform price equal to marginal costs because this would make it impossible to recover their fixed costs. In that case, and as explained by Ridyard, price discrimination could be a welfare enhancing solution for the fixed cost recovery problem.[355] Ridyard showed that if a firm with high fixed costs has prices equal to short-run marginal costs (which are equal or close to zero), it would fail to recover its fixed costs.[356] Consequently, such a firm must charge prices higher than the marginal cost. Higher prices mean less products sold because some customers will stop buying at the higher price. By charging different customers or markets with different price-cost margins, the firm will maximise its production volume while recovering its fixed costs.

In this scenario, price discrimination is a tool for recovering high fixed costs. A similar situation occurs when a firm has joint fixed costs for producing different products, selling them in different markets (economies of scope). In this case, the firm will charge higher prices in a market, with a lower elasticity of demand, and lower prices in the market with high elasticity of demand, the so-called Ramsey pricing.[357] This pricing strategy is the most efficient way for the firm to recover their joint fixed costs by earning different returns from the different markets.

These examples show that in some industries, price discrimination brings efficiencies that cannot be obtained by using linear pricing.[358] However, this assumes that the rebates imply true discount, which stimulate sales and that the condition of obtaining those rebates are linked to the purchased quantity.

[B] Stimulating Retailers' Efforts: The So-Called Hold-Up Problem

Some economic studies revealed how rebates might be used to stimulate retailers' efforts and to fix the so-called hold-up problem. The 'hold-up problem' is defined in the Guidelines on Vertical Restraints, as a situation in which:

> [t]here are client-specific investments to be made by either the supplier or the buyer, such as in special equipment or training. For instance, a component manufacturer that has to build new machines and tools in order to satisfy a particular requirement of one of its customers. The investor may not commit the necessary investments before particular supply arrangements are fixed.[359]

According to Rogerson, a hold-up problem occurs: (1) when two parties, i.e., the supplier and the customer must make some specific investments prior to the transaction in order to prepare for it; and (2) the parameters of the contract are not specified before the factual transactions.[360] From the hold-up problems' definition, it is obvious that first, there is some investment that has to be made by one part and second, there

355. Ridyard, 'Exclusionary pricing and price discrimination abuses under Article 82' (n. 4).
356. *Ibid.*
357. Bishop and Walker (n. 246) 254.
358. The same principles were recognized by the United Kingdom Office of Fair Trading, Draft competition law guideline for consultation, The Competition Act 1998 (April 2004) (3.6–3.7).
359. Guidelines on Vertical Restraints, para. 107(d).
360. William Rogerson, 'Contractual Solutions to the Hold-up Problem' (1992) 59(4) The Review of Economic Studies 777.

is some uncertainty on whether the other party will invest as well. In that case, both parties need an agreement to protect the return on the investment, e.g., by guaranteeing that a certain amount of units for a certain period will be sold.[361] A rebate system offered by a supplier to a customer could provide a certainty that the investment made before the agreement will be recovered. In addition, a rebate agreement could serve as an incentive for the supplier to invest in new technologies, new production or even to build a production plant.[362] Marvel, claims that:

> [I]ts [exclusive dealing] purpose is, instead, to protect suppliers' tie-in charges to dealers for the benefits of the supplier's intangible capital investments. Exclusive dealing will, indeed, be exclusionary, but that exclusion is required if the corresponding capital investment is to occur.[363]

In a similar study it was found that 'exclusivity has no effect when all investments are fully specific to the relationship'.[364]

[C] Preventing 'Free Riding'

A number of studies revealed that a possible economic rationale for using exclusive dealing or fidelity rebates with similar effect is to prevent dealers' free riding.[365] This possible pro-competitive rationale for using exclusivity obligations is closely related to the manufacturers' specific investments discussed above.

The economics of free riding is based on the assumption that manufacturers want their dealers to provide promotional activities and/or pre- or post sale services for their products, which are costly to provide.[366] Some dealers may invest and provide these services (or manufacturers may involve specific investment) whereas others may not but still be able to free ride on the promotional and service efforts. For example, customers might visit the full-service dealers' showroom for product demonstration and then buy the product from a low-cost dealer (low-cost because it does not incur costs for additional services). This might lead to losses for the full-service dealer, which would not only diminish their efforts but would decrease the demand for the product in general. To prevent free riding from the low-cost dealers (or to prevent the dealers using the manufacturer's investment to sell competitor products), the manufacturer may choose to sign an exclusive dealing agreement with their dealers.

This economic theory is supported by several studies – such as that conducted by Mills, who shows that market-share discounts can be pro-competitive by increasing the

361. Lang and O'Donoghue, 'Defining Legitimate Competition' (n. 4).
362. Geradin, 'A Proposed Test for Separating Pro-Competitive Loyalty Rebates from Anti-competitive Ones' (n. 4) 75.
363. Marvel (n. 56) 23.
364. Ilua Segal and Michael Whinston, 'Exclusive Contracts and the Protection of Investments' (2000) 31(4) RAND Journal of Economics 603.
365. David Mills, 'Inducing Downstream Selling Effort with Market Share Discounts' (2010) 17(2) International Journal of the Economics of Business 129; Marvel (n. 56); Klein and Lerner, 'The Expanded Economics of Free-Riding' (n. 56).
366. ABA Section of Antitrust Law, 'Antitrust Law and Economics of Product Distribution' (2006) 76, Chapter 2, 119.

efficiency of the distribution channels that might improve market performance while lessening the incentive to free ride on manufacturer-supplied promotions.[367] Similarly, Klein and Lerner demonstrate that exclusivity might minimise free riding in cases where dealers have a significant economic role in promoting manufacturer's products and the manufacturer compensates the dealers for these efforts.[368]

A manufacturer might prevent free riding through exclusive dealing or fidelity rebates agreements with some of the full-service dealers protecting their activities for example on certain territories.

[D] Reducing Prices for the Benefits of Final Consumers (i.e., Solving the 'Double Marginalisation Problem')

Double marginalisation occurs when two independent upstream and downstream firms with market power have mark-ups over marginal cost. Thus, the price to the final consumers has two mark-ups. As a result, the price to the end consumers may be higher than otherwise, which harms both the supplier and final consumers.[369] The problem of double marginalisation could be solved in two scenarios:

(1) If the two firms are vertically integrated, thus the supplier will charge a wholesale price equal to marginal cost to stimulate sales. As a result the first mark-up will be eliminated.
(2) If the two firms have an agreement involving fidelity rebates.

In the case of a fidelity rebates agreement, the client (downstream firm) has to reach the target threshold, which is the condition to be able to obtain the rebates from the upstream supplier. The downstream firm would have the incentive to sell more products to final consumers by lowering its prices by cutting the second mark-up. As a consequence of the fidelity rebates scheme, the double marginalisation problem will be solved in favour of the final consumers.

These theoretical statements are supported by an empirical study conducted by Kolay, Shaffer and Ordover that shows that 'all-units (or retroactive rebates) discounts can arise in the absence of any exclusionary motive, ... and they can eliminate double marginalisation but only "when demand is known at the time of contracting".[370] A recent empirical study shows that all units discounts "give the retailer a strong incentive to expand output to reach the discount threshold, while keeping upstream margins high enough to encourage upstream investment"' under bilateral monopoly assumption.[371]

367. Mills (n. 365) 130.
368. Klein and Lerner, 'The Expanded Economics of Free-Riding' (n. 56).
369. Bishop (n. 4).
370. Kolay, Shaffer and Ordover (n. 251); Spector, 'Loyalty Rebates and Related Pricing Practices' (n. 55).
371. Daniel O'Brien, 'All-Units Discounts and Double Moral Hazard' (2017) 170 Journal of Economic Theory 1.

[E] Providing Supplementary Services

In cases when a dominant company (upstream producer) offers fidelity rebates to a buyer (downstream distributor) on condition that the buyer will provide some additional supplementary services, rebates could create efficiencies, beneficial to final consumers.[372] Complementary services could include product promotion and/or demonstration of the product in the store. The EU Courts recognised the efficiency considerations of granting fidelity rebates related to complementary services, such as services, which the retailer performs for the undertaking by selling its products,[373] any marketing and transport costs paid by the customer, or any promotional, warehousing, servicing or other functions that the customer might have performed.[374]

According to the literature related to the possible efficiency claims of granting fidelity rebates, it seems that there are many pro-competitive rationales of granting fidelity rebates. Consequently, it cannot be claimed that any form of fidelity rebates is unlawful without analysing the possible efficiencies that they could give rise to.

Nevertheless, until now the European courts have accepted none of the efficiencies discussed here. There are several reasons why efficiency claims under Article 102 proceedings are less important than in Article 101, as explained by Geradin.[375] According to him, the first reason is that Article 102 does not contain an option for a conduct to be defended referring to efficiencies as is the case in Article 101(3). However, although there is no explicit efficiency defence for Article 102, throughout the years of jurisprudence, the Court of Justice effectively has created the possibility for efficiency defence for a dominant company.[376] The second reason, and arguably the better explanation, is that the welfare effect of a conduct by companies holding market power is often ambiguous and as such difficult to be justified under efficiency considerations.

§3.05 CONCLUSION

The aim of this chapter was to review the economic literature dealing with the possible effects of fidelity rebates in order to understand first, whether the classification of rebates and their different treatment made by the EU Courts, discussed in Chapter 2 make economic sense. Second, to identify under which circumstances fidelity rebates can be anticompetitive and whether these circumstances correspond to the facts pattern in the case law discussed in Chapter 2 in order to clarify whether the strict approach of fidelity rebates, developed by the EU Courts can be supported by the economic theories. Finally, whether the economic theories provide support for the implementation of a price-cost test to identify anticompetitive rebates.

372. Bishop (n. 4).
373. *Michelin* I, para. 45.
374. *Irish Sugar,* para. 173.
375. Damian Geradin, 'Efficiency Claims in EC Competition Law and Sector-specific Regulation' in H Ullrich (ed.), *The Evolution Of European Competition Law Whose Regulation, Which Competition?* (Edward Elgar 2004).
376. *See* Chapter 2.

The economic theories discussing anticompetitive exclusion do not contain any of the types of classification of rebates made by the EU Courts. Instead, the economic literature referring to a situation, in which, the dominant company is offering discounts to its customers in order to induce them to sign exclusive contracts, suggests that the rebates are granted for all units purchased, which is mathematically the same as offering fidelity/retroactive rebates. Next, the economic literature distinguishes between rebates with buyer commitment to purchase exclusively from the dominant company (which correspond to exclusivity rebates) and without buyer commitment to purchase exclusively (which correspond to 'other' category of rebates). All types of rebates have been referred collectively to as 'fidelity rebates' with the clarification that these variations do not play a significant role in their analysis.[377]

The review of the economic literature revealed that fidelity rebates could have anticompetitive effects only under certain circumstances. Likewise, rebates may have efficiency justifications that need to be taken into account. First, if rebates are linked to an obligation for the customer to buy exclusively all or a significant amount of their requirements from the dominant company they are more likely to be perceived as anticompetitive if the dominant company is an unavoidable trading partner and a significant part of demand is non-contestable due to the characteristics of the product, rebates are retroactive, there are economies of scale and barriers to entry. Under these circumstances only a small part of demand is open to competition, i.e., the contestable part. If a dominant company ties some part of the contestable share with fidelity rebates agreements, it might deprive a competitor from achieving MES and to compete effectively. The naked exclusion literature provides a theoretical foundation as to why rebates are anticompetitive under these circumstances, which suggests that if these circumstances exist, they are enough for a prima facie prohibition in the absence of efficiencies. These circumstances fit the fact pattern of the case law dealing with exclusivity rebates.[378]

Second, if fidelity rebate agreements do not contain commitments that customers will purchase their entire requirement from the dominant company, but instead are conditional on an achievement on specific threshold (target/growth rebates) or a certain share of customers' requirements, they nonetheless may have anticompetitive effects (according to the EU Courts terminology – 'fidelity-enhancing' effects) even if customers remain free to buy some part of their demand from competitors under the same circumstances relevant for fidelity rebates with buyer commitment for exclusivity.[379] However, the EU Courts considered that only if exclusivity obligations are not explicit, the effects of rebates require an evaluation of the circumstances mentioned above.

By presenting the different forms of rebates, their characteristics, and the possible effect that might arise from the implementation of each of them, this chapter showed

377. Greenlee and Reitman, 'Distinguishing Competitive and Exclusionary Uses of Loyalty Rebates' (n. 354) 442.
378. *See* Chapter 2, section 2.02 (the description of *Hoffmann-La Roche* and *British Gypsum*).
379. *See* Chapter 2, section 2.02 (the description of *Michelin I and II, Irish Sugar, British Airways* and *Tomra*).

that the clear-cut categorisation of rebates made by the EU Courts makes sense only as a starting point for the consideration of which category of rebates is more likely to create an anticompetitive effect and as such deserves more scrutiny. However, it does not make economic sense, because regardless of the types of rebates, the relevant economic theories identify that only under a certain set of circumstances can the conclusion that fidelity rebates are anticompetitive be supported.

Although the economic literature provides various models with different sets of variables and settings, which might lead to difficulties to reconcile which one is applicable to the fact pattern of each of the cases discussed in Chapter 2, it is safe to assume that anticompetitive effects are more likely if the dominant company has significant market power, the product is essential for the customers, rebates are retroactive and there are substantial economies of scale in manufacturing.[380] It can be also concluded that, even with the variations of the assumptions used in the economic models, they nonetheless arrived at similar conclusions – namely that fidelity rebates could have an exclusionary effect and that exclusion is possible without profit sacrifice, when the dominant company can deprive its rivals' access to crucial sales or input, which causes them to raise their price and it hinders their ability to compete.

These findings raised the question of the appropriateness of a price-cost test in situations in which the fidelity-enhancing effect is strong and whether this effect by itself can lead to anticompetitive exclusion regardless of whether the price is predatory or not? This chapter clarified that when incremental rebates apply or the whole demand is contestable, competition is based on prices. In this case, the dominant company can use the price as an exclusionary tool, if it is predatory. Thus, a traditional predatory pricing price-cost test is an important tool for the evaluation of the legality of rebates. On the other hand, rebates granted retroactively by a dominant company with an unavoidable trading partner status leads to the establishment of a non-contestable part of sales, for which competitors cannot compete. For that reason, some economists suggested a modified price-cost test, which aims to compare the price with the loyalty discount applied only for the contestable sales with the costs of providing these incremental units.

The analysis suggests that the modified test although economically rational is subject to implementation errors and cannot rule whether the conduct would lead to anticompetitive exclusion. In particular and based on the literature reviewed, this might be the case when the product is differentiated, when rebates are used as a punishment mechanism for disloyal customers and when competitors are deprived from achieving MES. In all those cases, the rebates can lead to anticompetitive exclusion even if the dominant company's price is above an appropriate measure of costs.

The relevant literature reviewed above in section 3.04, showed that fidelity rebates could have pro-competitive effects depending on the circumstances of each

380. Segal and Whinston, 'Naked Exclusion' (n. 277) 297; Michael Whinston, 'Tying, Foreclosure, and Exclusion' (1990) 80 American Economic Review 837, 839; Dennis Carlton, 'General Analysis of Exclusionary Conduct and Refusal to Deal-Why Aspen and Kodak are Misguided' (2001) 68 Antitrust Law Journal 659.

particular case. However, this literature also showed that fidelity rebates could only have pro-competitive effects in a limited set of circumstances. Moreover, this economic literature does not provide a detailed framework to distinguish between pro-competitive rebates from anticompetitive ones.[381] Furthermore, that theory has not dealt with the relevance of the price and whether the application of the price-cost test is useful to make this clear. As such, its importance for these studies is limited to identifying circumstances where it is plausible for prima facie anticompetitive rebates to have justifying efficiencies.

Having mapped the circumstances under which fidelity rebates might have anticompetitive or pro-competitive effects, drawn from the economic literature, and the relevance of the price-cost test to identify anticompetitive rebates, the next chapter will evaluate whether the reformed approach to Article 102, and the proposed assessment framework of fidelity rebates is in line with the economic theory.

381. Abbott and Wright (n. 321) 29. They claim that conflicting theories generate conflicting predictions regarding the competitive effects of exclusive dealing on output and consumer welfare.

CHAPTER 4

The Modernisation of Article 102 TFEU and the Concept of the 'Effects-Based' Approach

§4.01 INTRODUCTION

In the late 1990s, the European Commission started to modernise the EU competition law regime proclaiming a shift from a formalistic approach towards a more economic approach, which would focus on the effect of the conduct of companies on the market rather than the form of such conduct.[382] As discussed in Chapter 2, the 'form-based approach' had been broadly criticised by academics and practitioners for concentrating on the form of the company's conduct, ignoring its possible effect on competition, and failing to take into account the impact of impugned conduct on consumer welfare.[383] The aim of the new so-called effects-based approach was to guarantee effective competition policy by evaluating the impact of the conduct of companies on competition and consumer welfare. This approach was implemented through a reform of Article 101 and, later, of Merger Control with the adoption of Council Regulations and soft law instruments for the assessment of vertical restraints, horizontal agreements[384] and mergers.[385]

382. Green Paper on Vertical Restraints in EC Competition Policy, adopted 22 January 1997 http://europa.eu/documents/comm/green_papers/pdf/com96_721_en.pdf accessed 26 October 2016; White Paper on modernisation of the rules implementing Arts 85 and 86 of the Treaty, Commission Programme N 99/027, Brussels, 28 April 1999; *see also* The 'XXXth Report on Competition Policy 2000', SEC (2001) 694, 27; Commission Press Release IP/00/1376 of 29 November 2000 http://europa.eu/rapid/press-release_IP-00-1376_en.htm accessed 3 January 2017. The modernization of the EU competition law includes procedural changes which are beyond the scope of this book.
383. Text to (nn. 214–230) in Chapter 2.
384. *See* n. 7.
385. *See* n. 8.

In 2003, as a response to these criticisms, concerning its enforcement policy regarding Article 102,[386] the European Commission announced that it would undertake a modernisation effort to bring this policy in line with its previous reform of the other areas of the EU competition law regime.[387] The reform started in 2005 with the issuance of the EAGCP Report and the Discussion paper, and at the end of 2008, the Commission published the Guidance Paper. The aim of the reform was to introduce the 'effects-based' approach in applying Article 102 TFEU and to ensure coherence with the enforcement of Article 101 and Merger Control, following reforms in these areas. Importantly, the Guidance Paper adopted the AEC test as a tool to distinguish between pro-competitive and anticompetitive behaviour by a dominant company, which became the essence of the reformed approach to Article 102.

Whereas the modernisation of Article 102 was welcomed in general, many prominent commentators claimed that the way in which the effects-based approach was construed in the official statements and documents issued by the European Commission was vague and is clearly focused on the assessment of harm to competitors rather than consumer harm.[388] Moreover, it has been observed that although consumer welfare is presented as a main concern, a test for consumer harm cannot be found in a clear and systematic way in the Guidance Paper.[389] Some went as far as to state that the lack of a specific test for consumer harm in the Guidance Paper means that this Paper merely restates the case law,[390] based on how the case law stands, i.e., there is no requirement to establish harm to consumers in order to apply the Treaty's provisions.[391] It has also been argued that the Guidance Paper's approach on the application of Article 102 is in striking contrast with the guidelines regarding Article 101 and EU Merger Control where the 'effects-based' approach was previously

386. The criticism was mainly related with 'the gap between Art. 102 case law and the need to ensure that even dominant companies can compete where doing so would be beneficial for consumers,' as observed by Patrick Rey and James Venit, 'An Effects-Based Approach to Article 102: A Response to Wouter Wils' (2015) 38(1) World Competition 3, 5.
387. Philip Lowe, speech at the 30th Annual Conference on International Antitrust Law and Policy, Fordham Corporate, 23 October 2003.
388. Text to (n. 15) in Chapter 1.
389. Akman, 'The EC Discussion Paper on the Application of Article 82' (n. 15) 10; Petit, 'From Formalism to Effects? (n. 15) 489; Marsden and Gormsen, 'Guidance on Abuse in Europe: The Continued Concern for Rivalry and a Competitive Structure' (n. 15).
390. Marsden and Gormsen, 'Guidance on Abuse in Europe: The Continued Concern for Rivalry and a Competitive Structure' (n. 15) 891–892.
391. Philip Marsden and Peter Whelan, 'Consumer Detriment and Its Application in EC and UK Competition Law' (2006) 27(10) European Competition Law Review 569, 576. In their paper they demonstrated that neither 'consumer detriment' nor 'consumer benefit' are defined in the EC provisions or in the Merger Regulation. Moreover, in conducting a detailed research of both EC and UK competition case law, they concluded that there is no requirement to proof consumer harm in order to apply Treaty's provisions, because the protection of competitive structure is considered adequate to protect the interests of consumers, 588. *See also* Pablo Ibáñez Colomo and Alfonso Lamadrid. 'On the Notion of Restriction of Competition: What We Know and What We Don't Know We Know' (2016) https://papers.ssrn.com/sol3/papers.cfm?abstract_id=2849831 accessed 14 October 2016, who states that: 'Some judgments have made it clear that it is not necessary to show harm to consumers in order to establish a breach of Articles 101 or 102 TFEU, and that the competitive process is worthy of protection in and of itself. The EU courts have taken a similar position in relation to mergers'; Liza Lovdahl

adopted.[392] Lastly, others went as far as to conclude that there is a clear gap between the case law on Article 102 and the EU Commission's policy declarations proclaiming consumer welfare as a main objective.[393] According to this view, the Commission is trying to change the law when it has no power to do so.[394] Much of this criticism specifically reflects the proposed assessment of fidelity rebates.[395]

The aim of this chapter is to clarify the meaning attached to the notion of an 'effects-based' approach as an expression of the reform of Article 102 in order to allow us to understand whether the analytical framework proposed by the Commission is likely to satisfy those who criticise the Commission for their formalistic approach with regard to fidelity rebates, as outlined in Chapter 2. Consequently, this chapter builds on the economic theory of fidelity rebates discussed in Chapter 3 to clarify whether the proposed analytical framework for the assessment of fidelity rebates is appropriate.

The sections of this chapter systematically discuss three different sources to assess the exact meaning the Commission attaches to the term effects-based approach. Section 4.02 seeks to understand the meaning of effects-based approach by reference to the Commission's official statements (speeches, interviews and publications). Sections 4.03 and 4.04 will briefly review the reform of Article 101 and EU Merger Control which should provide further insight into the Commission's understanding of the meaning of the effects-based approach. Section 4.05 completes the review by evaluating the European Commission's official documents related to the reform of Article 102 itself to understand whether the meaning attached to the term effects-based approach in this context is in line with the reform in the other areas of EU competition law.

Section 4.05 also analyses critically the approach to the evaluation of the legality of fidelity rebates. The analysis suggests that most of the criticisms made by many commentators that the reform of Article 102 is less clear than the reform of Article 101 and Merger Control are based on a lack of sufficient clarity regarding the application of

---

Gormsen, 'The Conflict Between Economic Freedom and Consumer Welfare in the Modernisation of Article 82 EC' (2007) 3 European Competition Journal 329, 340. She states that: 'there was no serious analysis of consumer welfare loss in any of these cases (decisional and judicial practice under Art. 82)'.

392. Anne Witt, *The More Economic Approach to EU Antitrust Law* (Bloomsbury Publishing 2016) Ch. 5; Renato Nazzini, *The Foundations of European Union Competition Law* (OUP 2011) 155. *See also* Luc Peeperkorn, 'Coherence in the Application of Articles 101 and 102: A Realistic Prospect or an Elusive Goal?' (2016) 39(3) World Competition 389; Spector, 'From Harm to Competitors to Harm to Competition' (n. 15) 164.

393. Witt, *The More Economic Approach to EU Antitrust Law* (n. 392) Ch. 10; Pinar Akman, 'Consumer Welfare and Article 82EC: Practice and Rhetoric' (2009) 32(1) World Competition 71; *see also* Liza Lovdahl Gormsen, 'Why the European Commission's Enforcement Priorities on Article 82 EC Should Be Withdrawn' (2010) 31 European Competition Law Review 45; Petit, 'From Formalism to Effects?' (n. 15) 4; Crayencour and Lang (n. 14); Anne Witt, 'The Commission's Guidance Paper on Abusive Exclusionary Conduct–More Radical than It Appears?' (2010) 35 European Law Review 214, 216; *see also* CEPS Special Reports (n. 6) 31; Alison Jones and Liza Lovdahl Gormsen, 'Abuse Of Dominance: Exclusionary Pricing Abuses' in Ioannis Lianos and Damien Geradin (eds) *Handbook on European Competition Law: Substantive Aspects* (Edward Elgar 2013) 425.

394. John Temple Lang, 'Article 82 EC – The Problems and the Solution' (2009) presentation at the conference 'Ten years of Mercato Concorrenza Regole' (Milan, June 30, 2009).

395. Text to (n. 15) in Chapter 1.

the AEC test as an expression of the effects-based approach, in particular where the assessment of fidelity rebates is concerned.

§4.02 THE MEANING OF THE 'EFFECTS-BASED' APPROACH ACCORDING TO THE POLICY STATEMENTS OF THE COMMISSION

The introduction of a 'more economic' approach to EU competition law was initiated by the former Commissioner Monti as a main priority.[396] According to his statements, the shift to a more economic approach in the application of the competition rules would enhance the effectiveness of competition policy to the benefit of European consumers. Further, the Commissioner explicitly mentioned that protecting consumer welfare was a consequence of the protection of markets and competition.[397] This statement reflects the view that the main objective of EU competition law is the protection of competition, which guarantees consumer welfare. It further reflects Protocol (No. 27) on the Internal Market and Competition's statement that one of the activities necessary to achieve the objectives of the Community is a 'system ensuring that competition in the internal market is not distorted'.[398,399] Further policy statements recognized consumer welfare as the main priority of the EU competition policy, and expanded on the role that an effects-based approach could have in achieving this objective. As stated by Commissioner Croes in a speech in 2005:

> [C]onsumer welfare is now well established as the standard the Commission applies when assessing mergers and infringements of the Treaty rules on cartels and monopolies. Our aim is simple: to protect competition in the market as a means of enhancing consumer welfare and ensuring an efficient allocation of

396. Witt, *The More Economic Approach to EU Antitrust Law* (n. 392) Ch. 3; Mario Monti, *Introduction to the Commission's XXXth Report on Competition Policy* (2000) European Commission 9. This statement was repeated in a subsequent speeches between 2000–2004, such as: 'European Competition Policy for the 21st century', New York 20 October 2000, The Fordham Corporate Law Institute – Twenty-eight Annual Conference on International Antitrust Law and Policy (speech/00/389); 'Antitrust in the US and Europe: a History of convergence' Washington DC, 14 November 2001, General Counsel Roundtable American Bar Association (speech/01/540); 'The New EU Policy on Technology Transfer Agreement' Paris, 16 January 2004, Ecole des Mines (speech/04/19); 'EU competition policy after May 2004' New York, 24 October 2003, Fordham Annual Conference on International Antitrust Law and Policy (speech /03/489).
397. Monti, 'European Competition Policy for the 21st century' (n. 396).
398. *See* Protocol N 27 on the internal market and competition, OJ, 9 May 2008, C 115/309, annexed to the Treaty on European Union (TEU) and the Treaty on the Functioning of the European Union (TFEU). Before the Lisbon Treaty, this text was Art. 3(g) EEC, later Art. 3(1)(g) EC.
399. For similar interpretation *see* Wouter Wils, 'The Judgment of the EU General Court in Intel and the So-Called "More Economic Approach" to Abuse of Dominance' (2014) 37(4) World Competition, who states that: 'In any event, a system of undistorted competition as part of the internal market is the objective of Article 102 TFEU as determined by the EU Treaties. Whatever views this or that economist or other person or many or most of them may have as to what the objective of Article 102 TFEU should be is irrelevant, unless a debate were to be opened on changing the EU Treaties.'

> resources. An effects-based approach, grounded in solid economics, ensures that citizens enjoy the benefits of a competitive, dynamic market economy.[400]

The main policy objectives of Article 102 were thus formulated as consisting of the protection of competition on the market as a means of enhancing consumer welfare and ensuring an efficient allocation of resources.[401] These points were further elaborated in a subsequent speech in 2006, also delivered by Commissioner Kroes, according to which all that matters in competition enforcement is the potential harm to consumers, which requires the application of an effects-based approach through better use of economic analysis in the Commission's work.[402]

These statements indicate that the 'new' approach was focused on the evaluation of a possible negative effect of the conduct of a dominant company on competition and consumer welfare. Thus, what matters is the assessment of likely or actual effects from a conduct and not its form. However, this does not tell us how the effects-based approach is to be pursued in practice. To understand how the Commission actually interpreted the effects-based approach, one should look first at the reform of Article 101 and of the Merger Control regime, where the effects-based approach was adopted through soft law instruments.[403]

§4.03 THE REFORM OF ARTICLE 101 TFEU

The reform of Article 101 started with vertical agreements.[404] The effect on competition of these agreements has long been perceived as ambiguous. As such, a prohibition without proper evaluation of their possible effect on competition and consumers had been vigorously criticised in the academic literature.[405] As a result, and following the Green Paper, the European Commission adopted the Block Exemption Regulation

---

400. 'European Competition Policy – Delivering Better Markets and Better Choices', London, 15 September 2005 (speech 05/512); *see also* Symposium on 'Welfare Standard in Competition Policy' (2006) Competition Policy International.
401. Nellie Kroes, 'Preliminary Thoughts on Policy Review of Article 82', 23 September 2005, Fordham Corporate Law Institute, New York (speech 05/537).
402. Nellie Kroes, 'Competition Policy and Consumers', 16 November 2006, Fordham Corporate Law Institute (speech 06/691).
403. It is accepted that 'the general principles of the more economic approach were introduced by means of legally non-binding guidelines', *see* Witt, *The more Economic Approach to EU Antitrust Law* (n. 392) Ch. 3.
404. Green Paper on Vertical Restraints.
405. *See* in general Barry Hawk, 'System Failure: Vertical Restraints and EC Competition Law' (1995) 32(4) Common Market Law Review 973; *see also* David Deacon, *Vertical Restraints under EU Competition Law: New Directions* (Annual Proceedings-Fordham Corporate Law Institute, Transnational Juris Publications Incorporated 1996); Lyc Gyselen, 'Vertical Restraints in the Distribution Process: Strength and Weakness of the Free Rider Rationale Under EEC Competition Law' (1984) 21 Common Market Law Review 647; Valentine Korah, 'The Rise and Fall of Provisional Validity – The Need for a Rule of Reason in EEC Antitrust' (1981) 3 Northwestern Journal International Law and Business 320; Valentine Korah, 'The Judgement in Delimitis-A Milestone towards a Realistic Assessment of the Effects of an Agreement-or a Damp Squib?' (1993) 8 Tulane European and Civil Law Forum 17; Roger Van den Bergh, 'Modern Industrial Organisation Versus Old-Fashioned European Competition Law' (1996) 17 European Competition Law Review 75.

setting out a number of the conditions under which vertical agreements are exempt from Article 101(1). This Regulation was accompanied by soft-law instruments which aimed at providing guidelines for the appropriate assessment of certain categories of non-exempt vertical agreements.[406]

The new approach for the assessment of vertical restraint is focused on the overall effect of these practices through balancing their possible negative effects and efficiency gains.[407] The aim of the reform was to simplify the rules and to reduce the regulatory burden for companies, while simultaneously ensuring a more effective control of vertical restraints implemented by companies holding significant market power.[408] The key aspects of the reform could be summarised as follows: (1) vertical agreements might have pro-competitive or anticompetitive effects depending on the case and as such cannot be prohibited as a 'per se' restriction of competition, based on the legal form of the agreement; (2) the analysis should be focused on the effect of the agreement rather that its form; (3) anticompetitive effects are more likely when market power exists at one or more levels of trade; (4) negative effects on consumers are more likely if inter-brand competition is weak. In this sense, the reform of vertical agreements represents a radical departure from the previous approach, which condemned many of these agreements as illegal 'per se' based on their form rather than their actual effect.[409]

The Regulation introduced a market share threshold of 30% as a safe harbour. This reflects the Commission's position that the anticompetitive effects may exist only when the parties to the agreements (or one of the parties) possess market power.[410] Above this threshold, an individual assessment of the likely effects of the agreement is required.[411] Thus, one of the main benefits of the reform is the possibility for the Commission and the NCAs to avoid assessing agreements that are unlikely to create anticompetitive effects (market share below 30%) and to concentrate on agreements that are more likely to create harm to consumers because of the market power of the parties to the agreement. The main possible negative effect that could arise from a

406. Guidelines on Vertical Restraints.
407. Many commentators discussed the reform of Art. 101, *See* e.g., Ehlermann and Atanasiu (eds) *European Competition Law Annual 2000: The Modernisation of EC Antitrust Policy* (Hart Publishing 2001); Rein Wesseling, *The Modernisation of EC Antitrust Law* (Bloomsbury Publishing 2000); Richard Whish and Brenda Sufrin, *Community Competition Law: Notification and individual exemption – Goodbye to all that* (Hart Publishing 2000) 150; Claus-Dieter Ehlermann, 'The Modernization of EC Antitrust Policy: A Legal and Cultural Revolution' (2000) 37 Common Market Law Review 537; Wolfgang Kerber and Simonetta Vezzoso, 'EU Competition Policy, Vertical Restraints, and Innovation: An Analysis From an Evolutionary Perspective' (2005) 28(4) World Competition 507; Ekaterina Rousseva, 'Modernizing by Eradicating: How the Commission's New Approach to Article 81 EC Dispenses with the Need to Apply Article 82 EC to Vertical Restraints' (2005) 42(3) Common Market Law Review 587.
408. Report from the Commission – XXXth Report on Competition Policy 2000.
409. Nicolas Petit and David Henry, 'Vertical Restraints under EU Competition Law: Conceptual Foundations and Practical Framework' (2010) https://papers.ssrn.com/sol3/papers.cfm?abstract_id=1724891 accessed 25 October 2016.
410. Vincent Verouden, 'Vertical Agreements and Article 81 (1) EC: The Evolving Role of Economic Analysis' (2003) 71(2) Antitrust Law Journal 525, 567.
411. Guidelines on Vertical Restraints, para. 96.

vertical agreement is the foreclosure of competitors and harm to consumers.[412] It is argued that the elimination of competition is the most important criterion for the evaluation of vertical restraints and as such, if this criterion is not satisfied, 'the exemption is not possible whatever benefits might be claimed for the agreement'.[413]

The introduction of the 30% market share threshold by the European Commission indicates its position to treat dominant companies more harshly than non-dominant ones, which are free to practice vertical restraints (except hard-core restrictions). However, even below 30% market share, certain hard-core restraints,[414] listed in Article (4) of BER cannot benefit from the safe harbour.[415] Instead, hard-core restraints are subject to a non-rebuttable presumption of violation of Article 101 (1). This position was interpreted by some as not consistent with the effects-based approach and consumer welfare concerns.[416] Others interpreted this presumption of illegality for certain hard-core restraints, such as absolute territorial restrictions, as not based on economic efficiency grounds only but with the promotion of another objective of the EU competition law, market integration.[417]

Given the overlap of the application of Articles 101 and 102 to vertical restraints, for the purposes of this book, this section will focus on the Commission's proposed assessment criteria applicable to vertical agreements most like fidelity rebates, and in particular, at single branding – an agreement in which the buyer is obliged or induced to concentrate its orders for a particular type of product with one supplier.[418] A fidelity rebates scheme, which contains the same conditions, could be classified as being single branding obligation.

According to the Commission's Vertical Guidelines, single branding obligations could take the form of a non-compete agreement based on a condition, which makes the buyer purchase more than 80% of its requirements from the supplier. Thus, single branding obligations have a quantity-forcing component, based on an agreement between the supplier and the buyer, which makes the latter concentrate its purchases to a large extent with one supplier.[419] The Guidelines provide guidance for the evaluation of the possible harm that might result from these practices. The relevant criteria involve the evaluation of the condition of the market (i.e., market position of

412. The negative effects are listed at paras 100–105 of the Guidelines.
413. Martin Mendelsohn and Stephen Rose, *Guide to the EU Block Exemption for Vertical Agreements* (Vol. 4, Kluwer Law International 2002) 25.
414. Guidelines on Vertical Restraints established a presumption of incompatibility with Art. 101(1) TFEU for hard-core vertical agreements (Guidelines, para. 47), such resale price fixing, minimum resale price and restrictions of active sales from one territory to the other.
415. BER introduced that the threshold of 30% should be on the relevant market.
416. The New EU Rules On Vertical Restraints http://www.jonesday.com/files/Publication/408e0e9a-351f-4490-b881-06c805dce093/Presentation/PublicationAttachment/1d9cb38b-9251-4541-8d00-0a71b2d9acba/Law%20360%20%20New%20EU%20Rules%20on%20Vertical%20Restraints.smc.pdf accessed 25 October 2016.
417. Massimo Motta and Others, 'Hardcore Restrictions under the Block Exemption Regulation on Vertical Agreements: An Economic View', Report of the Economic Advisory Group on Competition Policy at the Directorate General for Competition, European Commission (2009).
418. Guidelines on Vertical Restraints, para. 129.
419. *Ibid.*

the supplier,[420] market position of the competitors,[421] entry barriers,[422] countervailing buyer power),[423] and the characteristics and nature of the agreement (duration,[424] coverage,[425] the level of trade subject to the agreement).[426] A cumulative assessment of all the parameters is required to consider the real risk of anticompetitive foreclosure.

The market position of a supplier is considered to be of main importance for the assessment of the possible anticompetitive effect of single branding obligations.[427] If the supplier is 'an unavoidable trading partner at least for part of the demand on the market, for instance because its brand is a "must-stock item" preferred by many final consumers', competitors cannot compete on equal terms for the entire demand of the customers because part of it is tied to the must-stock supplier.[428] The percentage of the tied part of demand can be equated with the market share of the dominant company. The higher the market share thus makes anticompetitive foreclosure more likely. The proposed assessment of the possible anticompetitive effect of single branding suggests that the unavoidable trading partner status of the supplier and the high percentage of the tied part of demand is likely to lead to anticompetitive foreclosure. This position reflects the definition of a fidelity-enhancing effect of fidelity rebates and the conclusion that this effect might be enough to create anticompetitive effects in certain circumstances that has been outlined in Chapter 3.

When the market share is really high, it is considered that 'even a modest tied market share may lead to significant anticompetitive effects'.[429] This statement might be interpreted as saying that it might not be necessary to consider the evaluation of the exact coverage of the agreement if the company possesses significant market power in line with the case law of fidelity rebates discussed in Chapter 2 where the EU Courts refused to evaluate the coverage of fidelity rebates. An alternative interpretation of why even a small foreclosure of a competitor's access to the market might create anticompetitive effects was addressed in Chapter 3. As can be recalled from the discussion of the evaluation of the possible anticompetitive effects of fidelity rebates, in some markets characterised by high fixed costs and constant demand, a rival needs to

420. *Ibid.*, para. 132.
421. *Ibid.*, para. 134.
422. *Ibid.*, para. 136.
423. *Ibid.*, para. 137.
424. *Ibid.*, para. 133 where it is stated that: 'Single branding obligations shorter than one year entered into by non-dominant companies are generally not considered to give rise to appreciable anti-competitive effects or net negative effects. Single branding obligations between one and five years entered into by non- dominant companies usually require a proper balancing of pro- and anti-competitive effects, while single branding obligations exceeding five years are for most types of investments not considered necessary to achieve the claimed efficiencies or the efficiencies are not sufficient to outweigh their foreclosure effect.'
425. *Ibid.*, para. 133.
426. *Ibid.*, paras 138–140, where the Commission make distinction between retail and wholesale level: 'For final products, foreclosure is in general more likely to occur at the retail level, given the significant entry barriers for most manufacturers to start retail outlets just for their own products. In addition, it is at the retail level that single branding agreements may lead to reduced in-store inter-brand competition.'
427. *Ibid.*, para. 134.
428. *Ibid.*, para. 132.
429. *Ibid.*, para. 140.

achieve MES in order to enter the market or to compete effectively with the dominant company if it is already in the market. In these markets, the dominant company might tie an insignificant part of demand, which might nonetheless be large enough to prevent the rivals achieving MES (*see* Chapter 3, section 3.03). Thus, if a competitor's ability to reach MES is restricted, the dominant company's conduct can exclude or marginalise competitors by raising their costs. In other words, the main concern is that the competition from rival suppliers may be restricted.[430]

Finally, the Guidelines provide examples of possible efficiencies and objective justifications in cases where appreciable anticompetitive effects are established. They could be summarised as follows: (1) lessening the incentive to free ride on manufacturer-supplied promotions;[431] (2) protecting market specific investments, thereby addressing the so-called hold-up problem;[432] (3) in case of capital market imperfection, it may be more efficient for the supplier of a product than for a bank to provide a loan;[433] (4) the transfer of substantial know-how.[434] In case there are restrictive vertical agreements that produce efficiencies, which may outweigh their anticompetitive effect, an assessment within the framework of Article 101 (3) is required.[435] These examples reflect the possible pro-competitive effect and efficiency explanations of granting fidelity rebates, and are broadly in line with the economic literature discussed in Chapter 3.

This analysis of the proposed treatment of single branding obligations demonstrates that the main focus of the reform was to concentrate on the Commission's analysis of the effect of an agreement and to ensure more effective control of vertical restraints implemented by companies holding significant market power.[436] In this respect at least, the reform of vertical restraints replaced the strict form-based approach with a more economic approach.[437]

This reform also influenced the courts. One can find good examples of this in the decisions of the *Delimitis*[438] and *Van den Bergh Foods*[439] cases. In *Delimitis*, the CJEU assessed whether exclusive purchases agreements covering beer distribution in Germany were contrary to Article 101 TFEU based on analyses of the possible foreclosure of other brewers from the market.[440] The Court recognised that an analysis of the

430. Valentine Korah and Denis O'Sullivan, *Distribution Agreements under the EC Competition Rules* (Bloomsbury Publishing 2002) 38.
431. Guidelines on Vertical Restraints, para. 144.
432. *Ibid.*, para. 146.
433. *Ibid.*, para. 147.
434. *Ibid.*, para. 148.
435. *Ibid.*, para. 122.
436. Verouden (n. 410).
437. Bishop and Walker (n. 246) 204; Witt, *The More Economic Approach to EU Antitrust Law* (n. 392) 45; Ekaterina Rousseva, 'Objective Justification and Article 82 EC in the Era of Modernisation' in Giuliano Amato and Claus-Dieter Ehlermann (eds) *EC Competition Law: A Critical Assessment* (Hart Publishing 2007).
438. Case C-234/89 *Delimitis v. HenningerBriu AG* (1991) ECR I-935 (hereinafter *Delimitis*).
439. Case T-65/98 *Van den Bergh Foods v. Commission* [2003] ECR II-4653 (hereinafter *Van den Bergh Foods*).
440. For the intensive comments on the Judgment, *see* in general Korah, 'Judgment in Delimitis' (n. 405).

number of the outlets tied, the quantity of the product and the duration of the agreement were necessary in order to find that the agreement is incompatible with the provision of Article 101 TFEU.[441] In this sense, the CJEU confirmed that the main concern with exclusive purchasing agreements is the anticompetitive foreclosure of competitors.[442] Moreover, the finding of foreclosure is not sufficient for the identification of restriction of competition; instead, the foreclosure must be of such a degree as to make it anticompetitive.[443] Thus, the analysis was focused on the possible anticompetitive effect of the agreement and its impact on the competitive structure in which case harm to consumers could be presumed. Similar conclusions were reached in the *Van den Bergh Foods* case, where the GC held that the dominant supplier of impulse ice cream had infringed both Articles 101 and 102. The Court relied on assessment of dominance, exclusivity and the extent of the share of supply affected (around 40% of the available outlets) in order to conclude that the exclusive agreement has an anticompetitive foreclosure effect.[444] Again, the analysis was focused on the possible anticompetitive effect of the agreement and its impact on competitive structure.[445]

These cases show that the anticompetitive foreclosure cannot be assumed at the outset simply because of the presence of exclusivity obligations.[446] In both judgments, the Courts adopted an approach based on the effect of the agreements on the competitive process, which was sufficient for an infringement decision even if it did not involve an evaluation of the impact of impugned conduct on consumer welfare. Both judgments have thus been used in the academic literature as an example of a successful implementation of the effects-based approach.[447]

The reform of Article 101 continued with the adoption of block exemptions concerning horizontal specialisation agreements, co-operation agreements and technology transfer agreements with accompanied Guidelines.[448] The next step for the Commission was then to incorporate the economic approach and efficiency justifications by adopting the Guidelines on the application of Article 101 (3).[449] In these Guidelines, the Commission provides that 'for an agreement to be restrictive by effect it must affect actual or potential competition to such an extent that on the relevant market negative effects on prices, output, innovation, variety or quality of goods and services can be expected within a reasonable degree of probability'.[450] The Commission explicitly placed consumer welfare at the core of the analyses under Article 101 (1) by stating that: 'the objective of Article 81 (now 101) is to protect competition on the market as a means of enhancing consumer welfare and of ensuring an efficient

441. *Delimitis*, para. 19.
442. Korah and O'Sullivan (n. 430) 38.
443. Giorgio Monti, *EC Competition Law* (CUP 2007) 31.
444. *Van den Bergh Foods*, paras 159–160.
445. O'Donoghue and Padilla (n. 13) 431–432.
446. Pablo Ibáñez Colomo, 'Beyond the "More Economics-Based Approach"' (n. 177) 728.
447. O'Donoghue and Padilla (n. 13).
448. *See* n. 7.
449. Guidelines on the application of Art. 81 (3), para. 5. *See also* Lars Kjølbye, 'The New Commission Guidelines on the Application of Article 81 (3): An Economic Approach to Article 81' (2004) 25 European Competition Law Review 566.
450. Guidelines on the application of Art. 81 (3), para. 24.

allocation of resources', which according to the Guidelines requires consumers to get a fair share of the benefits of any agreement to which Article 101 apply.[451] 'Fair share' means that the pass-on of benefits must at least compensate consumers for any actual or likely negative impact caused by the restriction of competition.[452] It should be clarified that the statement: 'consumers to get a fair share' does not mean evaluation of consumer harm; it means that 'consumers shall receive an appropriate share of wealth [...] that would be provided by a competitive market'.[453] In any event, the Guidelines on the application of Article 101 (3) express the Commission's understanding of competitive harm, one that focuses on the harmful effect on competition of certain agreements that might reduce consumer welfare.[454]

To determine whether an agreement can be justified under Article 101 (3), a two-phase analysis is necessary. The first phase assesses whether an agreement has an anticompetitive object or actual or potential anticompetitive effects.[455] When the agreement is found to be restrictive, the second step is to identify pro-competitive benefits produced by that agreement and to balance whether these pro-competitive effects outweigh the anticompetitive effects.[456] The analysis of the second step requires an assessment of four cumulative conditions, two positive and two negative: (1) The agreement must contribute to improving the production or distribution of goods or contribute to promoting technical or economic progress; (2) consumers must receive a fair share of the resulting benefits; (3) the restrictions must be indispensable to the attainment of these objectives; and (4) the agreement must not afford the parties the possibility of eliminating competition in respect of a substantial part of the products in question.[457] Hence, the assessment of Article 101 TFEU requires on the one hand an analysis of the negative effects on consumers through balancing the negative and positive effects of an agreement on consumers, and on the other the possibility of eliminating competition on a substantial part of the market.[458]

Because the conditions are cumulative, if a possibility of eliminating competition on a substantial part of the market is established there is no need for further assessment. Thus, the dominant company's inability to obtain exemption is related to the question of dominance. The importance of the 'no elimination of competition' condition over any pro-competitive efficiency was expressed in *Atlantic Container Line*.[459] If a dominant company is able to eliminate competitors and as such to harm effective competition, it cannot fulfil all four conditions for exemption under Article

451. *Ibid.*, para. 9.
452. *Ibid.*, para. 85.
453. Joseph Brodley, 'The Economic Goals of Antitrust: Efficiency, Consumer Welfare and Technological Progress' (1987) 62 NY University Law Review 1020, 1023.
454. Witt, *The more Economic Approach to EU Antitrust Law* (n. 392) 119–120.
455. Guidelines on the application of Art. 81(3), para. 11.
456. *Ibid.*
457. *Ibid.*, para. 34.
458. *Ibid.*, paras 24, 39 and 55. The same statement could be found in the Guidelines on the application of Art. 81 EC to technology transfer agreements, para. 7.
459. *See* Joined Cases T-191/98, 212/98 and 214/98 *Atlantic Container Line (TACA) v. Commission* [2003] ECR II-3275, para. 111.

101 (3) and the agreement may be unlawful even if it is welfare enhancing.[460] Since the ability to eliminate competition through an agreement requires the exercise of market power, the fulfilment of this condition has similarities with a dominance test to the point where authors have identified the market power of undertakings as a decisive factor in the analysis of this limb of Article 101 (3).[461] The presumption is that the negative effects on competition and a loss of consumer welfare are likely to occur when the parties possess market power and the agreement contributes to the creation, maintenance or strengthening of that market power.[462] Thus, the market power was considered as an indicator of potential anticompetitive effects.[463] That was also the Court's approach in *Delimitis* and *Van den Bergh Foods* discussed above.

§4.04 THE REFORM OF THE EU MERGER CONTROL

The Commission's reform of Merger Control was triggered when the European Courts overturned three prohibition decisions by the Commission.[464] In the annulment decisions, the Courts criticised the Commission's assessments for, among other things, failing to establish that the mergers would likely give rise to a negative effect on competition. The interpretation of the Courts was that the likelihood of harm to the structure of the market was not sufficient to establish that a merger is not compatible with the common market.[465] The assessment requires instead an evaluation of the impact of a merger on competition rather than their effect on the market structure.

Following this, in 2004 Regulation EC 139/2004 on the control of concentrations between undertakings was adopted, together with the Commission's Guidance on the assessment on horizontal mergers.[466] The new package introduced an effects-based approach that required the assessment of the impact of horizontal mergers on competition and consumers, rather than on market structure, based on economic analysis. Consequently, one of the key aspects of the reform of merger control was to move the assessment from a test based on the structure of the market and to adopt a 'significant impediment to effective competition' test – i.e., will the merger restrict

460. Luc Peeperkorn, 'EC Vertical Restraints Guidelines: Effects-Based or Per Se Policy? – A Reply' (2002) 23(1) European Competition Law Review 38.
461. Mario Monti, 'The Application of Community Competition Law by the National Courts in a Directly Applicable Exception System' ERA Forum (2001) 2(1) Springer-Verlag 6. *See also* Okeoghene Odudu, *The Boundaries of EC Competition Law: The Scope of Article 81* (OUP 2006).
462. Guidelines on the application of Art. 81 (3), para. 25.
463. Renato Nazzini, 'Article 81 EC Between Time Present and Time Past: A Normative Critique of Restriction of Competition in EU Law' (2006) 43 Common Market Law Review 497, 501.
464. Case T-342/99 *Airtours v. Commission* [2002] ECR II-2585; *Airtours/First Choice* (Case IV/M.1524) Commission Decision [1999] OJ L 93/1; Case T-310/01 *Schneider v. Commission* [2001] ECR II- 4071; Schneider (COMP/M.2283) Commission Decision [2002] OJ L 101/134; Case T-5/02 *Tetra Laval v. Commission* [2002] ECR II-4519; *Tetra Laval* (Case COMP/M. 2416) Commission Decision [2001] OJ 2004 L 38/1.
465. Witt, 'The Commission's Guidance Paper on Abusive Exclusionary Conduct–More Radical than It Appears?' (n. 393) 212, 215.
466. *See* n. 8.

competition substantially.[467] The new test asks whether the merger will create a significant impediment to the effective competition in the common market or in a substantial part of it, in particular as a result of the creation or strengthening of a dominant position.[468] The new test implies that dominance is no longer an essential condition for the prohibition of a merger, which suggests that the scope of Merger Control is extended to mergers that lead to oligopolies that might create significant impediment to the effective competition.[469]

At the same time the new Merger regulation came into force, the Horizontal Mergers Guidelines were published. The Guidelines elaborate the content of the new legal standard, and notice in particular that competitive harm may arise from mergers in two ways: unilateral and coordinated effects.[470] Both types of effects are problematic when they reduce consumer welfare,[471] which was widely perceived to be the ultimate legal standard for determining whether a merger should be approved or prohibited.[472] In the light of this, the reform of Merger Control also required the Commission to take into account any substantiated and likely efficiencies put forward by the undertakings concerned, and to assess whether those efficiencies would counteract the negative effect on competition, and in particular harm to consumers.[473] According to the Guidelines, efficiencies under EC merger control have to benefit consumers, have to result from the merger and have to be verifiable.[474] There are a variety of tools and techniques, which are used to assess quantitatively whether the claimed efficiencies will materialise after the merger.[475] Ultimately, the Guidelines require an assessment of whether effective competition is harmed to the detriment of consumers by horizontal mergers, and whether efficiency considerations are explicitly recognised as a part of the assessment of mergers.[476] However, while the protection of effective competition is for the benefit of consumers, this does not mean that consumer welfare must be measured directly. EU competition law does not require proof of direct harm to consumers in order to apply.[477] Instead, 'the need to protect the competitive process can coincide with the desire to protect consumers'.[478]

467. John Vickers, 'How Does the Prohibition of Abuse of Dominance Fit with the Rest of Competition Policy?' in Claus-Dieter Ehlermann and Isabela Atanasiu (eds) *European Competition Law Annual* 2003: *What is Abuse of Dominant Position* (Bloomsbury Publishing 2006) 147, 150. He also observes that the assessment of mergers *ex ante* is very different from the *ex post* intervention in abuse of dominance cases and as such, the threshold for the latter should be considerably higher than for the former.
468. Ioannis Kokkoris and Howard Shelanski, *EU Merger Control: A Legal and Economic Analysis* (OUP Catalogue 2014) 26.
469. Witt, *The more Economic Approach to EU Antitrust Law* (n. 392) 134.
470. Horizontal Mergers Guidelines, para. 22.
471. Witt, *The more Economic Approach to EU Antitrust Law* (n. 392) 136.
472. Kokkoris and Shelanski, *EU Merger Control: A Legal and Economic Analysis'* (n. 468) 35.
473. ECMR, para. 29.
474. Horizontal Mergers Guidelines, paras 76–88.
475. OECD Report, 'The Role of Efficiency Claims in Antitrust Proceedings' DAF/COMP(2012)23, 7.
476. Horizontal Mergers Guidelines, paras 79–84.
477. *See* in general Marsden and Whelan, 'Consumer Detriment and its Application in EC and UK Competition Law' (n. 391).
478. Kokkoris and Shelanski, *EU Merger Control: A Legal and Economic Analysis* (n. 468) 37.

The same approach can be observed in the non-horizontal merger guidelines.[479] Non-horizontal mergers take place between companies operating in a different level of the supply chain (vertical mergers) or between firms that are in a relationship which is neither horizontal nor vertical (conglomerate mergers) and are deemed more likely to create efficiencies than competitive harm.[480] However, a threat to effective competition might arise if the merged parties have a significant degree of market power. Thus, as in the assessment of horizontal mergers, the first step of the analysis is an evaluation of the degree of market power and of whether the merger would increase market power, which will harm effective competition and, as such, consumers would be harmed.[481] The Guidelines outline two situations where effective competition could be harmed: (1) where the merger is likely to raise the costs of downstream rivals by restricting their access to an important input (input foreclosure); and (2) where the merger is likely to foreclose upstream rivals by restricting their access to a sufficient customer base (customer foreclosure).[482] The assessment should focus on the evaluation of ability and the incentive of the merging parties to foreclose a rival and whether the foreclosure will have a significant detrimental effect on competition and consumers downstream.[483] The foreclosure will have a detrimental effect on consumers only if effective competition is distorted. Hence, the Guidelines envisage a three-step analysis for the assessment of non-horizontal mergers – ability, incentive and effect, in order to demonstrate whether the merger would have an anticompetitive effect.[484]

The understanding of competitive harm expressed in both sets of Guidelines is in contrast with the legal standard that applied before the reform, according to which a likely exclusion of a competitor was sufficient for a prohibition of a merger.[485] In this sense, the reform of Merger Control shifted the focus of analysis from the effect of the merger on the market structure to its effect on effective competition.

§4.05 THE MODERNISATION OF ARTICLE 102 TFEU

[A] 'The Report by the Economic Advisory Group for Competition Policy' (EAGCP Report)

The first step of the reform of Article 102 TFEU occurred in 2005 with the issuance of the EAGCP Report, which was commissioned by the DG Competition with the purpose of bringing Article 102 TFEU into line with Article 101 and the Merger Control regime. According to the EAGCP Report, a given practice is detrimental to competition only if

479. Non-horizontal Mergers Guidelines, para. 10.
480. *Ibid.*, para. 11.
481. *Ibid.*, paras 3–5 and 10. The Commission states that: 'An "increase in market power" in this context refers to the ability of one or more firms to profitably increase prices, reduce output, choice or quality of goods and services, diminish innovation, or otherwise negatively influence parameters of competition'
482. *Ibid.*, para. 30.
483. *Ibid.*, paras 32 and 59.
484. Carles Esteva Mosso, 'Non-Horizontal Mergers: A European Perspectives' (2007) 31 (5) Fordham International 1442, 1448.
485. Witt, *The more Economic Approach to EU Antitrust Law* (n. 392) 141.

leads to anticompetitive effects.[486] It is claimed throughout the Report that, under the effects-based approach, the focus of the antitrust assessment is to identify competitive harm.[487] The Report proposed abandoning the requirement to establish dominance, stating that an establishment of competitive harm 'is already proof of dominance'.[488] The Report further clarifies that the existence of competitive harm 'should be derived from the effect of the practice on consumers'.[489]

According to the Report, a proper effects-based analysis requires that: (1) a consumer harm should be identified in accordance with the specific relevant facts in a case (the possibility of consumer harm is not sufficient);[490] and (2) the balance between pro-competitive and anticompetitive effects should be assessed.[491] However, the Report recognises that in some cases an exclusionary effect can harm consumers in the medium to long run. It is not clear how consumer harm in the long run can be identified and, probably for that reason, the Commission subsequently abandoned the Report's statement that identifying consumer harm is required, as will be examined in the remainder of this section.

For the purpose of this book, the analysis below will focus on the EAGCP Report's proposal on how the Commission should deal with rebates. The EAGCP Report recognised that rebates may come in different forms: pure volume discounts, rebates based on growth in volume above certain thresholds, mixed bundling, and rebates conditional on the client buying all its quantities from the dominant supplier.[492] Further, the EAGCP recognised that rebates can exclude actual or potential competitors from the market in which the firm is dominant and that in most of these cases rebates are associated with predatory pricing because they induce short-run sacrifices and may have exclusionary effects either by inducing exit or by discouraging entry.[493] In the light of this, the proposed assessment of rebates includes several steps: (1) evidence that a negative externality is imposed on a third party; (2) evaluation of the magnitude of the penalty imposed on the entrant (i.e., what is the price that the entrant should offer to meet the rebates); (3) evidence that an efficient competitor is foreclosed; (4) evaluation of possible efficiency effects (if any) and how they are passed on to final consumers.[494] The EAGCP Report also emphasised that in some cases rebates can be associated with an exclusivity clause and as such, they could be similar to exclusive dealing.[495] Despite this observation, rebates and exclusive dealing are discussed in separate sections of the Report, and each is subject to a different standard of evaluation. The Report does not provide further clarity on how to distinguish between rebates that are associated with predatory pricing and those associated with an exclusive dealing.

---

486. EAGCP Report, p. 3.
487. *Ibid.*, pp. 3, 4, 6, 7, 13.
488. *Ibid.*, p. 4.
489. *Ibid.*, p. 8.
490. *Ibid.*, p. 13.
491. *Ibid.*, p. 30.
492. *Ibid.*, p. 34.
493. *Ibid.*, p. 35.
494. *Ibid.*, p. 38.
495. *Ibid.*, p. 35.

The EAGCP Report further emphasised that rebates can have pro-competitive or anticompetitive effects depending on the circumstances, in line with the criticisms of the case law discussed in Chapter 2. However, according to the Report 'rebates that take the form of pure quantity rebates are more likely to be motivated by efficiency considerations than fidelity rebates' and clarified that for that reason it is 'difficult to demonstrate that efficiency considerations motivate the rebate scheme'.[496] This observation would seem to provide support for the case law of fidelity rebates discussed in Chapter 2 according to which, where rebates were found to be fidelity-enhancing with the effect of hindering competitor's access to the market, they cannot be justified based on efficiency considerations.[497] It would also seem to be in line with the conclusions in Chapter 3 (*see* section 3.04) that the possible pro-competitive effects of fidelity rebates are only likely to occur in limited circumstances.

[B] The Discussion Paper

Soon after the publication of the EAGCP Report, the Commission introduced the Discussion Paper, which outlined possible principles for the application of Article 102 to exclusionary abuses. The Discussion Paper defined that exclusionary abuse is behaviour by a dominant firm, which is likely to have a foreclosure effect on the market and which ultimately harms consumers.[498] Protecting competition on the market means that consumer welfare is enhanced and the efficient allocation of resources is guaranteed.[499]

The Discussion Paper did not follow the EAGCP Report's proposal to drop the dominance screening; instead it used the *United Brands* definition of dominance as a position of economic strength enjoyed by an undertaking which enables it to prevent effective competition being maintained on the relevant market by affording it the power to behave to an appreciable extent independently of its competitors, its customers and ultimately of the consumers.[500] It further clarified that dominance means that an undertaking must not be subject to effective competitive constraint, i.e., it must have substantial market power, which is 'the power to influence market prices, output, innovation, the variety or quality of goods and services, or other parameters of competition'.[501] This interpretation of the economic concept of market power was seen by some as referring 'specifically to the ability to reduce consumer welfare', which is in line with the concept of a more economic approach to Article 101 and Merger Control.[502] However, it is accepted that the CJEU equated dominance with substantial

496. *Ibid.*, p..36.
497. *See* Chapter 2.
498. The Discussion Paper, para. 1.
499. *Ibid.*, para. 4.
500. Case 27/76 *United Brands v. Commission* [1978] ECR I -207, para. 65 (hereinafter *United Brands*).
501. The Discussion Paper, paras 23–24.
502. Witt, *The More Economic Approach to EU Antitrust Law* (n. 392) 155.

market power in the definition of dominance quoted above.[503] In this sense, the promotion of consumer welfare has been recognised by the EU Courts from the early days,[504] which makes the reform of Article 102 not as extensive as the reform of Article 101 and Merger Control.

The Discussion Paper also expresses the Commission's preference for an effects-based approach, according to which the main concern of Article 102 TFEU is to preclude 'an exclusionary conduct which produces actual or likely anticompetitive effects in the market and which can harm consumers in a direct or indirect way'.[505] This statement seems to refer to the second part of the definition of dominance – namely, a firm's ability to engage in exclusionary practices that prevent effective competition from being maintained. The power of a dominant company to exclude or deter its competitors from the market refers to its ability to prevent effective competition and as such, to exercise its substantial market power, which may harm consumers. Further, the Commission's definition of effects-based approach mentioned direct or indirect possible harm to consumers from an exclusionary conduct. This statement was interpreted by some as meaning that consumer harm needs to be shown as a requirement for the violation of the competitive rules.[506] Nevertheless, the Discussion Paper clearly states that to establish harm to consumers it is necessary to establish a market-distorting foreclosure, which means 'that actual or potential competitors are completely or partially denied profitable access to a market'.[507] The Discussion Paper emphasises that once the effective competition is harmed, the likely effect will be that prices will increase or remain at a supra-competitive level as a result of the foreclosure, which clearly constitutes consumer harm. Arguably, this is a presumption of the likely effects of a practice on consumers, which is quite different from the verification of direct or indirect consumer harm.

The Discussion Paper further makes it clear that, to establish a market-distorting foreclosure it is necessary to consider not only the form of the conduct, but also the market coverage of the conduct, market characteristics (i.e., economies of scale and scope) and the degree of dominance.[508] Hence, the Discussion Paper takes the position that what really matters is not the form of the conduct but rather its effect. Nonetheless, the Discussion Paper also envisages that for a certain form of exclusionary conduct, the abuse could be presumed without further assessment when such practices can only raise obstacles to competition and create no efficiencies.[509] In those cases, the

503. Damien Geradin and Others, *The Concept of Dominance in EC Competition Law* (2005) https://papers.ssrn.com/soL3/papers.cfm?abstract_id=770144 accessed 14 October 2015.
504. Richard Whish and David Bailey, *Competition Law* (8th edn, OUP 2015) 20.
505. The Discussion Paper, para. 55.
506. Philip Marsden and Simon Bishop, 'Article 82 Review: "What is Your Theory of Harm?" (2006) 2(2) European Competition Journal 257, 260; Akman, 'The EC Discussion Paper on the Application of Article 82' (n. 15); Petit, 'From Formalism to Effects?' (n. 15).
507. The Discussion Paper, para. 58.
508. *Ibid.*, para. 59.
509. *Ibid.*, para. 60.

possibility for objective justification being presented is nonetheless envisaged.[510] The Discussion Paper recognises a number of defences – including meeting competition, objective necessity and other efficiency defences under Article 102. The Discussion Paper then follows Article 101 (3) when identifying the criteria that a dominant company needs to meet to prevail in its defence: (1) efficiencies must be realised or be likely to be realised as a result of the conduct concerned; (2) the conduct is indispensable to realising these efficiencies; (3) the efficiencies benefit consumers and (4) competition in respect of a substantial part of the products concerned is not eliminated.[511]

The Discussion Paper then distinguishes between price and non-price exclusionary conducts, and indicates that different assessments should be adopted for each of them.[512] In assessing price-based conduct, anticompetitive foreclosure could arise only if the conduct excludes a hypothetical 'as efficient' competitor, which has the same costs as the dominant company.[513] The presumption is that a competitor is as efficient as the dominant company if its costs are the same. This means that if the dominant company's pricing is below costs, an as efficient competitor can be foreclosed, in which case, consumer harm (in terms of price, choice, quality and innovation) is presumed to follow. An exception to this rule is envisaged for cases when a not (yet) as efficient competitor should be protected, especially in markets where economies of scale and scope, learning curve effects or first-mover advantages are present.[514] In contrast, when assessing non-price based conduct, the assessment is directly on the possible anticompetitive effect on the market, rather than focusing on identifying how efficient competitors are or whether the dominant firm's conduct sacrifices profits in terms of above-cost pricing, which suggests an application of a price-cost test.

As regards rebates, the Discussion Paper distinguishes between three categories: single branding, conditional rebates and unconditional rebates. With regards to conditional rebates, it further distinguishes between incremental and retroactive rebates and proposes a different methodology for each category. The Paper further classifies single branding as non-price-based conduct and rebates conditional on all purchases as a price-based conduct. This classification is problematic because, as the Discussion Paper suggests, in some cases single branding and rebates may have the same effect as contractual exclusive dealing.[515] As was pointed out in section 4.03 above, single branding and fidelity rebates may for all practical purposes belong to the same category. If a rebate scheme with the effect of exclusive dealing is clearly a non-price-based conduct, it should be assessed by reference to a standard relevant to non-price conduct. Nonetheless, the Discussion Paper does not indicate how to distinguish between price and non-price-based rebates.

510. *Ibid.*, para. 77. The possibility for efficiency defence under Art. 102 is not new as far as the EU Courts have already considered that possibility. *See* cases *Michelin* I, para. 85; *Irish Sugar*, para. 189; *British Airways*, para. 88; *Michelin II*, para. 108.
511. The Discussion Paper, para. 84.
512. *Ibid.*, para. 61.
513. *Ibid.*, para. 63.
514. *Ibid.*, para. 67.
515. The Discussion Paper, para. 62.

[C] The Guidance Paper

Following the EAGCR Report and the Discussion Paper, it had been expected that the Commission would publish substantive guidelines regarding what it understood the law to be, along the same lines as the Guidelines it had drafted regarding Article 101 TFEU and EU Merger Control. Instead of issuing guidelines that interpret the introduction of the effects-based approach to Article 102, the Commission published enforcement priority guidance that cover only certain categories of potentially abusive conduct, such as predatory pricing, discrimination, fidelity rebates and tying. At the outset, the Commission stressed that the document is not intended to constitute a statement of the law and that was without prejudice to the interpretation of Article 102 by the EU Courts.[516]

In a similar way to the Discussion Paper, the Guidance Paper reiterates the definition of dominance from the case law, which equated dominance with substantial market power. The Commission further considered that competitive constraints might not be effective enough to prevent the dominant company from behaving independently even in the presence of some actual or potential competition.[517]

In elucidating the main objective of Article 102, the Guidance Paper emphasises that:

> [t]he Commission's enforcement activity in relation to exclusionary conduct is on safeguarding the competitive process in the internal market and ensuring that undertakings which hold a dominant position do not exclude their competitors by other means than competing on the merits of the products or services they provide. In doing so the Commission is mindful that what really matters is protecting an effective competitive process and not simply protecting competitors. This may well mean that competitors who deliver less to consumers in terms of price, choice, quality and innovation will leave the market.[518]

This statement explains in a meaningful way that the protection of the competitive process is the goal of the Commission's enforcement efforts, because effective competition is a guarantee that the consumers will not be harmed. Further, the Commission's Paper clarifies that the conduct of a dominant company should be considered abusive if it is likely to lead to an anticompetitive foreclosure.[519] For the Commission an 'anticompetitive foreclosure' means:

> [a] situation where effective access of actual or potential competitors to supplies or markets is hampered or eliminated as a result of the conduct of the dominant undertaking whereby the dominant undertaking is likely to be in a position to profitably increase prices to the detriment of consumers.[520]

According to this definition, in order to establish an anticompetitive foreclosure the Commission must find that a competitor is foreclosed and that consumers could be

516. The Guidance Paper, para. 3.
517. *Ibid.*, para. 10.
518. *Ibid.*, para. 6.
519. *Ibid.*, para. 20.
520. *Ibid.*, para. 19.

harmed as a result.[521] The Commission considers that consumers could be harmed if a dominant company is able to increase prices as a result of the conduct under consideration, or when other parameters of competition – such as prices, output, innovation, the variety (i.e., consumer choice) or quality of goods or services – are influenced.[522] However, these statements are not very clear on what consumer harm means. The first impression, rightly observed by some commentators, is that the Guidance Paper does not provide a clear test for consumer harm.[523] Arguably, the Guidance Paper does not contain such a test. The assessment of anticompetitive foreclosure, which became the essence of the effects-based approach, is testing the anticompetitive effect on the competitive structure rather than direct harm to consumers. Thus, only a foreclosure that is harmful for consumers can raise competition concerns. For that reason, the Guidance Paper does not contain a test for consumer harm.[524] More importantly, this interpretation clarified the European Commission's understanding of the effects-based approach, which is the standard guaranteeing the protection of competition on the market; it is also exactly the meaning of the effects-based approach that has been adopted in Council Regulations and soft law instruments for the assessment of vertical restraints and horizontal agreements and EU Merger Control as outlined in sections 3.03 and 3.04 above.

The Commission proposes that the assessment of foreclosure should start from an evaluation of the following factors: the position of the dominant undertaking; the conditions of the relevant market; the position of the dominant undertaking's competitors; the position of the customers or input suppliers; the extent of the allegedly abusive conduct; possible evidence of actual foreclosure; direct evidence of any exclusionary strategy.[525] These factors amount to a screening of possible anticompetitive foreclosure by looking at the market structure. Moreover, these factors mirror the evaluation of possible anticompetitive harm in the assessment of vertical restraints. This has been interpreted by some as eliminating the boundaries of Articles 101 and 102 in the area of vertical agreements;[526] and as creating a screening tool that looks at market structure instead of at consumer harm.[527] However, since Article 102 TFEU focuses on unilateral conduct, market structure is often used as a proxy for the possibility of consumer harm; furthermore, it is possible to apply Articles 101 and 102 TFEU simultaneously. Thus, this parallelism could also be welcomed as bringing coherence to the law while still

521. Petit, 'From Formalism to Effects?' (n. 15) 3.
522. The Guidance Paper, para. 11.
523. Akman, 'The EC Discussion Paper on the Application of Article 82' (n. 15); Petit, 'From Formalism to Effects?' (n. 15); Marsden and Gormsen, 'Guidance on Abuse in Europe: The Continued Concern for Rivalry and a Competitive Structure' (n. 180) 892.
524. Pinar Akman, *The Reform of the Application of Article 102 TFEU: Mission Accomplished?* (2015) 8 https://papers.ssrn.com/sol3/papers.cfm?abstract_id=2654679 accessed 6 October 2016.
525. The Guidance Paper, para. 20.
526. Ekaterina Rousseva, *Rethinking Exclusionary Abuses in EU Competition Law* (Hart Publishing 2010) 432.
527. Manuel Kellerbauer, 'The Commission's New Enforcement Priorities in Applying Article 82 EC to Dominant Companies' Exclusionary Conduct: A Shift Towards a More Economic Approach?' (2010) 31 European Competition Law Review 175, 183.

ensuring that the pursuit of consumer harm is at the forefront of competition enforcement.

The Commission further considers that foreclosure can be harmful for consumers if 'the conduct concerned has already been or is capable of hampering competition from competitors which are considered to be as efficient as the dominant undertaking'.[528] This foreclosure can be identified by reference to the 'as efficient competitor test'. According to the Commission, the consumers could be harmed only if the foreclosed competitor is as efficient as the dominant company. Further, the Commission considers that this could be evaluated through comparing costs and actual prices of a dominant company in order to assess whether the dominant company is sacrificing profits by its conduct. If the prices of the dominant company are below cost, a hypothetical as efficient competitor with the same cost structure would not be able to match its prices and, thus, to compete without incurring a loss. From this perspective, if a hypothetical as efficient competitor cannot survive, the aim of the conduct is anticompetitive foreclosure, regardless of how efficient the actual rivals are.[529] Thus, the test was considered as a screening devise.

The cost benchmarks that the Commission chooses to use are average avoidable costs (AAC) and long-run average incremental cost (LRAIC).[530] Failure to cover the AAC indicates that the dominant undertaking is sacrificing profits in the short term and that an equally efficient competitor cannot serve the targeted customers without incurring a loss. Failure to cover LRAIC indicates that the dominant undertaking is not recovering all the (attributable) fixed costs of producing the goods or service in question, and that an equally efficient competitor could be foreclosed from the market.

Thus, the Commission considers the price-cost test (requiring profit sacrifice as a key element) as a specific instrument to verify whether an as efficient competitor could survive or not. The Commission also considered that this test is applicable only for price-based exclusionary conduct. The logic of the test is that if a dominant company's pricing is below costs and sacrificing profits, its intention is to foreclose an as efficient competitor, which ultimately will harm the competitive structure in an anticompetitive way. In this sense, the test is a tool that measures harm to consumers in an indirect way, namely through evaluating the harm to competition; it is not a test evaluating direct consumer harm.

For the purpose of this book, the proposed assessment of fidelity rebates will be discussed in detail. The Guidance Paper places rebates into the general category of exclusive dealing and distinguishes between exclusive purchasing obligation, which requires a customer in a particular market to purchase exclusively or to a large extent

528. The Guidance Paper, para. 23.
529. Nicholas Banasevic and Per Hellström, 'When the Chips are Down: Some Reflections on the European Commission's Intel Decision' (2010) 1(4) Journal of European Competition Law and Practice 301, 304.
530. The Guidance Paper, para. 26. LRAIC is usually above AAC because, in contrast to AAC (which only includes fixed costs if incurred during the period under examination), LRAIC includes product specific fixed costs made before the period in which allegedly abusive conduct took place.

only from the dominant undertaking[531] and conditional rebates, which are granted if customer's purchases over a defined reference period exceed a certain threshold. Further, the Paper distinguishes between rebates granted on all purchases (retroactive rebates) or only on those made in excess of those required to achieve the threshold (incremental rebates).[532] The Guidance Paper proposes a different assessment for each category, which will be discussed in turn.

The Commission considers that the evaluation of the possible risk of anticompetitive foreclosure in cases of exclusive purchasing obligation (which covers fidelity rebates with similar characteristics) should be based on the following assessment. First, the Commission considers that the capacity for exclusive purchasing obligations to result in anticompetitive foreclosure arises when competitors may not be able to compete for an individual customer's entire demand because the dominant undertaking is an unavoidable trading partner at least for part of the demand on the market, for instance because its brand is a 'must-stock item' preferred by many final consumers or because the capacity constraints on the other suppliers are such that a part of demand can only be provided by the dominant supplier. Further, it is considered that the duration of the exclusive purchasing obligation is important. If the duration of the obligation is lengthy, customers would find it difficult to switch suppliers, which means that a foreclosure effect is more likely. In addition, the Commission considered that, 'if the dominant undertaking is an unavoidable trading partner for all or most customers, even an exclusive purchasing obligation of short duration can lead to an anti-competitive foreclosure'.[533] These considerations reflect the proposed assessment of the possible anticompetitive effect of single branding under Article 101 as discussed in section 4.03 above. The proposed assessment of exclusive purchasing obligation and fidelity rebates with similar effect does not contain a price-cost test, which suggests that the Commission considered these practices as a non-price conduct even though this is not mentioned explicitly.

For the assessment of conditional rebates, the Commission considered as a first step an assessment of the general factors related to market conditions.[534] Next, it was considered that conditional rebates might have actual or potential foreclosing effects similar to exclusive purchasing obligations without necessarily requiring a sacrifice for the dominant undertaking.[535] This observation is of great importance because it indicates that the assessment of rebates with effects similar to exclusive dealing differs from that of predation, which always entails a sacrifice and as such, requires that a price-cost test should be utilised. It also means that the treatment of such rebates can be effects-based without carrying out a price-cost test. However, the European Commission did not emphasise this, and referred to it only in an accompanying footnote to paragraph 37. Thus, the Commission recognised that proving sacrifice through a price-cost test might not be necessary for the evaluation of conditional

531. The Guidance Paper, para. 33.
532. *Ibid.*, para. 37.
533. *Ibid.*, para. 35.
534. *Ibid.*, para. 20.
535. *Ibid.*, para. 37.

rebates with effects similar to exclusive purchasing obligation effects. The Commission also observed that in cases when the effect of conditional rebates is similar to exclusive purchasing obligations, the rebates are likely to have an anticompetitive foreclosure if the dominant company is an unavoidable trading partner and customers obtain a significant part of their demand (the assured base of sales) from it and at the same time the dominant company is in a position to use the assured portion of the demand of each customer as leverage to decrease the price to be paid for the non-assured portion of demand.[536] In this regard, the Commission observed that 'the assessment of loyalty-enhancing effect of a rebate is not simply the effect on competition to provide the last individual unit, but the foreclosing effect of the rebate system on (actual or potential) competitors of the dominant supplier'.[537] This statement suggests that the fidelity-enhancing effect of conditional rebates might be enough to foreclose an as efficient competitor, which would be anticompetitive. In such a case, the foreclosure of an efficient competitor is due to the fidelity-enhancing effect of rebates (non-price conduct) and not to pricing below cost (price conduct). This explanation resembles the interpretation of the fidelity-enhancing effect of rebates as outlined in Chapter 3. However, the Commission failed to clarify explicitly that in these cases, the fidelity-enhancing effect of fidelity rebates makes them similar to exclusive purchasing obligations, i.e., non-price conduct.

Notwithstanding the observation that conditional rebates can have actual or potential anticompetitive foreclosure effects similar to exclusive dealing without necessarily entailing profit sacrifice, the Guidance Paper proposed the application of a price-cost test to fidelity rebates.[538] The Commission thus seemed to consider, contrary to what was described in the previous paragraphs, that conditional rebates are always price-based conduct without any clarification of why and when they should be regarded as price conduct. Recalling the discussion in Chapter 3, conditional rebates might appear in many different forms depending on the condition to be obtained and moreover, depending on the circumstances, they might amount to pricing or non-pricing conduct. Thus, a clear-cut categorisation of when conditional rebates are price or non-price conduct is crucial for the proper assessment of their legality.[539] However, the Commission proposed a price-cost test for the assessment of the legality of conditional rebates and did not provide any guidance as to when they should be assessed as exclusive purchasing obligations or as a potentially anticompetitive pricing conduct.

Whereas the price-cost test has a strong pedigree under Article 102 in predatory pricing and margin squeeze cases;[540] in the area of fidelity rebates it represents an innovation and it was not used in the case law discussed in Chapter 2. Moreover, the test proposed by the Commission is not the same as that applied in a plain-vanilla predatory pricing cases but is a 'modified' test, which is more complex as can be

536. *Ibid.*, para. 39.
537. *Ibid.*, para. 40.
538. *Ibid.*, para. 41.
539. On this point *see* in general Jessen (n. 257) Ch. 5.
540. O'Donoghue and Padilla (n. 13) 231.

recalled from the discussion in Chapter 3. This modified test operates in two stages. The first one starts with an evaluation of whether the price discount of the dominant undertaking covers the costs of producing the same goods/services produced by the equally efficient competitor, allowing the latter to compete effectively with the dominant undertaking. The purpose of the first step is to establish the effective price that the competitor will have to offer in order to compensate the customer for the loss of the conditional rebate if the latter switched part of its demand ('the relevant range') away from the dominant undertaking. The effective price is not the average price of the dominant undertaking, but the normal (list) price minus the rebate the customer loses by switching, calculated over the relevant range of sales for the relevant period of time. Next, an estimation of the relevant range is required. The relevant range depends on whether rebates are incremental or retroactive. For incremental rebates, the relevant range is the incremental purchases above the threshold. For retroactive rebates, the relevant range depends on how much of a customer's purchase requirements can realistically be switched to a competitor (the 'contestable share'). Presuming that each customer has a different requirement, the contestable share should be different for each customer. Thus, the relevant range should be estimated for each customer separately.

The second step would require the Commission to compare the effective price with the appropriate measure of costs. If the effective price is below AAC, as a general rule the rebate scheme is capable of foreclosing even equally efficient competitors. Where the effective price is between AAC and LRAIC, the Commission will investigate whether other factors point to the conclusion that entry or expansion even by equally efficient competitors is likely to be affected. The Commission was aware that the modified price-cost test is prone to errors and uncertainties and considers that it will 'take into account the margin of error that may be caused by the uncertainties inherent in this kind of analysis'.[541]

The Commission also observes that the application of a price-cost test is only part of the assessment, since low prices do not in themselves harm competition. The Commission clarifies that the result of the test should be combined with the other circumstances of the case in order to assess whether the exclusion is anticompetitive and might harm consumers.[542] This observation suggests that the Commission was aware that the price-cost test is not a sufficient condition for finding an abuse.[543] It also confirms that the concept of the AEC test is broader and contains not only a price-cost test but also an evaluation of all other circumstances.

The price-cost test was developed by some economists to provide rules for anticompetitive pricing conduct such as predatory pricing and margin squeeze.[544] However, it cannot be identified as a single tool for the evaluation of an anticompetitive effect in all cases, even less can it be equated with the effects-based approach. Recalling

541. The Guidance Paper, para. 41.
542. *Ibid.*, para. 45.
543. Geradin, 'A Proposed Test for Separating Pro-Competitive Conditional Rebates from Anti-Competitive (n. 4) 47; Martin Mandorff and Johan Sahl, 'The Role of the 'Equally Efficient Competitor' in the Assessment of Abuse of Dominance' (2013) 1 Konkurrensverket (Swedish Competition Authority).
544. Lang, 'Article 82 EC – The Problems and The Solution' (n. 394) 9.

the discussion in section 4.02 above, the effects-based approach is focused on the evaluation of a possible negative effect (anticompetitive foreclosure) of the conduct of a dominant company on competition and consumer welfare. Foreclosure is anticompetitive if a competitor at least as efficient as the dominant company is foreclosed, which can occur even if prices are above costs. Thus, an effects-based approach can be equated with an anticompetitive effect due to an exclusion of an as efficient competitor, which is not reliant exclusively on a price-cost test. Consequently, the effects-based approach covers the concept of the AEC test, which is not limited to a price- cost test.

Further, the Commission considers that, in some circumstances a less efficient rival can stimulate competition, and that this should be taken into account.[545] This observation is very important because it indicates that the Commission was aware that in certain circumstances (as e.g., but not limited to cases of economy of scale and scope and/or first-mover advantages), competitors cannot become as efficient as the incumbent. In such cases, even a less efficient competitor can create competitive constraints to the dominant company.[546] Hence, a less efficient competitor can stimulate competition and lower prices if an incumbent dominant firm is charging monopoly prices. In those cases, harm to the less efficient competitor might be seen as harm to competition. This observation also suggests that the Commission considers that the AEC test is not suitable to identify anticompetitive effects in all cases. Still, the assessment of the conduct accounts for the effects-based approach because the focus is on the possible harm to competition, and this can be evaluated without a price-cost test. Arguably, the CJEU in *Post Danmark II* (which will be discussed in Chapter 5) expressed exactly the same view when it stated that the market in this particular case could not accommodate a competitor as efficient as Post Danmark, in which case 'the presence of a less efficient competitor might contribute to intensifying the competitive pressure on that market and, therefore, to exerting a constraint on the conduct of the dominant undertaking'.[547]

Finally, and in line with the Discussion Paper, the Commission considers that some unilateral conducts should be expected to result in consumer harm, in which case it might not be necessary for a detailed assessment to be carried out.[548] In other words, the Commission would not deviate significantly from the case law of Article 102 and keep prohibiting some 'by object' restrictions when enforcing Article 102.[549] As has been shown in Chapter 2, in certain circumstances the alleged conduct could be at least prima facie abusive and, hence, it is reasonable for it to be condemned as abusive 'by object' without engaging in further analysis of the possible effect.[550] Further, the

545. The Guidance Paper, para. 24.
546. Many commentators criticised the AEC test on that ground, *see* Lang and O'Donoghue 'The Concept of an Exclusionary abuse under Article 82 EC' (n. 14); Gavil (n. 298); Steven Salop, *Avoiding Error in the Antitrust Analysis of Unilateral Refusals to Deal* (2005) V written submission to AMC, Statement for the hearing at the Antitrust Modernization Commission.
547. *Post Danmark II*, para. 60.
548. The Guidance Paper, para. 22.
549. Richard Whish, *Competition Law* (6th edn, OUP 2009) 120.
550. O'Donoghue and Padilla (n. 13) 225. They claimed that when the: [E]xperience and logic suggest that the benefit/harm resulting from a practice is so clear and unambiguous that there is no point in wasting court or regulatory resources in investigating its effects; *see also* Petit, 'From formalism to effect' (n.15) 496, who states that: 'a full-fledged effects-based approach

Commission provides limited examples of when this might be the case, as for example in cases:

> when the dominant undertaking prevents its customers from testing the products of competitors or provides financial incentives to its customers on condition that they do not test such products, or pays a distributor or a customer to delay the introduction of a competitor's product.[551]

Finally, the Guidance Paper explains that a dominant undertaking may demonstrate that its conduct is objectively necessary, or produces substantial efficiencies which outweigh any anticompetitive effects.[552] In this sense, the Guidance Paper reproduces the position from the Discussion Paper, as discussed above.

§4.06 CONCLUSION

European competition policy acknowledged consumer welfare as its ultimate goal.[553] This position is reflected in the modernisation of European competition law through the adoption of the 'effects-based' approach. While the adoption of this approach to vertical and horizontal agreements and mergers is widely perceived as successful,[554] the modernisation of Article 102 has been subject to harsh criticism from academics, commentators and practitioners alike.

The aim of this chapter has been to clarify the meaning of the 'effects-based' approach, in an attempt to understand what the appropriate treatment of fidelity rebates should be under this approach. Another goal was to understand whether the proposed approach reflects first, the reform of Article 101 and Merger Control regime, and, second, whether it reflects criticisms that the Commission discarded the possible pro-competitive effects of fidelity rebates. This has been done by examining the Commission's understanding of the effects-based approach as reflected in its policy statements, in the reform of Article 101 and of Merger control. Next, by evaluating the European Commission's official documents related to the reform of Article 102 to understand whether the effects-based approach is in line with the reform attributed to the other areas of EU competition law.

As discussed throughout the chapter, when modernising Article 101 and Merger Control the European Commission defined its objectives as the protection of an effective competitive process, which guarantees the protection of consumer welfare and the efficient allocation of resources. This is supported by the content of the Commission's soft law instruments related to the reform of Article 101 and Merger Control. Accordingly, under the reformed approach, a conduct is considered to breach Article 101 only if it results in an anticompetitive effect on the market that is likely to harm consumers, and that concomitant efficiencies cannot overcome the conduct's

might not be warranted in all Article 82 EC cases. This is especially true of cases where a dominant firm has blatantly sought to foreclose competition.'

551. The Guidance Paper, para. 22.
552. The Guidance Paper, paras 28–30.
553. Alhborn and Padilla (n. 6) 57.
554. *See* in general Witt, *The More Economic Approach to EU Antitrust Law* (n. 392).

anticompetitive effect. In contrast, before the reform, agreements could be deemed anticompetitive based on their form rather than their actual effect.

Similarly, a merger will only be anticompetitive if it is likely to result in a substantial lessening of competition – which is in contrast to the legal standard applicable before the reform, according to which the impact of a merger on the market structure was sufficient to establish that a merger is not compatible with the common market. The new approach requires an examination of a wide range of economic facts and circumstances in order to identify the conditions of competition as well as in what way efficiencies might arise. In this sense, the reformed approach to Article 101 and Merger Control is focused on the creation of rules that guarantee the maintenance of an effective competitive process. While the ultimate goal is to benefit consumers, this does not mean that consumer welfare should be measured directly because the EU competition law does not require proof of direct harm to consumers in order to apply.[555]

The reform did not significantly amend the Commission's interpretation of Article 102. First, in its Guidance Paper, the Commission reiterated the significance of the concepts of dominance and special responsibility from the settled case law and stressed that the protection of the competitive process is a main objective of Article 102. This reflects the 'traditional' approach of the EU Courts. In this sense, as observed by Monti, 'the seeds for reform of Article 102 are already inherent in the case law, which suggests that the Commission's reform programme envisages incremental change rather than radical revolution'.[556]

Instead, the Commission focuses on its enforcement priorities – with enforcement being directed against conduct that is likely to result in anticompetitive foreclose, since this is an outcome that is likely to result in harm to effective competition that will lead to consumer harm. The Commission defined what type of conduct might result in anticompetitive foreclosure, and clarified that exclusion is anticompetitive if a competitor that is at least as efficient as the dominant company is foreclosed – a principle known as the AEC test. Further, the Commission considered that anticompetitive foreclosure could be evaluated through a price-cost test as a specific instrument that would determine whether an as efficient competitor could survive or not.

The Commission observes that the application of a price-cost test is only a part of the assessment identifying anticompetitive foreclosure, since the low prices do not in themselves harm competition and the result of the test should be combined with the other evidence, which suggests that the price-cost test cannot be equated with the general concept of the AEC test. However, the concept of the AEC test can be interpreted more broadly than a price-cost test. Anticompetitive foreclosure might occur if an as efficient competitor is foreclosed but as described in Chapter 3, anticompetitive foreclosure might arise due to the fidelity-enhancing effect of rebates that maintain prices above cost. In this case, a price-cost test is not appropriate. The Commission's own definition of anticompetitive foreclosure suggests that, in order to amount to an anticompetitive practice, the conduct must foreclose competitors leading to a harmful effect on competition, which would in turn harm consumers. Thus, what

555. *See* text to (n. 394) in Chapter 4.
556. Monti, *EC Competition Law* (n. 443) 162.

matters is an exclusion of a competitor that is at least as efficient as the dominant one, regardless of whether a price-cost test is met or not. The Guidance Paper recognises this, and proposes that the assessment of anticompetitive foreclosure in cases of non-price conduct, such as exclusive purchasing, refusal to supply and tying should be evaluated without a price-cost test. Arguably, the case law has long recognized that some forms of conduct can be exclusionary without involving below-cost pricing.[557] Still, the approach is effects-based because it requires an assessment of the effect of the conduct on the competitive structure that might harm consumers. In this sense, it could be assumed that the effects-based approach is a standard that minimizes type I errors, which occur when a practice is deemed abusive despite being pro-competitive – as can be the case with prohibiting fidelity rebates granted by a dominant company as abusive without assessing their effects.[558]

Thus, if the concept of the AEC test is that only an exclusion of an as efficient competitor is capable of harming consumers, it still can be an effects-based approach even if the assessment is carried out without a formal price-cost test. In this sense, the concept of the AEC test might be more broadly interpreted than the view that the AEC test is only a price-cost test. Moreover, the concept of an AEC test, not the price-cost test in itself, can be correctly equated with the effects-based approach.

In the context of efficiency considerations, the Commission proposes the concept of objective justification; a concept that had always been recognised as a principle under Article 102, that an abusive conduct could be objectively justified if it creates efficiencies.

However, the Guidance Paper lacks clarity as to how to differentiate between conditional rebates that have effects similar to exclusive purchasing obligation (non-price conduct) and those that might be regarded as pricing conduct. Some forms of conduct, such as tying and refusal to deal can easily be categorised as non-price conduct, while predatory pricing and margin squeeze can be categorised as pricing conduct but for conditional rebates it might not be so obvious.[559] But it is unclear when conditional rebates fall within a pricing or non-pricing category, which is crucial for the choice of the appropriate framework for their assessment. If conditional rebates are regarded as pricing conduct, an application of a price-cost test would be relevant for the evaluation of their anticompetitive effect; whereas if they are regarded as non-price conduct, an evaluation of qualitative evidence rather than comparing price and cost would be relevant.

From the above, it is doubtful, however, that the Guidance Paper's classification of some rebates as amounting to exclusive dealing (non-price conduct) while proposing to evaluate their effect in applying an innovative price-cost test, which is extremely complex, prone to implementation errors,[560] which no court endorses so far[561] is

557. Case C-53/92 P *Hilti v. Commission* [1994] ECR I-667 (hereinafter *Hilti*); Case C-333/94 P *Tetra Pak International SA v. Commission* [1996] ECR I-5951, para 41 (hereinafter *Tetra Pak II*).
558. The symmetrical situation occurs when a practice is considered legal despite being anticompetitive – this is known as a Type II error.
559. Jessen (n. 257) 104.
560. *See* Chapter 3, section 3.04.
561. US submission for the OECD Report (2008).

appropriate – a matter which has come to the fore when the Commission's approach has been subject to judicial scrutiny. To illustrate this, the next chapter of this book will look at the recent case law on fidelity rebates, where the applicability of a modified price-cost test in relation to the anticompetitive effects of fidelity rebates has been raised as a central issue.

CHAPTER 5

Recent Case Law on Fidelity Rebates

§5.01 INTRODUCTION

As indicated in the previous chapters, the effects-based approach requires an assessment of the effect of the conduct on competition in order to distinguish anticompetitive conduct from legitimate competition. A conduct is considered anticompetitive if a competitor that is at least as efficient as the dominant company is foreclosed, which can be assessed through the evaluation of all the circumstances including a price-cost test depending on the circumstances of the case, as a part of the assessment.

This chapter will focus on recent case law on fidelity rebates, and in particular on two cases where the effects-based approach and the application of a price-cost test in particular in relation to the anticompetitive effects of fidelity rebates have been raised as a central issue. The first case is *Intel*, in which the Commission for the first time followed the provisions of the Guidance Paper and conducted an in-depth assessment to assess the effect of fidelity rebates granted by an undertaking possessing market power under Article 102 – including a price-cost test.[562] However, the Commission based its decision on the settled case law of fidelity rebates and emphasised that the assessment of the rebates at issue, including the price-cost test, was conducted merely for completeness. In short, it was unnecessary to conduct a price-cost test in order to find an abuse of dominant position. On appeal, the GC upheld the Commission's decision and reasserted settled case law concerning fidelity rebates under Article 102 TFEU.[563] The GC concluded that a price-cost test was not required for an infringement of Article 102 to be found. In contrast to the reasoning of the GC in Intel, Advocate General (AG) Wahl – in an Opinion provided in the context of Intel's appeal of the GC decision before the CJEU– suggested that the evaluation of fidelity rebates should

562. Commission Decision.
563. GC judgment.

consider the rebates economic and legal context before condemning them as abusive.[564] AG Wahl's Opinion also endorsed the application of the AEC test. With these two contrasting viewpoints, the *Intel* judgment has led to deeper controversy about the appropriate treatment of fidelity rebates. On Intel's further appeal, the CJEU referred the case back to the GC, ordering it to examine the arguments as regard the validity of the price-cost test put forward by Intel.[565] In its decision, the CJEU did not clarify whether the application of a price-cost test is a necessary element of an assessment of fidelity rebates.

The second key ruling on rebates is *Post Danmark II*. The CJEU was asked to clarify, in the context of a preliminary reference, the framework that has to be applied in order to determine whether a rebate scheme is liable to have an exclusionary effect on the market contrary to Article 102 TFEU. The Court was also asked to clarify the relevance of the AEC test (in terms of price-cost test) in the context of this framework.[566] In its decision, the CJEU deemed the application of the AEC test as irrelevant in that particular case, but suggested that the test could be used as one tool amongst others, which means that the application of the test is not rejected in general. The CJEU nonetheless left the question open about under which circumstances the AEC test could be useful.

Against this backdrop, this chapter aims to evaluate recent case law on fidelity rebates and the academic debate that follows in order to clarify why the controversy regarding the treatment of fidelity rebates is still a live issue. The critical discussion of the case law is centred on the idea as to whether the standard needs to reflect economic analysis and particularly the AEC test, in an attempt to clarify why the treatment of fidelity rebates is still unclear.

This chapter will first review the Commission's decision on Intel and the judgment of the GC. It will contrast the GC judgment with the opinion of AG Wahl issued in the context of Intel's appeal to the CJEU, before finally reviewing the CJEU's judgment. Next, the chapter will review the *Post Danmark II* judgment, devoting particular attention to the reasons underpinning the CJEU's assessment of the AEC test. Lastly, a review of the academic debates following these judgments will be pursued before their critical assessment, which will be focused on the role that the courts have attributed to economic analysis and price-cost tests in assessing fidelity rebates.

§5.02 THE INTEL COMMISSION'S DECISION

In its decision of 13 May 2009, the European Commission found that Intel violated Article 102 TFEU, and fined it in an amount of over a billion euros, the highest penalty ever imposed by the European Commission up to that point.

564. Case C-413/14 *Intel v. Commission* [2017] ECR I-632, Opinion of AG Wahl (hereinafter Opinion of AG Wahl).
565. CJEU judgment, para. 150.
566. Pablo Ibáñez Colomo, *Post Danmark II, or the Quest for Administrability and Coherence in Article 102 TFEU* (2015) http://papers.ssrn.com/sol3/Papers.cfm?abstract_id=2636407 accessed 8 December 2015.

[A] Background

Intel is the 'world's largest semiconductor chip maker based on revenue' and it operates worldwide, including in locations within the EEA.[567] It produces microprocessors, known as central processing units (CPUs), which are integrated into computers, servers, and networking and communications products. The CPUs are a key component in the overall performance of a computer, and its cost represents a significant part of the final price of a computer. Intel sells its CPUs primarily to original equipment manufacturers (OEMs) such as Dell, HP, NEC and Lenovo, and occasionally to retailers such as Media-Saturn Holding GmbH (MSH). Intel's customers manufacture computers and sell them to the final consumers and, as such, they compete among themselves in a downstream market. In this sense, the CPUs are an intermediate product. The main competitor of Intel in the production of CPUs is AMD.

[B] The Product

The CPUs manufactured by both Intel and AMD are destined for different segments of the computer industry such as desktop computers, laptop computers and server computers. CPUs used in computers can be sub-divided into two categories: the x86 and non-x86 architecture.[568] In its decision, the European Commission analysed the demand and supply-side substitution between x86 and non-x86 CPUs and concluded that they form two separate relevant markets based on their lack of substitutability.[569]

In the 1980s, IBM adopted a PC standard, based on Intel's CPUs, which was known as the x86 architecture CPUs. The x86 instruction was the subject of substantial intellectual property right protection. As a result, in order to access the x86 market a potential entrant had to develop a basic x86 CPU design, which requires 'an enormous combination of ingenuity, time and capital to develop the required know how to design x86 CPUs or to obtain a license from Intel'.[570] Over the years, both AMD and Intel developed know-how to design x86 CPUs and obtained a cross license agreement 'with both parties guaranteeing mutual non-exclusive, non-transferable licences to the applicable intellectual property rights required to produce [...], without the right to sublicense'.[571] At that time, Intel and AMD were the main manufacturers of x86 architecture CPUs.[572]

[C] Competition Between Intel and AMD

In its decision, the European Commission found that the main dimensions of competition between Intel and AMD were price and innovation. In order to reach this

567. Commission Decision, para. 1.
568. *Ibid.*, para. 120.
569. *Ibid.*, paras 808 and 831.
570. *Ibid.*, para. 129.
571. *Ibid.*, para. 130.
572. *Ibid.*, para. 123.

conclusion, the European Commission analysed the pricing policy of Intel and AMD and concluded that Intel's average selling price for CPUs has historically been higher than that of AMD.[573] Subsequently, it analysed the importance of innovation in this market. The Commission observed that 'the very high research and development (R&D) and production costs can usually only be recovered if new inventions can be sold before the competitor responds with a more innovative product'.[574] The Commission further summarised that the main innovations in recent years were related to: (i) the speed of the internal CPU calculations (clock rate); (ii) the width of the connections between the CPU and other devices of the motherboard; and (iii) the number of processor cores and the ability of several CPUs to work together on a single motherboard.[575]

In 2003, AMD launched its improved x86 CPUs with 64-bit architecture, namely the Opteron, Athlon 64, and Mobile Athlon 64 CPUs. At the same time, Intel announced its first 64-bit processor with an x86 architecture called Xeon-64 (EM64-T). The Commission's analysis showed that AMD's CPUs had the advantage in terms of price and performance over the existing Intel's CPUs.[576] Therefore, AMD's developed CPUs became the first significant competitive threat to Intel's dominant position in the CPUs market.

Further, the Commission analysed Intel's response to the changed condition of competition in the market. It examined various arrangements between Intel and its main clients, namely the OEMs Dell, HP, NEC and Lenovo, and one retailer (MSH) in regard to the terms of price and supply, including the various rebates.[577] In its decision, the Commission found that the level of Intel's rebates granted to Dell, HP, NEC and Lenovo and one retailer (MSH) was de facto conditional upon those companies purchasing all or nearly all of their x86 CPUs from Intel.[578] Furthermore, the Commission found that the agreements between Intel and HP,[579] ACER[580] and Lenovo,[581] were subject to unwritten conditions regarding the launch and other parameters of the commercial policy regarding x86 CPUs AMD-based products. The agreement between Intel and MSH was also subject to an unwritten agreement regarding the setting of prices in exchange for exclusivity. Moreover, the Commission found that the exclusivity agreement was kept secret and that Intel requested the wording 'non-exclusive' to be introduced into the agreement for optical purposes.[582] Further, the Commission demonstrated that Intel was in a position to monitor MSH's sales in order to find deviation from its exclusionary commitment.[583]

573. *Ibid.*, para. 136.
574. *Ibid.*, para. 139.
575. *Ibid.*, para. 142.
576. *Ibid.*, paras 150–164.
577. *Ibid.*, paras 165 et seq.
578. *Ibid.*, paras 323, 413, 450, 501, 579, 788, 924.
579. *Ibid.*, para. 413.
580. *Ibid.*, para. 450.
581. *Ibid.*, para. 579.
582. *Ibid.*, para. 788.
583. *Ibid.*, para. 789.

[D] The Assessment of Intel's Dominant Position

In its assessment of Intel's dominance, the European Commission based its analysis on settled case law, stating that 'holding a dominant position confers a special responsibility on the firm concerned, the scope of which must be considered in the light of the specific circumstances of each case'.[584]

The European Commission concluded that Intel held very high market shares in excess of 80% in an overall x86 CPUs market, and in excess of 70% in any of the sub-markets throughout the six-year observation period.[585] Based on the case law, the Commission concluded that market shares between 70% and 80% were a clear indication of the existence of a dominant position.[586]

The Commission further assessed the barriers to expansion and entry in the relevant market. These barriers related mainly to the nature and size of sunk investment, combined with capacity constraints and significant product differentiation, in particular through brands.[587] After a thorough evaluation of the conditions needed to develop the technology and design of x86 CPUs, the cost of production, and the role of economies of scale, the European Commission concluded that there are significant barriers to entry related to substantial intellectual property barriers, initial research and development and production investments, as well as significant economies of scale.[588] The Commission also found that Intel's strong must-stock brand, and the resulting product differentiation, should be considered as factors that provide Intel with additional market power.[589] Further, as a part of the assessment of dominance, the Commission evaluated the possibility of the OEM's to exert significant buyer power and concluded that in this case buyer power did not provide a sufficiently effective constraint to Intel's market power.[590] The Commission also examined the price trends in the relevant market and found that the prices of CPUs have fallen over time, which was not seen as a factor susceptible to negating the existence of dominance.[591]

[E] The Legal Assessment of Intel's Conduct

The European Commission based its legal assessment of Intel's conduct on existing EU case law regarding fidelity rebates. The Commission commenced its analysis by using the classical definition of abuse from *Hoffmann-La Roche*, where the CJEU equated the effect of the conduct on the competitive structure of the market with abuse.[592] Further, the Commission stated that according to the Courts, Article 102 of the Treaty:

584. *Ibid.*, para. 837.
585. *Ibid.*, para. 852.
586. *Ibid.*, para. 852.
587. *Ibid.*, para. 853.
588. *Ibid.*, para. 866.
589. *Ibid.*, para. 881.
590. *Ibid.*, paras 885–905.
591. *Ibid.*, paras 907–910.
592. *Hoffmann-La Roche*, para. 91.

> [p]rohibits a dominant undertaking from eliminating a competitor and thereby reinforcing its position by having recourse to means other than those within the scope of competition on the merits. From that point of view, not all competition on price can be regarded as legitimate.[593]

The Commission further made clear that, according to settled case law, there is no requirement to demonstrate actual foreclosure (concrete effect) in order to prove an infringement of Article 102 of the Treaty;[594] it is sufficient to demonstrate that the conduct of the dominant undertaking is capable or likely to restrict competition.[595] If a dominant company ties its customers to obtain all or most of their requirements exclusively from it, this conduct constitutes an abuse of dominant position within the meaning of Article 102 TFEU.[596] A violation of Article 102 may also result from a dominant company's conduct, which is anticompetitive by object.[597]

According to the European Commission, Intel engaged in two separate types of exclusionary abuses of its dominant position, namely: conditional rebates and payments; and so-called naked restrictions. The effects of each conduct reinforced the other.[598]

The Commission concluded that the first type of exclusionary conduct amounted to Intel's conditional rebates to Dell, HP, NEC and Lenovo, as well as Intel's payments to MSH to source almost all of their x86 CPUs requirements from Intel.[599] The rebates had the effect of restricting those companies' freedom to choose their source of supply and prevented other competitors from supplying them with corporate desktop x86 CPUs over the period in question.[600] In its decision, the Commission stated that 'those practices were capable of having or likely to have had an even greater negative impact overall on the market, which harmed consumers by depriving them of choices of computers based on AMD x86 CPUs'.[601]

The second type of exclusionary conduct, i.e., naked restrictions, amounted to Intel's conduct to restrict the commercialisation of specific AMD-based products by HP, Acer and Lenovo, related to payments in order for the OEM in question to delay, cancel or in some other way restrict the commercialisation of specific AMD-based products.[602] The two types of conduct complement each other, forming a part of a single strategy to foreclose AMD, resulting in a reduction of consumer choice and in lower incentives to innovate.[603] The Commission did not credit the observation that AMD substantially increased its market share and performance during the period covered by the decision

593. Case C-62/86 *AKZO Chemie BV v. Commission* [1991] ECR I-3359, para. 70 (hereinafter *AKZO*); *Irish Sugar*, para. 111.
594. Commission decision, para. 919.
595. *Ibid.*, para. 922.
596. *Ibid.*, para. 920.
597. *Ibid.*, para. 923.
598. *Ibid.*, para. 917.
599. *Ibid.*, para. 1001.
600. *Ibid.*, para. 972.
601. *Ibid.*, para. 1747.
602. *Ibid.*, para. 1641.
603. *Ibid.*, paras 1598 et seq.

because, according to the relevant case law of conditional rebates, the performance of rivals in the market is not relevant for the application of Article 102.[604]

When answering the Commission's statement of objections, Intel argued that the Commission's approach was contrary to the case law and to the Commission's Guidance on Article 102, where it is stated that, in order to establish an infringement, an actual foreclosure had to be shown.[605] The Commission considered that the Guidance paper was not applicable to this decision because it was published after the proceedings were opened against Intel, and that nevertheless, the Commission's conclusions were in line with the orientations set out in the Guidance paper.[606] The Commission stated that, according to the case law, it is not necessary to conduct an as efficient competitor analysis for finding an infringement under Article 102 TFEU. It further clarified that the test is only one possible way of showing whether Intel's rebates and payments were capable of causing, or were likely to cause anticompetitive foreclosure;[607] and that the test 'should not be regarded as a necessary or absolute test'.[608] However, in addition to its legal analysis based on the settled case law, the Commission conducted an AEC test to assess the effect of fidelity rebates granted by a dominant company under Article 102 TFEU for the first time.

[F] The Relevance of the AEC Test

The starting point for the Commission in conducting the AEC test was the observation that Intel is an unavoidable trading partner (because its product is must-stock for the customers). Hence, part of the demand of each customer was inelastic (non-contestable), because the customer would anyhow purchase that amount from Intel. The Commission observed that, in granting rebates, Intel could use the non-contestable part of the demand from each customer to decrease the price for the elastic part of demand, which the customer may prefer to obtain from Intel's competitor.[609] Then, the Commission identified the contestable share of demand for each of the OEMs and the PC retailer (Dell, HP, NEC, Lenovo and MSH), and found that the contestable share was relatively low.[610] Consequently, the Commission also assessed the relevant time horizon on which the OEMs based their decisions as to whether to change the supplier and found that it was at most one year.[611] The final parameter of the test was the relevant measure of viable cost to be chosen. The Commission selected average avoidable costs (AAC) as a benchmark to assess the exclusionary effect of Intel's rebate schemes.[612] Then, the Commission estimated the effective price for each buyer in order

604. *Ibid.*, para. 1685.
605. *Ibid.*, para. 918.
606. *Ibid.*, para. 916. The Guidance Paper was published on 24 February 2009 whereas in the proceeding against Intel the first Statement of Objection was sent on 26 July 2007.
607. *Ibid.*, para. 925.
608. *Ibid.*, para. 1155.
609. *Ibid.*, para. 1005.
610. *Ibid.*, para. 1012.
611. *Ibid.*, para. 1014.
612. *Ibid.*, para. 1037.

to assess whether the rebates were capable of hindering the entry or performance of an as efficient competitor. The Commission accepted that, in general, if the effective price is below AAC, then the rebate scheme is capable of foreclosing an as efficient competitor.[613] After conducting the AEC test for each of the OEMs and the retailer MSH, the Commission concluded that:

> [t]he Intel payments are capable of having or likely to have anticompetitive foreclosure effects, since even an as efficient competitor would be prevented from supplying the OEM's x86 CPU requirements or ensuring that MSH sells PCs based on its x86 CPUs.[614]

The Commission explicitly mentioned the possible consumer harm of the conduct stating that: 'Intel's conduct would harm final consumers by depriving them of choices of computers based on AMD x86 CPUs.'[615]

§5.03 THE JUDGMENT OF THE GENERAL COURT

Intel appealed the Commission's Decision. This section of the chapter summarizes the substantive analysis of the GC judgment concerning the legal test that the Court applied to exclusivity rebates. The GC's analysis of jurisdiction, rights of defence and amount of the fine is beyond the scope of this book.

[A] The Categorization of Rebates

In its reasoning, the GC distinguished between three categories of rebates – quantity rebates, exclusivity rebates and 'other' rebates.[616] The GC made clear that the first category of rebates is linked solely to the volume of purchases made from an undertaking occupying a dominant position and it is generally considered lawful.[617]

The second category is linked to rebates granted on the condition that customers obtain all or most of their requirements from the undertaking in a dominant position.[618] This corresponds to the traditional definition of fidelity rebates, but the GC emphasized their exclusive nature, renaming them 'exclusivity rebates'. The GC confirmed the Commission's position that the rebates granted to Dell, HP, NEC and Lenovo fell within this second category.[619]

The third category of rebates comprised 'other rebates systems', granted on the basis of certain non-exclusivity related conditions, e.g., when customers' purchases during the current year exceed their previous year's purchases. These rebates are granted not on particular purchased volume (in which would fall under the first category of rebates) but when this volume exceeds the volume purchased from the

613. *Ibid.*, para. 1006.
614. *Ibid.*, para. 1575.
615. *Ibid.*, para. 1154.
616. GC judgment, paras 74–78.
617. *Ibid.*, para. 75.
618. *Ibid.*, para. 76.
619. *Ibid.*, para. 79.

dominant company in a previous period. Such rebates are not applied exclusively or quasi-exclusively either. The effect of this third category of rebates cannot be presumed *ex ante*, and as such it is necessary to consider all the circumstances in order to assess whether they may have anticompetitive effects. The GC considered that all the circumstances should include:

> [t]he criteria and rules governing the grant of the rebate, and to investigate whether, in providing an advantage not based on any economic service justifying it, that rebate tends to remove or restrict the buyer's freedom to choose his sources of supply, to bar competitors from access to the market, or to strengthen the dominant position by distorting competition.[620]

The GC made it clear that 'it is only in the case of rebates falling within the third category that it is necessary to assess all the circumstances, and not in the case of exclusivity rebates falling within the second category'.[621] Thus, only for the third category of rebates is a detailed analysis of their anticompetitive effects required.

[B] The Presumption of Illegality of Exclusivity Rebates and the Assessment of Their Effect

Referring to settled case law, the GC stated that the second category of rebates is abusive 'per se' if there is no objective justification for granting it, because such rebates 'are by their very nature capable of foreclosing competitors'[622] and 'are designed to remove or restrict the purchaser's freedom to choose his sources of supply and to deny other producers access to the market'.[623] For that reason, the GC considered that it is 'not necessary to examine the circumstances of the case in order to determine whether that rebate is designed to prevent customers from obtaining their supplies from competitors'.[624] This presumption of illegality of exclusivity rebates has become exceedingly controversial, as will be seen in the remainder of this chapter.

In its reasoning, the GC took into account the strong dominant position of Intel – which means that for a substantial part of demand (the so-called non-contestable share) there are no substitutes to Intel's products and as such, Intel is an unavoidable trading partner.[625] This dominant position means that a competitor can compete only for that portion of demand that exceeds Intel's non-contestable share, the so-called contestable share.[626] The GC observed that the mechanism of exclusivity rebates granted by Intel makes it possible 'to use the non-contestable share of the demand of the customer as leverage to secure also the contestable share'.[627] In doing so, Intel made it more difficult for its competitor to compete for the contestable share of demand

620. *Ibid.*, para. 78.
621. *Ibid.*, para. 84.
622. *Ibid.*, para. 87.
623. *Ibid.*, para. 77.
624. *Ibid.*, para. 86.
625. *Ibid.*, para. 91.
626. *Ibid.*, para. 92.
627. *Ibid.*, para. 103.

because the competitor not only has to make an attractive offer for the contestable portion of the market, but also has to compensate the customer for the loss of the exclusivity rebate.[628] The GC also observed that the anticompetitive effect occurs 'not only where access to the market is made impossible for competitors, but also where that access is made more difficult'.[629] The GC concluded that anticompetitive effects can thus be presumed and, for that reason, 'it is unnecessary to undertake an analysis of the actual effects of the rebates on competition'.[630]

As regards exclusivity conditions, the GC clarified that in certain circumstances it may have beneficial effects for competition in competitive markets in which case, it is necessary for an assessment of their effect on the market to be carried out.[631] The GC referred to *Delimitis* where the analysis of the CJEU was focused on the possible anticompetitive effect of the agreement in their specific context.[632] According to the GC, those considerations cannot be accepted in the case of a market where competition is already restricted because of the dominant position of Intel.[633] The GC justified its approach by claiming that, given the special responsibility that an undertaking in a dominant position has, Intel's conduct is not allowed to impair genuine undistorted competition in the common market.[634] According to the GC's reasoning, exclusivity rebates granted by a dominant company 'constitute an unacceptable obstacle to access to the market'.[635]

To further reinforce the point that the Commission is not required to prove consumer harm, the GC held, following the decision in *British Airways*, that:

> [T]he Court would point out that, a fortiori, the Commission is not required to prove either direct damage to consumers or a causal link between such damage and the practices at issue in the contested decision. It is apparent from the case-law that Article 82 EC is aimed not only at practices, which may cause damage to consumers directly, but also at those, which are detrimental to them through their impact on an effective competition structure.[636]

[C] The Relevance of the AEC Test

Although the Commission stated that the AEC test is not necessary for finding an infringement under Article 102, but was only one possible way of showing whether rebates were capable of causing or likely to cause anticompetitive foreclosure,[637] the Commission carried out the ACE test in 150 pages of its decision. In its reasoning of the relevance of the AEC test, the GC reasserted settled case law according to which the

628. *Ibid.*, para. 93.
629. *Ibid.*, para. 88.
630. *Ibid.*, para. 103.
631. *Ibid.*, para. 88.
632. *Delimitis*, paras 14–27.
633. GC judgment, para. 89.
634. *Ibid.*, para. 90.
635. *Ibid.*, para. 90. To that effect, the GC referred to *British Gypsum*, paras 65–68.
636. GC Judgment, para. 105.
637. *Ibid.*, para. 925.

Commission is not required to assess the circumstances of the case in order to demonstrate the effect of exclusivity and as such, pursuing an the AEC test is not required for finding an infringement of Article 102 TFEU.[638] Moreover, the GC also held that: 'even in the case of rebates falling within the third category, for which an examination of the circumstances of the case is necessary, it is not essential to carry out an AEC test'.[639] The GC further explained that, in order to find anticompetitive effects, it is not necessary for a rebate system to force an as efficient competitor to charge 'negative' prices, but only to demonstrate the existence of a loyalty mechanism.[640] In this sense, the GC accepted that an assessment of all the circumstances was necessary to demonstrate a loyalty mechanism, which would amount to an anticompetitive effect. However, such a mechanism needs not to be demonstrated by means of an AEC test.[641]

Regarding the usefulness of the AEC test, the GC observed that this test is relevant only in situations where access to the market was made impossible, but not in a situation where access was made more difficult.[642] As a result of rebates from the dominant company, an as efficient competitor may be forced to sell its products below cost in order to compensate a customer for the loss of exclusivity rebates. In that case, the AEC test would be met, since 'it is economically impossible for an as-efficient competitor to secure the contestable share of a customer's demand'.[643] However, according to the GC, even if the AEC test demonstrates that a competitor is able to cover its costs, and hence access to the market is technically possible, this does not mean that there is no foreclosure effect. This is so because the mechanism of exclusivity rebates 'is still capable of making access to the market more difficult for competitors of the undertaking in a dominant position, even if that access is not economically impossible'.[644]

Furthermore, the GC made it clear that in price-cost abuses, the AEC test could be applied unlike in the case of exclusivity rebates. In price-cost abuses such as margin squeeze practices (*TeliaSonera* and *Deutsche Telekom*) or low price practices (*Post Danmark I*), there is an obligation for a price-cost test to be carried out because 'it is impossible to assess whether a price is abusive without comparing it to other prices and costs'.[645] The GC clarified that the scope of that case law is limited to pricing practices, whereas the case under consideration did not relate to a pricing practice, where the level of a price could be regarded as unlawful in itself.[646] In this sense, the AEC test may be a necessary part of the assessment of price-based abuses, whereas in the case of exclusivity rebates it is the condition of exclusive or quasi-exclusive supply that makes

638. *Ibid.*, para. 143.
639. *Ibid.*, para. 144.
640. *Ibid.*, para. 145.
641. *Ibid.*, para. 146.
642. *Ibid.*, para. 150.
643. *Ibid.*, para. 150.
644. *Ibid.*, para. 150.
645. *Ibid.*, para. 152.
646. *Ibid.*, para. 99.

access to the market more difficult and as such abusive, rather than the amount of the rebate.[647]

In addition to holding that the AEC test is not relevant for the assessment of exclusivity rebates because it cannot fully capture their anticompetitive nature, the GC observed also that 'it is not therefore necessary to consider whether the contested decision is in line with the Article [102] Guidance',[648] because 'the fact that the Article [102] Guidance was published after the adoption of the contested decision does not mean that it [the Guidance] was applicable'.

[D] The Relevance of the Market Coverage of Rebates

The GC rejected Intel's arguments that the 'practices at issue in the contested decision concerned only a small part of the x86 CPU market, namely between 0.3 % and 2 % per year and considered the market coverage of the rebates granted by Intel as irrelevant'.[649] The GC justified its reasoning by the fact that, in markets where a company possessing dominant position operates and where the structure of competition is already weakened, even a small further weakening of the degree of competition may constitute an abuse of dominant position.[650]

[E] The Relevance of the Duration of the Supply Contracts

The GC considered Intel's arguments that the agreements with the OEMs and the MSH were for a short duration and could be terminated at thirty days' notice, but rejected its relevance for a number of reasons. First, in practice the exclusivity contracts were not short term because they lasted between one and more than five years for different customers, regardless of the possibility of termination. Second, the GC pointed out that the possibility of termination is not related to the duration of the contracts because 'the right to terminate a contract in no way prevents its actual application until such time as the right to terminate it has been exercised'.[651] In that context, the GC stated that the incentive for customers to purchase exclusively from Intel was based on the existence of a financial incentive, which in practice would prevent them from terminating the contract.[652]

[F] Objective Justification

The GC stated that, if a dominant company can justify the use of an exclusivity rebate system, in particular by showing that its conduct is objectively necessary or that the potential foreclosure effect that it brings about may be counterbalanced, or outweighed

647. *Ibid.*, para. 152.
648. *Ibid.*, para. 156.
649. *Ibid.*, para. 114.
650. *Ibid.*, para. 116.
651. *Ibid.*, para. 112.
652. *Ibid.*, para. 113.

even, by advantages in terms of efficiency that also benefit consumers, then the rebate may be warranted.[653] In short, this means that discounting practices can be justified if they create efficiencies and consumers are not harmed.[654] The fact that Intel did not put forward an argument in this regard does not mean that exclusivity rebates are abusive 'per se' without consideration of their positive effect.

§5.04 THE OPINION OF ADVOCATE GENERAL WAHL

Intel appealed the GC's judgment relying on six grounds of appeal namely: the legal test to be applied for the assessment of the rebates at issue; market coverage in determining whether an undertaking has abused its dominant position; classification of certain rebates as 'exclusivity rebates'; rights of defence; jurisdiction; and the amount of the fine. For the purpose of this book, only the first three grounds of appeal, which relate to the legal test applied to exclusivity rebates by the GC, and in particular to whether the GC was justified in finding that there is no need to evaluate all the circumstances of the case in order to determine whether Intel's rebates were capable of having an anticompetitive effect, will be discussed.

In the context of this appeal, AG Wahl was tasked with producing an opinion in which he advised the CJEU to overthrow the GC judgment on all grounds. In AG Wahl's view, the case law distinguishes between two, not three, categories of rebates, i.e., volume-based rebates, which are presumptively lawful, and fidelity rebates, which are presumptively unlawful and which should be examined in their legal and economic context so as to exclude any other plausible explanation for the dominant company's conduct.[655] In addition, he considers that the GC erred in law when distinguishing 'exclusivity rebates' from other types of fidelity rebates and in deeming them anticompetitive without giving consideration to 'all the circumstances'.[656]

AG Wahl points out that the GC referred to *Hoffmann-La Roche*[657] when deciding that: (i) rebates conditional on the customer purchasing all or most of its requirements from the dominant undertaking are exclusivity rebates; and (ii) there is no need to take into account all the circumstances of the case when assessing the potential of such a rebate to restrict competition.[658] AG Wahl holds that unlike what the GC held, the Court in *Hoffmann-La Roche* assessed the unlawfulness of the rebates on the basis of a thorough analysis of the circumstances of the case, including market coverage.[659] However, because the Court in *Hoffmann-La Roche* made no mention of the need to consider all the circumstances of the case when setting out its legal test, there is a

653. *Ibid.*, para. 94.
654. Federico Etro and Ioannis Kokkoris, 'Towards an Economic Approach to Art. 102' in Federico Etro and Ioannis Kokkoris (eds) *Competition Law and the Enforcement of Article 102* (OUP, USA 2010) 9.
655. Opinion of AG Wahl, paras 81–82.
656. *Ibid.*, para. 84.
657. *Hoffmann-La Roche*, paras 89–90.
658. Opinion of AG Wahl, para. 62.
659. *Ibid.*, para. 66.

discrepancy between what the Court held and what it actually did.[660] In subsequent case law, the Court kept considering 'all the circumstances' of a case when establishing whether rebates constitute an abuse of dominant position contrary to Article 102 TFEU.[661] AG Wahl argues that because the GC applied the statement of the Court in *Hoffmann-La Roche* to Intel's rebates without placing that statement in its proper context, it created a sub-category of rebates, which was termed 'exclusivity rebates'.[662] Thus, AG Wahl argues that the GC judgment is 'one of the very few cases where the Court's statement in *Hoffmann-La Roche* has been applied *verbatim*, without examining the circumstances of the case'.[663] In the light of this, AG Wahl proposes that an assessment of 'all the circumstances' of a case should be an obligatory part of the legal test for the assessment of fidelity rebates, regardless of whether these rebates are linked to exclusivity or other conditions.

When assessing the specific rebates under consideration in this case, AG Wahl focused his analysis on the conditions for the grant of the rebates, market coverage, the duration of the rebate schemes, and the performance of competitors. AG Wahl considers the relevance of the market coverage to be of a particular importance, because the likelihood of negative effects increases with the size of the tied market share. These considerations are necessary for an assessment that seeks to determine whether Intel's behaviour had anticompetitive effects.

According to this view, what matters is not the form of the practices in consideration but their anticompetitive effect.[664] The core idea of AG Wahl's opinion is that the anticompetitive effects cannot be presumed in the abstract, which means that it is of a 'particular importance to consider all the circumstances in order to determine whether the impugned conduct amounts to an abuse of a dominant position contrary to Article 102 TFEU'.[665] For AG Wahl, this test should be applied to all fidelity rebates regardless of their form because they are not harmful as a rule even when offered by dominant undertakings.[666] For that reason, AG Wahl argues that there is no objective reason that exclusivity rebates should receive a stricter treatment than fidelity rebates falling under category 3.[667]

Lastly, AG Wahl considers the application of the AEC test as a tool that can help to identify conduct that has anticompetitive effects.[668] In his opinion, in each particular case it is necessary for exclusionary effects to be demonstrated; and the AEC test could be considered as a part of the all the circumstances test. Further, he observes that because the test cannot simply be disregarded in the context of rebate cases just because it was validated by the Courts in the context of other types of price-based exclusion.[669] AG Wahl justified this conclusion referring to *Post Danmark II* where the

660. *Ibid.*, paras 64–65.
661. *Ibid.*, paras 67–69.
662. *Ibid.*, para. 84.
663. *Ibid.*, para. 70.
664. *Ibid.*, para. 43.
665. *Ibid.*, para. 76.
666. *Ibid.*, para. 90.
667. *Ibid.*, para. 93.
668. *Ibid.*, para. 165.
669. *Ibid.*, para. 166.

Court considered that the AEC test 'may prove useful in the context of assessing a fidelity rebates scheme too'.[670] In addition, he observes that in *Post Danmark II* the Court was careful to qualify its position on the AEC test when it held that, while it considered the test useful, it observed that there is no legal obligation to make use of that test.[671] From the above, AG Wahl concludes that in the present case, there is no need for the AEC test to be carried out.[672] However, because the Commission did carry out the AEC test, AG Wahl argues that it cannot be ignored as irrelevant.[673]

§5.05 THE INTEL JUDGMENT OF THE COURT OF JUSTICE

In a judgment released on 6 September 2017, the CJEU set aside the judgment of the GC and referred the case back for further assessment of the arguments put forward by Intel regarding whether the rebates at issue are capable of restricting competition.[674]

In its reasoning, the CJEU starts with reiterating that the purpose of Article 102 is to ensure that effective competition is not distorted, clarifying that a dominant company is not prevented from competing on the merits, and that only if a competitor at least as efficient as the dominant company in terms of, among other things, price, choice, quality or innovation is excluded, the conduct should be considered abusive; a principle already established in the case law in *Post Danmark I*.[675] Next, the CJEU reiterated settled case law on the concept of dominance and the special responsibility.[676] The special responsibility means that a dominant company can be prohibited from adopting pricing practices that can exclude a competitor as efficient as the dominant company and it strengthens its dominant position, this constitutes an abuse of that position. As a result, 'not all competition by means of price may be regarded as legitimate'.[677]

The CJEU also reiterated settled case law on fidelity rebates according to which if a dominant company ties its purchasers to obtain all or most of their requirements exclusively from that undertaking, it abuses its dominant position within the meaning of Article 102 TFEU.[678] However, it clarified this line of case law in the case where the dominant company submits supporting evidence that its conduct is not capable of restricting competition, in which case the Commission is required to analyse all the circumstances including the extent of the undertaking's dominant position on the relevant market, the coverage and the duration of the practice, the conditions and arrangements for granting the rebates. The Commission must also assess the possible existence of a strategy aiming to exclude competitors that are at least as efficient as the

670. *Ibid.*, para. 166.
671. *Ibid.*, para. 167.
672. *Ibid.*, para. 168.
673. *Ibid.*, para. 170.
674. CJEU judgment, para. 149.
675. *Ibid.*, paras 133–134.
676. *Ibid.*, para. 135.
677. *Ibid.*, para. 136.
678. *Ibid.*, para. 137.

dominant undertaking from the market.[679] In this respect, the CJEU stressed the importance of trading off efficiency benefits against foreclosure risks.[680]

The Court further clarified that, in cases when the Commission carries out an in-depth analyses of all the circumstances, including an AEC test and the defendant is able to present evidence to put into question the validity of the Commission's findings, the GC must examine all of these arguments.[681] Moreover, the Court noted, that although the Commission considered the evaluation of all the circumstances and, in particular the AEC test as unnecessary in order to find an abuse of dominant position, it nevertheless chose to carry out such an analysis. As a result, the AEC test played an important role in the Commission's assessment.[682] For that reason, the GC was required to examine all of Intel's arguments concerning the AEC test.[683]

§5.06 THE *POST DANMARK II* JUDGMENT OF THE COURT OF JUSTICE

The *Post Danmark II* judgment is the second key ruling on rebates issued by the EU court where the relevance of the AEC test has been raised. While it was adopted after the Commission's and GC's decisions in Intel, it preceded the CJEU's decision on it.

[A] Background

Post Danmark is a company controlled by the Danish State, which operates a one-day delivery universal postal service for letters and parcels, including bulk mail weighing less than 2 kilogram throughout Danish territory. Post Danmark also had a statutory monopoly on a number of market segments for the distribution of letters, including the distribution of bulk direct advertising mail weighing up to 50 grams. In 2003, Post Danmark implemented a rebate scheme for the services provided in this particular segment, at a time when there was no competition on the market for the distribution of bulk mail. The rebates contained a scale from 6% to 16% depending on the amount of purchases, and were granted to all customers on the basis of their aggregate purchases over one year periods.

In 2007, Bring Citymail Danmark A/S, a subsidiary of Poste Norge AS, entered the Danish postal market, including into the direct advertising mail market. It thus became the only serious competitor to Post Danmark in the bulk mail market. In 2010, Bring Citymail left the market after suffering heavy losses.

During the period in which Bring Citymail Danmark was in the market, it made a complaint to the Konkurrencerådet, which led to a decision against Post Danmark. The Konkurrencerådet found that Post Danmark was an unavoidable trading partner on the bulk mail market because of its very high market share (over 95%), the presence of high barriers of entry and economies of scale, and Post Danmark's significant

679. *Ibid.*, para. 139.
680. *Ibid.*, para. 140.
681. *Ibid.*, paras 141–142.
682. *Ibid.*, para. 143.
683. *Ibid.*, para. 144.

structural advantages arising from the fact that over 70% of all bulk mail in Denmark was covered by Post Danmark's monopoly and from Post Danmark's unique geographical coverage encompassing all of Denmark. Its rebates in respect of the direct advertising mail market were deemed to constitute an abuse of dominant position which had the effect of tying customers and 'foreclosing' the market, without providing efficiency gains that might have benefited consumers and neutralised those rebates' restrictive effects on competition.

In 2010 the decision was upheld by the Konkurrenceankenævnet (Competition Appeals Tribunal). Post Danmark appealed before the Sø-og Handelsretten (Maritime and Commercial Court), which decided to stay the proceedings and to refer to the CJEU for a preliminary ruling. The CJEU was asked to clarify what framework has to be applied in order to determine whether a rebate scheme is liable to have an exclusionary effect on the market contrary to Article 102 TFEU. Further, the CJEU was asked to clarify the relevance to the AEC test in assessing a rebate scheme.

[B] The Opinion of the Advocate General Kokott

In her opinion, AG Kokott began by discussing the criteria for assessing rebate schemes operated by a dominant company.[684] AG Kokott considered the categories of rebates elaborated more recently by the GC in *Intel* – which decision preceded this opinion – and accepted that quantity rebates linked solely to the volume of purchases are not abusive even when granted by dominant undertakings, whereas loyalty rebates or target discounts, by which dominant undertakings attempt to tie their own customers and attract the customers of their competitors, are presumably abusive.[685] At the same time, the AG stated that the different categories are ultimately immaterial when considering whether a rebate scheme is abusive, because the decisive criterion is not the category but whether the rebates are capable of producing an exclusionary effect on the market which is not economically justified.[686] The assessment of whether the rebates are capable of having such an effect depends on the evaluation of all the relevant circumstances of the individual case,[687] which cannot be provided in an exhaustive list 'since each market and each rebate scheme may have features which are peculiar to it'.[688]

According to the AG's opinion (which follows the traditional approach on rebates), the first step of the assessment is to determine whether the rebates are incremental or retroactive, which means assessing whether the rebates are granted for the quantities above certain thresholds only or for the whole purchases during a given reference period.[689] The AG observed that retroactive rebate schemes usually have a loyalty-building effect, which makes it easy for the dominant company to tie its

684. Case C-23/14 *Post Danmark A/S v. Konkurrencerådet*, Opinion of AG Kokott.
685. *Ibid.*, para. 28.
686. *Ibid.*, para. 29.
687. *Ibid.*, para. 31.
688. *Ibid.*, para. 34.
689. *Ibid.*, para. 36.

customers or to attract the customers of its competitors due to their 'suction effect'.[690] AG Kokott considered that the high rebates granted by Post Danmark, which were between 6% and 16%, and the relatively long reference period, which was one year, made the suction effect stronger.[691] The next step of the assessment, according to the AG is an evaluation of the conditions of competition. Given Post Danmark's strong dominance on the relevant market (Post Danmark held 95% market share of the market), and the weak position of current and potential competitors, the AG suggested that 'a rebate scheme such as that operated by Post Danmark was capable of producing considerable exclusionary effects, without further assessment'.[692]

As regards the applicability of the AEC test, AG Kokott held that: (i) the invoicing of prices below cost to customers is not a prerequisite to a finding that a retroactive rebates scheme operated by a dominant undertaking is abusive;[693] (ii) there is no legal requirement that a price-cost analysis, such as the AEC test, must be undertaken to determine whether a rebate scheme operated by a dominant undertaking constitutes abuse.[694] Hence, the AG suggested that the Court should not require an AEC test to be pursued in the present case.[695] AG Kokott further raised questions concerning the administrability of the AEC test, arguing that 'the added value of expensive economic analyses is not always apparent' because the evaluation of the relevant circumstances may be much more informative than the AEC test.[696] In her view, the abusive nature of rebates in this particular case can be immediately shown by the evaluation of the circumstances of the case and as such, there is no need for the AEC test to be carried out.[697]

Lastly, AG Kokott held that the exclusionary effect of a rebate scheme must not be purely hypothetical, but must in practice be capable of having anticompetitive effects such as making it difficult or impossible for the dominant undertaking's competitors to gain access to the market and for its co-contractors to choose between various sources of supply or trading partners.[698] Yet, the opinion of AG Kokott clarified that it is not necessary for the actual effect to be observed because the potential exclusionary effect also constitutes an abuse.[699]

[C] Considerations by the CJEU

The CJEU stated that the observed scheme is neither a simple quantity rebate (because the rebates were not granted in respect of the volume of purchase of each individual order), nor an exclusivity rebate (because there is no obligation for purchasers to

690. *Ibid.*, para. 37.
691. *Ibid.*, para. 38.
692. *Ibid.*, para. 50.
693. *Ibid.*, para. 48.
694. *Ibid.*, para. 61.
695. *Ibid.*, para. 64.
696. *Ibid.*, paras 66–68.
697. *Ibid.*, para. 70.
698. *Ibid.*, para. 80.
699. *Ibid.*, para. 81.

obtain all or a given proportion of their supplies from Post Danmark). Thus, the CJEU classified the rebate schemes as falling into a category for which 'all the circumstances of the case should be examined, including the rules for granting the rebates, the extent of the dominant position, and the conditions of competition on the relevant market',[700] including the duration of the reference period.[701] In this sense, the CJEU developed the 'all the circumstances test' proposed by the GC in the earlier case law.[702] Thus, the extended criteria that the test entails requires a complete and profound economic analysis of the actual or probable effect on competition of this type of rebate. Having evaluated all the circumstances, the CJEU concluded that the rebate scheme under review produced an anticompetitive exclusionary effect.

As regard the application of the AEC test, the CJEU stated that charging a price below cost to customers is not a prerequisite of a finding of abuse regarding a rebate scheme.[703] Further, the CJEU considered that the characteristics of the market under consideration in this particular case, such as high market share, barriers to entry, etc., meant that the market could not accommodate a competitor as efficient as Post Danmark, in which case 'the presence of a less efficient competitor might contribute to intensifying the competitive pressure on that market and, therefore, to exerting a constraint on the conduct of the dominant undertaking'.[704] Consequently, the application of the AEC test was considered inappropriate in this particular case.

In short, the CJEU held that the application of the AEC test does not constitute a necessary condition for a finding of abuse but it must instead be regarded as one tool amongst others to assess whether there is an abuse. The CJEU thus confirmed the GC's conclusions in *Intel* that the AEC test need not be applied even for rebates that fall into the third category of rebates, for which an examination of 'all the circumstances' of the case is necessary.

§5.07 THE RECENT CONTROVERSY REGARDING THE TREATMENT OF FIDELITY REBATES UNDER ARTICLE 102 TFEU

[A] The Renewed Academic Debate

As Chapter 2 showed, the presumption of illegality of fidelity rebates has been a controversial topic for the last decades, and has been heavily criticised by many for being similar to a strict akin to 'per se' approach; however no judgments generated such an intense discussion between academics, practitioners and commentators as like

700. *Post Danmark II*, para. 50.
701. *Ibid.*, para. 34.
702. The GC referred to *Michelin I*, para. 73; *British Airways*, paras 65–67 and *Tomra*, para. 71.
703. *Post Danmark II*, para. 56. The CJEU referred to *Tompa*, paras 73 and 80.
704. *Ibid.*, para. 60.

Intel and *Post Danmark II*.[705] Two particular areas where controversy has increased as a result of these decisions concerned the assessment of fidelity rebates according to their effect (whether or to what extent their effect requires evaluation); and whether the application of the AEC test (in terms of price-cost test) must be part of the evaluation of a possible anticompetitive effect of fidelity rebates.

The review of the academic literature shows that two opposing views have been advanced, dividing the academic scholarship into two camps. The first one holds that the application of Article 102 to rebates can only be in line with economic theory if the AEC test is a part of the legal standard.[706] In this view, if a dominant company passes the AEC test 'there is no need for regulatory intrusion', whereas failing the test would be an indication of foreclosure, which would require a further assessment for an anticompetitive effect to be demonstrated.[707]

705. The *Intel* judgment has been discussed in many papers. *See*, e.g., Wils, 'The Judgment of the EU General Court in Intel and the So-Called "More Economic Approach' to Abuse of Dominance" (n. 399); Andrea Usai, 'The Intel Case: Between Tomra Systems ASA, the Commission's Guidance on Enforcement Priorities, and the Alleged Infringement of Procedural Requirements – No Fat Left on the Bone' (2014) 35(8) European Competition Law Review 387; Venit, 'Case T-286/09 Intel v. Commission' (n. 40); Rey and Venit (n. 386); Christian Ahlborn and Daniel Piccinin, 'The Intel judgment and Consumer Welfare – A Response to Wouter Wils' (2015) 1(1) Competition Law and Policy Debate 60; Damian Geradin, 'Loyalty Rebates after Intel: Time for the European Court of Justice to Overrule Hoffmann-La Roche' (2015) 11(3) Journal of Competition Law and Economics 579; Lars Kjølbye, Jorge Padilla and Robbert Snelders, 'The Intel Controversy: An Introduction' (2015) 1(1) Competition Law and Policy Debate 28; Alison Jones and Brenda Sufrin, 'The European Way – Reflections on the Intel judgment' (2015) 1(1) Competition Law and Policy Debate 32; Bill Allan, 'Loyalty and Fidelity Rebates: A Sense of déjà vu again' (2015) 1(1) Competition Law and Policy Debate 50; Maurits Dolmans and Thomas Graf, 'Dealing with Intel Intelligently Delineating the Scope and Limits of the Court's Ruling' (2015) 1(1) Competition Law and Policy Debate 76; Damien Neven, 'A Structured Assessment of Rebates Contingent on Exclusivity' (2015) 1(1) Competition Law and Policy Debate 86; Sher, 'Keep Calm – Yes; Carry on – No!' (n. 204); Pablo Ibáñez Colomo, 'Intel and Article 102 TFEU Case Law: Making Sense of a Perpetual Controversy' LSE Law, Society and Economy Working Papers 29/2014 http://eprints.lse.ac.uk/60585/1/WPS2014-29_Colomo.pdf accessed 19 January 2016; Nicolas Petit, 'Intel, Leveraging Rebates and the Goals of Article 102 TFEU' (2015) 11(1) European Competition Journal 26; Luk Peeperkorn, 'Conditional pricing: Why the General Court is Wrong in Intel and What the Court of Justice Can Do to Rebalance the Assessment of Rebates' (2015) 1 Concurrences 43; Bill Batchelor and Fientje Moerman, 'A Practical Approach to Rebates' (2016) 37(12) European Competition Law Review 479; Derek Ridyard, 'Calibration and Consistency in Article 102: Effects-based Enforcement after the Intel and Post Danmark judgments' (2016) 3 Concurrences 29; Bill Batchelor and Benedikt Meyer, 'The Question of Intel' (2014) Competition Law Insight; Damien Geradin, 'The Opinion of AG Wahl in Intel: Bringing Coherence and Wisdom into the CJEU's Pricing Abuses Case-Law' (2016) Tilburg Law School Legal Studies Research Paper Series No. 18/2016; Frederik Preetz, 'Does the Notion of Legal Certainty Prohibit an Effects-Based Approach to Rebates?' (2017) 38(3) European Competition Law Review 99; Damian Neven, and others, 'Intel: Analysing the Advocate General's opinion' (2017) 1 Concurrences 16.

706. Geradin, 'A Proposed Test for Separating Pro-Competitive Loyalty Rebates from Anti-Competitive Ones' (n. 4) 31; Waelbroeck (n. 4); Geradin, 'Loyalty Rebates after Intel (n. 705); Venit, 'Case T-286/09 Intel v Commission' (n. 40) 202; Peeperkorn, 'Conditional Pricing: Why the General Court Is Wrong in Intel' (n. 705).

707. Damien Geradin, 'The Decision of the Commission of 13 may 2009 in the Intel Case: Where Is the Foreclosure and Consumer Harm?' (2010) 1(2) Journal of European Competition Law and Practice 112, 122.

The proponents of the first camp interpreted the rejection of the AEC test in *Intel* as a rejection of the effects-based approach in European competition law,[708] 'a return to the dark ages',[709] 'all steps backward and no steps forward'.[710] Those criticisms were often coupled with support for AG Wahl's Opinion, which 'vindicates the approach taken by the Commission in the Guidance Paper'.[711] Some questioned why the Court continued to resist the Commission's adoption of a more economics-based approach as regards fidelity rebates arguing that 'if the Commission wishes to depart from the AEC framework, it must officially withdraw its Guidance Paper'.[712] Others expressed doubt about the correctness of the test arguing that:

> [T]he Commission's guidance on the enforcement of article 102 is dead and should be withdrawn, because the balancing test, which was based on article 101 (3), has been demolished and the main contribution of the guidance – the as efficient competitor test – is considered unnecessary and, more importantly, incorrect.[713]

A noticeable feature of these criticisms was that they seemed to equate the AEC test with a formal price-cost test and claimed that, by rejecting the AEC test, the EU Courts were choosing to support the form-based approach adopted in the previous case law instead of the effects-based approach. For that reason, the prevailing view was that the case law on fidelity rebates is not in line with this reformed approach of the EU competition law regime.

However, others took more nuanced view arguing that fidelity rebates should be evaluated under an effects-based approach in the light of all the circumstances without necessarily conducting a price-cost test.[714] In their view, the AEC test is one but not an indispensable part of the effects-based approach.[715] Similarly, others argue that the AEC test should not be 'a mandatory test in all abuse cases' but should remain as one tool amongst others in line with the position of the CJEU in *Post Danmark II*.[716]

The proponent of the second camp supports the opposite view arguing that the treatment of fidelity rebates should be in line with GC's position in *Intel*. According to them, two main arguments advocating the strict treatment of fidelity rebates has been advanced. First, the assessment of fidelity rebates does not require a price-cost test in order to establish that rebates are anticompetitive and its rejection by the GC is reasonable because the 'exclusivity rebates are not price-based abuse and the problem

708. Nicolas Petit, 'Rebates and Article 102 TFEU: The European Commission's Duty to Apply the Guidance Paper' (2015) http://papers.ssrn.com/sol3/Papers.cfm?abstract_id=2695732 accessed 1 December 2015.
709. As cited by Whish, 'Intel v Commission: Keep Calm and Carry on!' (n. 42) 2.
710. Venit, 'Case T-286/09 Intel v Commission' (n. 40) 203.
711. Geradin, 'The Opinion of AG Wahl in Intel: Bringing Coherence and Wisdom into the CJEU's Pricing Abuses Case-Law' (n. 705) 10.
712. Petit, 'Rebates and Article 102 TFEU: The European Commission's Duty to Apply the Guidance Paper' (n. 708).
713. Jorge Padilla's presentation at the ACE webinar, The Economic Consequences of the Intel Judgment, 20 June 2014.
714. Rey and Venit (n. 386).
715. *Ibid.*, (n. 714) 23.
716. Nicolas Petit, *The Advocate General's Opinion in Intel v Commission: Eight Points of Common Sense for Consideration by the CJEU* (2016) https://papers.ssrn.com/sol3/papers.cfm?abstract_id=2875422 accessed 1 December 2016.

is the exclusivity, not the price'.[717] Similar arguments were provided by Wils, who argues that in the case of exclusivity rebates, 'there is not only a price but also exclusivity, which is a distinct source of harm to the competitive process'.[718] In his view, fidelity rebates in their nature and effect are very different from price-based conduct.[719] Similar conclusions were made by a prominent US antitrust analyst who claimed that a price-cost test is not relevant for evaluating fidelity rebates as will be seen in the next chapter of this book where the academic debate among the leading US commentators and academics will be discussed.[720]

Second, fidelity rebates are not condemned as 'per se' illegal, because the dominant firm has the right to provide objective justification.[721] In supporting this position, Wils argues that fidelity rebates granted by a dominant company with unavoidable partner status should be prohibited in the absence of objective justification, because of their distortive effects on competition.[722] From this perspective, applying a general prohibition rule for these practices enhances predictability and legal certainty and saves enforcement costs, 'while allocating the responsibility of showing any possible objective justification to the dominant undertaking'.[723] In line with these arguments, Nihoul substantiates the rationale behind the GC's strict approach arguing that the ruling is adopted with reference to the capacity of fidelity rebates to produce anticompetitive effects because: 'the effect of exclusivity based rebates is to compel clients not to deal with competitors; to impede competitors from dealing with clients; and to prevent clients from choosing the products or services best corresponding to their needs'.[724] In his view, the anticompetitive effects of Intel's rebates were clearly produced which makes the approach 'effects-based' without requirement for specific qualitative tools to be used (i.e., price-cost test). In view of this, if the record of the case shows that the practice has a capacity to foreclose competitors, the practice has as its object to hurt them and, as a result to deprive customers of their freedom to choose.[725] In those cases, the practice should be considered harmful without a requirement of full-effects based analysis and would at the same time minimise enforcement errors, 'while limiting the administrative cost and delay associated with a detailed AEC analysis in cases where other factors suggest harm is likely'.[726]

717. Whish, 'Intel v Commission: Keep Calm and Carry on!' (n. 42).
718. Wils, 'The Judgment of the EU General Court in Intel and the So-Called "More Economic Approach" to Abuse of Dominance' (n. 399).
719. *Ibid.*, (n. 718) 429.
720. Text to (n. 43) in Chapter 1.
721. Whish, 'Intel v Commission: Keep Calm and Carry on!' (n. 42).
722. Wils 'The Judgment of the EU General Court in Intel and the So-Called "More Economic Approach" to Abuse of Dominance' (n. 399).
723. *Ibid.*
724. Paul Nihoul, 'The Ruling of the General Court in Intel: Towards the end of an Effect-Based Approach in European Competition Law?' (2014) 5(8) Journal of European Competition Law and Practice 521, 528.
725. Nihoul (n. 724) 528.
726. Julie Clarke, 'The Opinion of AG Wahl in the Intel Rebates Case: A Triumph of Substance over Form?' (2017) 40(2) World Competition 241, 268.

The next few subsections of this chapter will discuss the recent case law of fidelity rebates in an attempt to frame the controversy underlining the academic debated outlined above.

[B] The Treatment of Fidelity Rebates and the Application of the AEC Test in the Commission's Decision

In its decision, the Commission analysed carefully Intel's market position, the market dimensions of competition between Intel and its only competitor AMD and examined various agreements between Intel and its customers. It further conducted a price-cost test in order to assess whether the rebates were capable of hindering the entry or performance of an as efficient competitor, while simultaneously clarifying that the test is not necessary or absolute but arrived at conclusions that supported its decision and therefore it was in line with the orientations set out in the Guidance paper. However, instead of basing the unlawfulness of the rebates on a detailed analysis of the circumstances, the Commission grounded its legal assessment on the settled case law, according to which, there is no requirement to demonstrate the negative effect of the conduct. Instead, given their form the illegality of the rebates at issue is presumed as anticompetitive by object in the absence of objective justifications.

Thus, the Commission followed the 'per se' approach adopted by the EU Courts, even if the Commission then decided to conduct a price-cost test clarifying that the test was conducted for completeness, without explaining for completeness of what, having in mind that the rebates at issue had been considered as abusive 'by object' without the need for their effect to be demonstrated. From this perspective, the Commission's position is in striking contrast to the Guidance Paper, where it is stated that in order to establish an infringement an actual foreclosure has to be identified or in other words, the anticompetitive effect has to be demonstrated based on a coherent theory of harm. Thus, it seems that there is a discrepancy between what the Commission stated in the Guidance Paper and what it actually did in its Intel decision.

As can be recalled from the previous chapter, anticompetitive foreclosure means the exclusion of an at least as efficient as the dominant company competitor. This can be demonstrated through examination of the circumstances of the case and, in some cases, the application of a price-cost test, which is one of the possible tools to show a possible or likely anticompetitive foreclosure. In this sense, a price-cost test might be a supportive but not decisive factor in finding an infringement of Article 102. As the analysis in Chapter 4 also suggested, the conceptual economic framework of the AEC test encompasses evaluation of all the circumstances that can demonstrate a possible strategy aiming to exclude an as efficient competitor and as such, it is broader and cannot be limited to a formal price-cost test.

From this perspective, carrying out a price-cost test as a technical exercise evaluated in isolation from the assessment of the other circumstances of the case cannot constitute a fully flagged effects-based approach. As indicated in the Commission's Guidance Paper, a price-cost test ought to be evaluated in addition to the factors related to the market conditions, since low prices do not in themselves harm competition. An argument supporting this view is the position consolidated in the *Post Danmark I* judgment, where the Court clarified that the low prices (prices below average total costs, but above average variable costs) 'must be regarded as abusive if they are part of a plan for eliminating a competitor'.[727] In this sense, the price-cost test itself can be used only as a proxy and as such, it cannot rule out the existence of abusive conduct. Thus, the main message of the judgment is that not the price in itself but an existence of a strategy aiming to exclude an as efficient competitor is the basis for finding infringement. In the Guidance Paper the Commission clarifies that the result of the AEC test would be combined with the other circumstances of the case in order to assess whether the exclusion is anticompetitive and might harm consumers.[728] As observed in Chapter 4, the Commission was aware that the price-cost test, i.e., negative pricing, is not a sufficient condition for finding an abuse.[729] The same was made clear by the Court in cases of margin squeeze where it is stated that the prices in themselves cannot be abusive on account of their predatory (or excessive) nature but on whether they have an exclusionary effect.[730] This observation gives support to the conclusion that carrying out a price-cost test in itself without taking into consideration the evaluation of other circumstances of the case cannot be considered as a sufficient condition for liability. In the light of this, if the Commission were following the Guidance Paper orientation it should have incorporated the assessment of the general factors related to the market conditions (as listed in paragraph 20 of the Guidance Paper) with the results of the price-cost test.

Next, the Commission should have explained why the rebates under consideration were to be assessed as price conduct instead of exclusive purchasing obligations in order to substantiate why it chose to conduct a price-cost test. Instead, the Commission chose to conduct a price-cost test without mentioning supportive arguments in economic terms in order to explain what differentiates Intel's rebates from an exclusive dealing (or single branding obligation). Moreover, in an academic paper, the Commission's officials (engaged with the case) argue that in its decision, the European Commission makes 'clear, the issue was not with the rebates themselves, but with the conditions associated with the rebates',[731] which suggests that the Commission actually considered Intel's rebates similar to exclusive purchasing obligation. From this perspective, it might be suggested that the Commission wrongly chose to apply a price-cost test to evaluate the anticompetitive effect of rebates that do not constitute price conduct.

As recalled from Chapter 4, the Commission in its Guidance Paper seemed to consider that fidelity rebates might be similar to exclusive purchasing obligation, which would require an assessment of the circumstances of the case, which does not contain a price-cost test, because these practices are non-price conduct. In those cases,

727. *Post Danmark I*, para. 27.
728. The Guidance Paper, para. 45.
729. Damien Geradin, 'Proposed Test for Separating Pro-Competitive Conditional Rebates from Anti-Competitive Ones' (n. 4) 47; Mandorff and Sahl (n. 543).
730. *Deutsche Telekom*, para. 183; *TeliaSonera*, para. 98.
731. Banasevic and Hellström (n. 529) 307.

the Commission considers an assessment of the possible anticompetitive effect in a similar way to single branding under Article 101 TFEU.[732] The evaluation of the proposed assessment of the possible anticompetitive effect of single branding conducted in Chapter 4 suggests that the unavoidable trading partner status of the supplier and the high percentage of the tied part of the demand is likely to lead to anticompetitive foreclosure. For that reason, the Commission stated that 'even a modest tied market share may lead to significant anti-competitive effects'.[733] Ultimately, the assessment of a single branding under Article 101 is clearly based on the evaluation of the possible anticompetitive effects and this can be done without conducting a formal price-cost test.

In short, the Commission failed to explain why it considered Intel's rebate as a pricing conduct and pursued a price-cost test. In a way, this reflects the Guidance Paper's failure to provide clarity as to how to differentiate between conditional rebates that have similar to exclusive purchasing obligation (non-price conduct) and those that might be regarded as pricing conduct.[734]

[C] The Treatment of Fidelity Rebates and the Rejection of the AEC Test in the GC's Judgment in Intel and the CJEU's Judgment in *Post Danmark II*

In the light of the Commissions' failure to substantiate why it considered Intel's rebates as price conduct and its decision to carry out a price-cost test, the GC's judgment in *Intel* came as no surprise. On appeal, the GC upheld the Commission's decision and rejected the implementation of the AEC test as irrelevant. The GC affirmed that, under settled case law, there are three categories of rebates – volume rebates, fidelity (exclusivity) rebates and 'other' rebates, each requiring a different standard for assessment as outlined in section 5.03[A] above. The Court holds that Intel's rebates were fidelity rebates, and as such, abusive by their very nature in the absence of objective justification. Thus, it is not necessary that their effect be examined. This position of the GC has led to extensive debate as discussed in section 5.07[A].

In contrast, AG Wahl challenged the GC's position about the categorisation of rebates, identifying only two, categories of rebates, i.e., volume-based rebates and fidelity rebates.[735] In addition, and unlike the GC, AG Wahl proposed that all types of fidelity rebates should be subject to an evaluation of all the circumstance of the case. In should be noticed, that Wahl's position on this point is entirely with the conclusions in Chapter 3, where it was outlined that economic theories do not distinguish between rebates with exclusivity obligations and those without commitment for exclusive purchases, because in both cases rebates can be anticompetitive only under specific set of circumstances.[736]

732. *See* Chapter 4, section 4.03.
733. Guidelines on Vertical Restraints, para. 140.
734. *See* Chapter 4, section 4.04[C].
735. Opinion of AG Wahl, paras 81–82.
736. *See* Chapter 3, section 3.03.

The opposite view was expressed by others, and most prominently by Wils, who claim that categorization of rebates adopted by the GC is legally and economically sound.[737] According to him, the GC's categorisation did not look at a rebate's form, but at the different risk of competitive harm that they might create. A similar interpretation was adopted by AG Kokott in her opinion in *Post Danmark II.* AG Kokott considered that the different categories of rebate are ultimately immaterial when considering whether a rebate scheme is abusive, because the decisive criterion is not the category but whether the rebates are capable of producing an exclusionary effect on the market, which is not economically justifiable.[738] From this perspective, the categories outlined by the GC do not identify different forms of rebates based on their form but merely reflect the likelihood of each category creating anticompetitive harm. On the other hand, the categorization of fidelity rebates in Intel's judgment as exclusivity rebates for which it is not necessary to evaluate further their effect corresponds to the Commission's position in its Guidance Paper as discussed in Chapter 4, where it is considered that in some cases, where the conduct in consideration is likely to result in consumer harm, 'it is not necessary for the Commission to carry out a detailed assessment'.[739]

In short, according to this view, the different forms of rebate create different risks of competitive harm.[740] In some cases, the conduct of a dominant company is prima facie abusive and the anticompetitive effect of rebates might be presumed with a high degree of probability, which substantiate their prohibition without engaging in further assessment of its possible effects, as the GC did in Intel with regard to exclusivity rebates (and the Commission suggested in paragraph 22, as mentioned above). This position supports the arguments of the proponents of the second camp discussed in section 5.07[A] above. In other cases, the conduct is less likely to cause harm (as rebates categorized in the third category by the CG in *Intel*) and it should be evaluated according to their legal and economic context taking into account all the circumstances.

This approach seems to focus on the practical implications of adopting certain types of rules on enforcement, particularly in terms of saving enforcement costs, instead of merely focusing on the accuracy of the applicable rules. From this perspective, it might not be appropriate to apply a single legal test to rebates that have different risks of competitive harm in terms of saving enforcement costs.[741] This would ignore the different concerns that different types of rebates have and could lead to false positives and false negatives.[742] From this perspective, and for the sake of legitimacy and legal certainty, it is important that a single test be used for similar practices that create the same risk of competitive harm, as the GC seems to have done.

737. Wils, 'The Judgment of the EU General Court in Intel and the So-Called 'More Economic Approach' to Abuse of Dominance' (n. 399) 21.
738. Opinion of AG Kokott, para. 29.
739. The Guidance Paper, para. 22.
740. For support to that point, *see* Gavil (n. 298) 75.
741. Wils 'The Judgment of the EU General Court in Intel and the So-Called "More Economic Approach" to Abuse of Dominance' (n. 399).
742. Marina Lao, 'Defining Exclusionary Conduct under Section 2: The Case for Non-universal Standards' in Barry Hawk (ed.) *International Antitrust Law & Policy: Fordham Competition Law* (Ch. 19, Juris Publishing 2006) 433.

These different approaches – detailed economic analysis and rules that reflect competition risks – have implications for a number of topics of analysis. A good example is the relevance of market coverage of exclusivity rebates. The GC refused to grant importance to the market coverage of exclusivity rebates in *Intel* (which was approximately 14%), considering that in markets where a company possessing a dominant position operates and where the structure of competition is already weakened, even a small further weakening of the degree of competition may constitute an abuse of dominant position. This is in line with the development of rules by reference to the potential risk of a conduct. On the other hand, AG Wahl considered the size of the tied part of the market as relevant, because the likelihood of anticompetitive effects increases with the size of the tied share of the market.[743] AG Wahl did not say that the 14% coverage may or may not be sufficient to bring about anticompetitive foreclosure but that the position of the GC was inconclusive.[744] This is in line with the view that the economic effects of a conduct need to be established, which require a particular degree of foreclosure to be shown. A half-way position seems to have been adopted in the *Post Danmark II* judgment, where CJEU stated that a large proportion of customers covered by the rebate scheme 'does not, in itself, constitute evidence of abusive conduct by that undertaking'[745] but that it might be considered as a 'useful indication as to the extent of that practice and its impact on the market, which may bear out the likelihood of an anti-competitive exclusionary effect'.[746] Thus, the CJEU held that it was not appropriate to create a *de minimis* threshold above which a practice should be considered anticompetitive merely because competition was already weakened by the presence of the dominant company.[747] Nonetheless, this position of the Court has been criticised by some commentators.[748]

A contrasting point of view can be found in the Commission's proposed assessment criteria applicable to single branding obligation in its Guidelines on Vertical Restraints, as discussed in detail in Chapter 4 of this book and mentioned above.[749] When considering single branding (which can be equated with exclusivity rebates), the European Commission observed that if the dominant supplier is 'an unavoidable trading partner at least for part of the demand on the market – for instance, because its brand is a "must stock item" preferred by many final consumers – competitors cannot compete on equal terms for the entire demand of the customers because part of it is tied

743. Opinion of AG Wahl, para. 140.
744. *Ibid.*, paras 141–146.
745. *Post Danmark II*, para. 44.
746. *Ibid.*, para. 46.
747. *Ibid.*, paras 70–73. The position of the CJEU in *Intel* not to consider the second ground of Intel's appeal which dealt with the market coverage 'may be a signal that it still rejects, or is at least uncertain about, the possibility of a de minimis threshold under Article 102' as rightly observed by James Venit, 'The judgment of the European Court of Justice in Intel v Commission: a procedural answer to a substantive question?' (2017) 13(2), 3 European Competition Journal 172, 186.
748. Venit, 'The judgment of the European Court of Justice in Intel v Commission' (n. 747). *See also* Whish, 'Intel v Commission: Keep Calm and Carry on!' (n. 42) who criticise the GC's judgment only on this point.
749. *See* Chapter 4, section 4.03.

to the must-stock supplier'.[750] When the market share is really high it is further considered that 'even a modest tied market share may lead to significant anti-competitive effects'.[751] In this sense, the unavoidable trading partner status of the dominant company and the share of the tied market were considered as a decisive factor in finding an infringement. Besides this explanation relevant to the market coverage in cases of single branding, this position seems to be in line with the economic theory of raising rivals costs discussed in Chapter 3, according to which a dominant company may tie a small part of the market, which might in practice be large enough to deprive a competitor from achieving minimum efficient scale (MES) and from remaining in the market. In this case, even a small amount of foreclosure might create strategic barriers and as such, be enough to marginalise competitors of a dominant company by preventing them from reaching MES. In other cases, rivals may be excluded from a large share of market but nonetheless they may be able to overcome the exclusionary effect, as for example by sponsoring entry by a new producer.[752] According to this economic theory, the degree of foreclosure does not make economic sense.[753] Thus, as Jacobson argues, an intervention might be appropriate irrespective of the percentage of the foreclosed market.[754] As such, the GC reasoning regarding the significance of the market coverage seems to be in line with the economic theory, which would seem to indicate that it may be more appropriate for a limited rather than a detailed economic analysis to be conducted for the evaluation of the possible anticompetitive effects of fidelity rebates in these circumstances.

The GC also refused to accept the duration of exclusivity rebates as short, based on the duration of individual agreements, accepting the Commission's position that the cumulation of multiple agreements exists, which can be contrasted with the AG Wahl's position. Arguably, the relevance of the reference period had been acknowledged by the EU Courts, although the case law does not provide clear indications on how long is enough for an anticompetitive effect to be presumed.[755] However, according to some empirical studies in the economic literature, the duration of the reference period (even that it is an essential part of any rebate system) cannot be endorsed as a part of the economic assessment of retroactive rebates and their potential foreclosure effect, because the rebate percentage, the threshold and the amount already bought is sufficient for the conclusion in that respect.[756] Other empirical models reported that looking only at the length of the contract is misleading; instead, it is important to assess 'to what extent a contract of a given length locks the parties into a relationship' due to

750. Guidelines on Vertical Restraints, para. 132.
751. *Ibid.*, para. 140.
752. Meese (n. 326) 422.
753. *Ibid.*, 417.
754. Jacobson, 'Exclusive Dealing, Market Foreclosure and Consumer Harm' (n. 324) 369.
755. *Michelin I*, para. 81; *Michelin II*, para. 88.
756. Maier-Rigaud, 'Switching Costs in Retroactive Rebates-What's Time Got to Do with It?' (n. 302); Faella (n. 4) 405; *see also* Jacobson, 'Exclusive Dealing, Foreclosure, and Consumer Harm' (n. 324) 352. According to Jacobson, in some of the recent US cases, 'the duration of the agreements had little to do with the real-world lack of any credible ability of the affected customers to switch to alternatives'.

the penalties that a customer have to incur in order to terminate a contract.[757] According to this, 'liquidated damages constitute an implicit measure of the effective length of the contract'.[758] These statements could be interpreted as suggesting that the reference period in itself is not a sufficient indicator to be taken into account; instead the possibility for termination of the agreement with short notice without penalties, such as a termination of the contract or requirement to return the rebates would suggest that the practice is capable of harming competition.[759] From this perspective, the GC's reasoning not to accept the duration as short was based on the existence of a financial incentive, which in practice prevented customers from terminating the contract.[760] From this perspective, an evaluation of the reference period in itself seems redundant.

As regard the rejection of the AEC test for the evaluation of fidelity rebates, the GC in *Intel* considered the price-cost test as irrelevant for the assessment of exclusivity rebates for two reasons. First, the GC clarified that the AEC test is limited to pricing practices and as such not relevant for the evaluation of exclusivity rebates, which in the Intel case were considered not related to pricing conduct. Second, the GC clarified that the AEC test cannot capture the rebates' anticompetitive nature and the foreclosure effects could arise even if an as efficient competitor could theoretically enter the market. This statement indicates that the GC considered that the AEC test is prone to false negatives in holding that even if a competitor is able to cover its costs, this does not mean that there is no foreclosure effect.[761] This statement could be interpreted as suggesting that even if the AEC test is passed by the dominant company, the existence of other evidence, such as unavoidable trading partner status, significant part of demand secured for the dominant company, retroactivity of rebates in combination with additional anticompetitive conditions – the naked restrictions, would be sufficient for considering Intel's practice as capable to harm competition. As can be recalled from Chapter 3, the relevant economic theories also provide support for the conclusion that under these circumstances, fidelity rebates can be anticompetitive even if prices are above appropriate measure of cost.

However, although the GC substantiated the reasons for rejecting the need of the price-cost test in *Intel*, it then somehow contradictorily observed that this test is relevant only in situations where access to the market was made impossible, and not for situations where the access was made more difficult. This position is in striking contrast to the GC's statement that a foreclosure effect occurs not only where access to the market is made impossible for competitors, but also where that access is made more difficult; and with the GC's explanation that a price-cost test cannot capture the rebates' anticompetitive nature because even 'a positive AEC test result would not be

757. Aghion and Bolton (n. 277) 389.
758. *Ibid.*, (n. 757).
759. Jacobson, 'Exclusive Dealing, Foreclosure and Consumer Harm' (n. 324) 352; *see also* Pablo Ibanes Colomo, *The Future of Article 102 TFEU After Intel* (2018) https://papers.ssrn.com/sol3/papers.cfm?abstract_id=3125468 accessed 19 February 2018.
760. GC judgment, para. 113.
761. *Ibid.*, para. 150.

capable of ruling out the potential foreclosure effect'.[762] Thus, if the AEC test cannot capture an anticompetitive foreclosure, this should be relevant for both situations – when access to the market is impossible or it is more difficult, as in both cases the foreclosure is anticompetitive. As outlined in Chapter 3, the economic theory of raising rival's cost (RRC) can accommodate a reasonable explanation in understanding why the AEC test is not relevant even in situations when the access to the market is more difficult, which the GC failed to clarify.

Next, the GC held that the price-cost test is also not required for the evaluation of the 'other' types of rebates because the assessment of all the circumstances was considered enough to demonstrate the existence of a loyalty mechanism, which was deemed to amount to an anticompetitive effect, that did not have to be demonstrated by means of a price-cost test. This position was adopted in AG Kokott's opinion[763] and repeated in the *Post Danmark II* judgment where the CJEU considered the AEC test neither legally required nor decisive for establishing an abuse, which might be seen as limiting its usefulness in general.[764] The CJEU considered the application of a price-cost test as irrelevant for this particular case for two main reasons. First, the Court considered that the characteristics of the market under consideration in this particular case could not accommodate a competitor as efficient as Post Danmark, in which case the presence of a less efficient competitor still might impose a competitive constraint on the dominant company. This position might be interpreted as suggesting that the rejection of the test in this particular case is more as an exception rather than a rule but also that the test cannot be accepted as absolute, which reflects the criticism of the AEC test, discussed in Chapter 7. Second, the CJEU held that the application of the AEC test does not constitute a necessary condition for a finding of abuse, which means that there is no legal obligation to make use of that test. However, the CJEU held that the test could be used as one tool amongst others without providing much clarity when this might be the case, 'which creates additional questions in a field already strewn with significant academic dispute'.[765] Nonetheless, the CJEU extended the criteria of 'all the circumstances' test from the settled case law – stating that not only the rules of granting rebates should be evaluated but also their duration, the extent of the dominant position and the conditions of competition on the relevant market. In this sense, the CJEU departed significantly from settled case law by introducing an in-depth effects analysis of the possible exclusionary effect of rebates.[766] The evaluation of these factors reflects the assessment of vertical agreements under Article 101 TFEU as discussed in Chapter 4. Thus, the *Post Danmark II* judgment endorsed the effects-based approach for the

762. GC Judgment, para. 151.
763. Opinion of AG Kokott, para. 56.
764. James Venit, 'Making Sense of Post Danmark I and II: Keeping the Hell Fires Well Stoked and Burning' (2016) 7(3) Journal of European Competition Law and Practice 165.
765. Christian Ahlborn and Will Leslie, 'The Post Danmark II Case: The ECJ's Decision Leaves Major Questions Unanswered' (2015) Competition Law Insight, https://www.competitionlawinsight.com/competition-issues/abuse-of-dominance/the-post-danmark-ii-case-113678.htm, accessed 1 February 2016.
766. Colomo, 'Post Danmark II: The Emergence of a Distinct "Effects-Based" Approach to Article 102 TFEU' (2016) 7(2) Journal of European Competition Law and Practice 113, 114.

evaluation of the legality of the third category of rebates regardless of the rejection of the AEC test.

[D] The Treatment of Fidelity Rebates and the Role of the AEC Test in the CJEU's Judgment in *Intel*

In any event, the Commission conducted the AEC test. On appeal, Intel submitted evidence putting into question the Commission's performance of the price-cost test, which the GC did not examine. The CJEU accepted these arguments and referred the case back to the GC for further assessment of the arguments (concerning the test) put forward by Intel, of whether the rebates at issue are capable of restricting competition. The CJEU further stated that in cases in which the defendant provides supportive evidence that its conduct is not capable of restricting competition, the Commission is required to evaluate all the circumstances in order to assess the possible existence of a strategy aiming to exclude an as efficient competitor, mentioning explicitly the extent of the undertaking's dominant position on the relevant market, the coverage and the duration of the practice, the conditions and arrangements for granting the rebates. However the CJEU did not clarify whether in the evaluation of a strategy aiming to exclude an as efficient competitor a price-cost test is required. Some commentators have argued[767] that when the CJEU mentioned that 'Art. 102 TFEU prohibits a dominant undertaking from, among other things, adopting pricing practices that have an exclusionary effect on competitors considered to be as efficient as it is itself' and that 'not all competition by means of price may be regarded as legitimate', it meant that the rebates under consideration were pricing practices.[768] However, as Petit clarified, the French version of the judgment does not contain explicit mention of 'pricing practices' but only 'adopting practices that have an exclusionary effect', which means that it is not clear whether Intel's rebates were considered by the CJEU as pricing or non-pricing practices, which is of great importance for the relevance of a price-cost test.[769] Moreover, it is not clear whether the CJEU considered the application of the price-cost test to be a requirement for finding an abuse or it has to be considered because the Commission decided to apply it and Intel raised it as a defence.

However, if the Commission had not applied the test and Intel contested its decision on the grounds that the Commission was required to conduct the test, the GC's judgment seems reasonably argumentative.[770] Because the Commission chose to carry out the test, the GC was required to examine Intel's arguments in the name of the right of defence. From this perspective, this position of the CJEU might be interpreted as

767. Assimakis Komninos and others, 'New Era Dawning in EU Competition Law? CJEU Endorse an Effects-Based Assessment of Rebates and Sets Aside Lower Court's Judgment in Intel https://www.whitecase.com/publications/alert/new-era-dawning-eu-competition-law-cjeu-endorses accessed 3 November 2017.
768. CJEU judgment, para. 136.
769. Nicolas Petit, *The Judgment of the EU Court of Justice in Intel and the Rule of Reason in Abuse of Dominance Cases* (2017) https://papers.ssrn.com/sol3/papers.cfm?abstract_id=3086402 accessed 12 December 2017.
770. On this point, *see Tomra*, paras 258–259.

saying that the case is sent back to the GC on procedural grounds, instead of providing clarification on whether the test is a necessary part of the legal assessment of fidelity rebates. Thus, clear and predictable rules under which circumstances a price-cost is a relevant tool for the evaluation of the legality of rebates is required in the name of legal certainty; an issue, which is still outstanding and it is not clear what position the GC will take.[771]

Further, in referring to the settled case law of rebates, the CJEU also made clear that the presumption of illegality of fidelity rebates stands, which might be seen as a position in line with the GC's categorisation of rebates.[772] As can be recalled from the discussion in Chapter 2, the reason behind the Court's view in creating an abbreviated test for the evaluation of this type of rebates condemning them as a 'by object' restriction is based on the presumption that there is a certain degree of probability that the practice will have an anticompetitive effect and as such there is no need for the effect to be shown. Instead, the CJEU clarified that now this presumption can be rebutted if the defendant provides supportive evidence that its conduct is not capable of restricting competition. Rebutting the presumption of capability to restrict competition would require a similar level of evidence that the dominant company have to satisfy, such as, a short reference period and a possibility for a customer to breach the contract without penalty, evidence that the dominant company is not an unavoidable trading partner and competitors are able to compete for the whole demand, instead of only for the contestable share and that rebates are not retroactive but incremental.[773] If the dominant company is unavoidable trading partner, evidence that the contestable share of the market is sufficient to allow a rival to reach MES can also be used.[774] However, it may be even more difficult for Intel to rebut the Commission's findings of the existence of a strategy aiming to exclude an as efficient competitor including the existence of the 'naked restrictions' (which was not subject to appeal, which suggests that these aspects could still prove problematic for Intel) and the unwritten conditions regarding the launch of Intel's customers x86 CPUs AMD-based products and the fact that the agreements were kept secret and Intel requested the wording 'non-exclusive' to be introduced into the agreement for optical purposes.

From this perspective, it can be assumed that the settled case law of fidelity rebates was not overruled explicitly by the CJEU in Intel but now it is clear that this presumption can be rebutted if the dominant company can provide supportive evidence; the possibility that was already established under Article 101 TFEU.[775]

Further, the GC relied on the existence of the cumulation of multiple agreements and accepted the concept of single continuous infringement, in order to expand the Commission's jurisdiction to apply Article 102 as regard agreement concluded outside the European Union, which was confirmed by the CJEU. Although the discussion of

771. Appeal case before the GC T-286/09.
772. CJEU judgment, para. 137.
773. Colomo, 'The Future of Article 102 TFEU After Intel' (n. 759) 25.
774. Ridyard, 'Exclusive Contracts and Article 82 Enforcement' (n. 258) 594.
775. Case C-429/08 *Karen Murphy v. Media Protection Services Ltd* [2011] ECR I-9083, paras 140 and 143; Case C-67/13 P *Groupement des Cartes Bancaires v. European Commission* [2014] ECR I-2204, para. 69.

this ground of appeal is beyond the scope of this book it will be briefly discussed for the proper interpretation of the judgment in order to understand the rationale of the CJEU to set aside the judgment of the GC. The GC held that Intel's conduct satisfied both the implementation test (the arrangements had taken place within the EEA) and the qualified effects test (that it is foreseeable that the effects of the arrangements will have an immediate and substantial anticompetitive effect in the EEA). The CJEU held that the two tests are an alternative, rather than cumulative and confirmed the GC's position that it is sufficient to take account only of the probable effects of a conduct on competition.[776] In contrast, AG Wahl took the view that the GC failed to assess whether the agreements had the capacity to produce any immediate, substantial and foreseeable anticompetitive effect in the EEA and as such, the cumulation of short-term agreement cannot be assumed to show that the rebates in question are capable of restricting competition; a position that was explicitly rejected by the CJEU.

In this respect, the CJEU confirmed that the effect of Intel's agreements is expected to affect in a material manner competition in Europe, and moreover, that it is sufficient only for the probable effects of the conduct on competition to be taken into account, which might be seen as a position in line with the GC's acceptance of an exclusionary abuse. However, even if the GC's conclusions were correct that Intel's rebates are capable of having anticompetitive effects, these findings must have been based on the assessment of all the circumstances.

Having in mind that defendants in dominance cases routinely raise such defence, the clear message of the Court is that all the arguments put forward by the defendant must be assessed, which means that even if the GC might reach the same conclusion, its findings have to be based on the assessment of all the circumstances. This statement might also be interpreted as a clear endorsement of the effects-based approach for the second category of rebates. In this sense, the conclusion as to whether the rebates at issue are capable of having anticompetitive effects requires an evaluation of their legal and economic context, which represents a clear departure from the statement that rebates are abusive by their very nature and for that reason, there is no need for an assessment to be carried out. This assumption reflects the AG Wahl's interpretation of *Hoffmann-La Roche* and his position that the Court actually did consider all the circumstances of the case but made no mention of the need for it to be considered when setting out the legal standard.

From the above, it can be concluded that although the judgment endorsed the effects-based approach, it did not clarify whether and under which circumstances an application of the AEC test (in terms of a price-cost test) is required.

§5.08 CONCLUSION

The description of the judgments in this chapter showed that the case law of fidelity rebates fail to provide clarity of the appropriate legal standard for the assessment of

776. CJEU judgment, paras 51–52.

fidelity rebates. The controversy is mainly related as to whether the price-cost test is relevant for the assessment of fidelity rebates.

An academic trend is to see the AEC test (in terms of price-cost test) as an expression of the effects-based approach, arguing that the application of Article 102 to rebates can only be in line with the economic theory if the AEC test is a part of the legal standard. From this perspective, the proponents of this position equated the AEC test with a formal price-cost test. The discussion of the judgments above revealed that the position of the CJEU in both *Intel* and *Post Danmark II* might be interpreted as being contra the view that the AEC test can be equated with a price-cost test. In *Post Danmark II*, the CJEU made it explicit that the treatment of fidelity rebates should be based on the evaluation of all the circumstance, which represents a clear effects-based approach, although the application of the price-cost test was considered irrelevant. Similarly, the CJEU in *Intel* held that if a defendant disputes the Commission's assessment, the Commission is required to evaluate all the circumstances in order to assess the possible existence of a strategy aiming to exclude an as efficient competitor without mentioning the outcome of a price-cost test. It seems that according to the CJEU, this can be done through the evaluation of the circumstances of the case, which represents an assessment of the possible anticompetitive effect, which means an exclusion of a competitor at least as efficient as the dominant company. Thus, in both judgments, the CJEU clearly endorsed an approach based on the evaluation of the possible negative effects of fidelity rebates. From this perspective, the proponents of the first camp equated wrongly the AEC test with a formal price-cost test. This position is also in line with the conclusion in Chapter 4.

However, despite the change of direction towards an effects-based approach, the relevance of the price-cost test to determine the anticompetitive effects of fidelity rebates remains an outstanding issue. In particular, it remains unclear when a price-cost test should be deployed. In equating the AEC test with a formal price-cost test, the proponents of the first camp did not question the relevance of the price-cost test in cases where the conduct is similar to exclusive dealing and as such, constitute non-price conduct. In contrast, the proponent of the second camp went further, putting into question the relevance of the application of a price-cost test in cases of fidelity rebates with a similar to exclusive dealing effect, suggesting that the application of the test is not relevant; an issue that has not been addressed by the Commission and the EU Courts. However, it has been a central topic of contention in the US courts and US academic debate. Thus, the next chapter of this book will focus on recent case law development in the US, and on the academic dispute following these judgments, in an attempt to clarify under which circumstances the price-cost test can or should be used to identify the anticompetitive effect of fidelity rebates.

Chapter 6

The Treatment of Fidelity Rebates under US Antitrust Law: Predatory Pricing or Exclusive Dealing?

§6.01 INTRODUCTION

It is accepted that the treatment of fidelity rebates is one of the most difficult and controversial topics in EU competition law and US antitrust law. It is also suggested by some that it is an area where there is a larger divergence of opinion than with other topics.[777] This divergence derives from the different historical development and the different goals of the two antitrust regimes.[778] The US approach emphasies the importance of allowing dominant firms to compete aggressively and only condemns unilateral conduct with actual foreclosure effects. This emphasis leads to a rule of reason approach, in contrast to 'the special responsibility not to allow its conduct to impair genuine undistorted competition in the common market' under EU competition law, which can arguably be said to constitute a stricter approach.[779] However, both antitrust regimes target the same type of conduct in which a company with market power is engaged in practices that might harm effective competition.[780]

777. William Kolasky, 'What is Competition-A Comparison of US and European Perspectives' (2004) 49 The Antitrust Bulletin 29, 40.
778. *Ibid.*, 41, According to Kolasky: 'In Europe, national markets were formerly protected by internal trade barriers, resulting in more local monopolies, and many more government-owned monopolies. As a result, there may be more undertakings with dominant positions that are not the natural result of market dynamics than exist in the United States. If so, greater vigilance by competition authorities may well be warranted to assure that the competitive process can operate freely to restore or create competitive conditions.'
779. *Michelin I*, para. 57.
780. Francisco Marcos, *The Prohibition of Single-Firm Market Abuses: US Monopolization Versus EU Abuse of Dominance* (2017) https://papers.ssrn.com/sol3/papers.cfm?abstract_id=3028629 accessed 1 December 2017.

The discussion of the development of recent EU case law of fidelity rebates in the previous chapter revealed that this divergence is getting blurred reflecting the clear position of the CJEU in both the *Intel* and *Post Danmark II* judgments to depart from the strict form-based approach and to endorse an approach based on an evaluation of the possible anticompetitive effects of fidelity rebates; an approach, which seems to be more is in line with the rule of reason standard applied traditionally in the US.[781] However, as indicated in Chapter 5, the legal assessment of fidelity rebates still lacks clarity, particular as regards the application of the price-cost test as a tool to determine the anticompetitive effect of fidelity rebates. This issue remains outstanding despite the attention devoted to the application of the test in both the case law and academic debate following the judgments.

Similarly, the application of a price-cost test to determine the anticompetitive effect of fidelity rebates has been raised as a central issue in the recent case law of fidelity rebates in the US. The Third Circuit Court in both *ZF Meritor* and *Eisai* also rejected the relevance of the price-cost test under the facts of each of case, while clearly stating that the application of the test depends on whether the price is the mechanism of exclusion. The Court further clarified that in both cases the test was not relevant because the rebates were more similar to exclusive dealing than to predatory pricing. In this sense, case law from the other side of the Atlantic deals with similar questions regarding the place of the price-cost test in the assessment of fidelity rebates.

The application of the price-cost test is a topic of intense academic debate in US scholarship. Leading US commentators and academics have been engaged in controversies about whether the price-cost test is applicable only in predation cases – where the price is the mechanism for exclusion – or whether it should also apply to fidelity rebate cases. According to some leading commentators, in the US there are two paradigms for exclusionary conduct – predatory pricing (where the price-cost test is appropriate) and raising rivals cost (RRC) (where the foreclosure should be analysed under exclusive dealing law).[782] These authors argue that fidelity rebates should be evaluated under the exclusive dealing standard because they can exclude a competitor without profit sacrifice, which means that a price-cost test is not relevant for evaluating fidelity rebates falling outside the scope of predatory behaviour.[783] The opposite view argues that exclusive dealing (and loyalty discounts) do require profit sacrifice to achieve exclusion in very similar circumstances to predation.[784] Thus, they support the view that a predatory pricing standard and the use of a price-cost test as a safe harbour is required as an appropriate measure to distinguish pro-competitive from anticompetitive rebates.

Against this backdrop, this chapter aims to evaluate recent US federal case law and the academic debate among US scholars and practitioners on fidelity rebates

781. For similar interpretation *see* Petit, 'The Judgment of the EU Court of Justice in Intel and The Rule of Reason in Abuse of Dominance Cases' (n. 769).
782. Text to (n. 43) in Chapter 1.
783. *Ibid.*, (n. 782).
784. Thomas Lambert, 'Evaluating Bundled Discounts' (2004) 89 Minnesota Law Review 1688; Herbert Hovenkamp, 'Discounts and Exclusions' (2006) Utah Law Review 841; Daniel Crane, 'Bargaining Over Loyalty' (2013) 92 Texas Law Review 253.

concerning the circumstances under which the price-cost test can be used as a tool to identify a possible anticompetitive effect of fidelity rebates. This chapter will devote particular attention to case law, that clarifies under which circumstances a price-cost test might be relevant as a part of the assessment of the legality of fidelity rebates; an issue which has not been addressed by the Commission and the EU Courts in the *Intel* and *Post Danmark II* judgments.

For that reason, section 6.02 will provide a detailed description of the background and the legal assessment of the two cases mentioned above, before reviewing the academic debate in US scholarship comparing the two paradigms for exclusionary conduct – predatory pricing and exclusive dealing – through the prism of this case law. The goal is to shed light on to which circumstances a price-cost test should be used as a tool to determine an anticompetitive effect of fidelity rebates and how this clarification can inform the EU approach. Finally, this chapter will compare the US and EU approach to price-cost tests in the assessment of fidelity rebates. Ultimately, this chapter aims to understand whether the economic theory of 'raising rivals' costs may underlie the reasoning of the *Intel* and *Post Danmark II* judgments.

§6.02 THE RECENT US CASE LAW ON FIDELITY REBATES

[A] *ZF Meritor v. Eaton*

[1] Background

Eaton was the leading supplier of heavy-duty-truck transmissions in North America. Transmissions are an important component of heavy-duty trucks, which are used to travel long distances on highways, and 'performance' vehicles such as cement mixers, garbage trucks, and dump trucks. There were only four truck manufacturers purchasing heavy-duty-truck transmissions in North America. These manufacturers sell trucks to final consumers.

Truck buyers have the ability to choose many of the components used in their trucks, including transmissions, from manufacturers catalogues called 'data books'. These catalogues list 'standard' offerings of components that will be provided to final truck buyers unless such buyers expressly select another supplier's product. Catalogues also list 'preferred' offerings, which are the lowest priced components in the data book among comparable products. Truck buyers may also request components that are not published in a data book, even though such requests will tend to increase the cost of the component. Analysis of the retail market found that data book positioning is essential in the industry.

Eaton dominated the transmissions market from 1950 to 1989, when Meritor entered the market. By 1999, Meritor had achieved a 17% market share. In mid-1999, Meritor formed a joint venture with ZF, which was the leading supplier of heavy-duty-truck transmissions in Europe. This joint venture aimed to introduce innovative transmissions called 'FreedomLine' into the North American market – which occurred in 2001.

Shortly thereafter, the trucking industry experienced a 40%–50% decline in demand for new heavy-duty trucks, which was followed by changes in Eaton's trade policy towards its customers. In particular, Eaton entered into new long-term agreements (LTAs) with truck manufacturers that were unprecedented in terms of their duration – at least five years – and market coverage. The LTAs included up-front payments and a conditional rebate provision according to which a purchaser would receive rebates only if its purchases reached a specified percentage of its requirements from Eaton. Such requirements were between 70% to more than 90% depending on the manufacturer. The LTAs could be terminated if the target requirements were not met, upon which all payments and contractual saving had to be paid back to Eaton.

Before the renewed LTAs were adopted, Meritor's products were listed in the component data books of all manufacturers, in some cases with preferred positioning. All LTAs required the truck manufacturers to include Eaton as the standard offering in its data book; two of the four LTAs required the truck manufacturers to remove competitors' products from their data books entirely. Finally, each LTA contained a 'competitiveness' clause according to which each of the manufacturers could purchase transmissions from another supplier if that supplier offered a lower price or a better product which Eaton was unable to match.

Following these agreements being entered into, Meritor suffered a significant erosion of its market shares. By 2003 Meritor's market share had dropped to 8%, which resulted in a decision to dissolve the joint venture with ZF. At the end of 2005, Meritor's market share had dropped to 4%. In January 2007, Meritor exited the market.

[2] Assessment

In its decision, the US Court of Appeal for the Third Circuit found that the most significant issue was whether the antitrust analysis of rebates should be subject to the price-cost test applicable to predation, or to the 'rule of reason' approach applicable to exclusive dealing. Under the price-cost test, Meritor had to prove that Eaton's prices were below an appropriate measure of costs – and although Eaton's prices during the period following the LTAs having been entered into were lower than Meritor's, Eaton never priced below its costs. On the other hand, under the rule of reason applicable to exclusive dealing the agreements would be unlawful only if their 'probable effect' was to substantially lessen competition in the relevant market.[785]

The majority of the Third Circuit court rejected the application of the price-cost test in this case, stating that the test is appropriate only in 'a case in which price is the clearly predominant mechanism of exclusion'.[786] The Third Circuit distinguished between pricing practices, which are 'unlikely to exclude equally efficient rivals unless they are below-cost', and non-pricing practices/exclusive dealing arrangements which 'can exclude equally efficient rivals, and thereby harm competition, irrespective of

785. *Meritor*, para. 269.
786. *Ibid.*, para. 275.

below-cost pricing'.[787] In this regard, the Court identified a number of anticompetitive provisions in the LTAs, in order to to classify the conduct as non-price practice in showing that price was not the predominant mechanism of exclusion. First, Eaton was an unavoidable trading partner. Second, the contracts lasted at least five years and the LTAs covered all four purchasers in the market. Third, some of the agreements required Meritor's products to be removed from the manufacturers' data books, thereby preventing competing products – and particularly FreedomLine transmissions – from being promoted.[788] Fourth, if the manufacturers failed to meet the target sale requirements the contract could be terminated. Thus, the cost of breaching the agreement was very high, which amounted not only to a penalty in the form of a rebate but losing Eaton as an unavoidable supplier. Lastly, the market was highly concentrated, with no significant external supplier having entered the market during the last twenty years. The market had very high barriers to entry, and access to the intermediate market in which the truck manufacturers operate was crucial to successful entry.

The majority therefore reached the conclusion that Eaton's conduct constituted an unlawful exclusive-dealing arrangement.[789] Further, the Court considered that 'exclusive dealing will generally only be unlawful where the market is highly concentrated, the defendant possesses significant market power, and there is some element of coercion present'.[790] For that reason, the Court declined to apply a price-cost test, clarifying that in this case Eaton's competitors 'may be driven out not because they cannot compete on a price basis, but because they are never given an opportunity to compete, despite their ability to offer products with significant customer demand'.[791] Thus, the application of a price-cost test in this case was refused because the defendant's price was not 'the clear driving force' and the customers were not free to walk away if a competitor offered a better price, which means that the application of a price-cost test 'would place a significant portion of anti-competitive conduct outside the reach of the antitrust laws without adequate justification'.[792] Further, the Court observed that in those cases, a dominant firm may be able to hinder rivals ability to reach a large enough portion of the market to achieve the minimum economies of scale necessary to compete by locking up a sufficient part of demand, which would allow the discounter to successfully protect or enhance its market power.[793]

Judge Greenberg disagreed with the majority's decision to reject the price-cost test, and issued a dissenting opinion that concluded that Meritor did not suffer antitrust injury. The reasons for this conclusion were as follows. First, the price-cost test is relevant and had a dispositive effect in this case[794] because of 'the fundamental and broader principle that above-cost pricing practices, even those embodied in discount

787. *Ibid.*, para. 281.
788. *Ibid.*, para. 277.
789. *Ibid.*, paras 282–283.
790. *Ibid.*, para. 284.
791. *Ibid.*, para. 281.
792. *Ibid.*, para. 278.
793. *Ibid.*
794. *Ibid.*, paras 311–312.

and rebate programs memorialized in written agreements, generally are not anticompetitive'.[795] It is true that a price-cost test would not preclude the possibility of a non-price aspect of a conduct being anticompetitive, even in the absence of below-cost pricing. In such cases, the price-cost test 'would operate only as one element, though a significant one, of a court's and jury's inquiry under rule of reason'.[796] Second, the non-price aspects of the LTAs – such as market-share targets and the data book placement provisions – would not have been adopted without the reduced prices offered as an incentive for the truck manufacturers to accept entering into the LTAs.[797]

Contrary to the majority's conclusion that the price was not the predominant mechanism of exclusion, the dissenting opinion holds that the prices were 'the crux of the rebate program and are an inextricable element of the LTAs'.[798] If single-product market share rebates do not require exclusivity as a condition, as occurred in this case, then such rebates are pro-competitive and lawful as long as they are not predatory, i.e., remain above cost – which means that they can be matched by an equally efficient competitor.[799] However, he recognized that in concentrated markets with high barriers to entry and long-term buying commitments, as well as when the large firm can offer a larger variety of products than competitors, above-cost rebates are most plausible for competitive injury.[800] In this sense, he distinguished between single-item rebates, which can be anticompetitive only if they are predatory and rebates conditional on purchasing different products produced by a single producer or when they are aggregated over a longer period, which can be problematic even when they remain above cost.[801]

Lastly, Judge Greenberg reviewed whether a rule of reason standard should apply to an evaluation of the lawfulness of Eaton's LTAs, notwithstanding their above-cost prices. He suggested that the share of the market which is foreclosed should be established in order to determine whether this is a substantial share of the relevant market. Other elements that should be taken into account when assessing the effect of the LTAs is their duration, how easy it was to terminate them, whether there were entry barriers, what alternative outlets competitors could have employed to sell their products, and the buyer's and seller's business justifications for entering into the LTAs.[802] Since the LTAs did not contain a condition for the purchasing of 100% of customers requirement from Eaton, they were not on their terms exclusive dealing contracts and, as such, they did not preclude manufacturers from purchasing from competitors.[803] Consequently, the LTAs were not exclusive agreements; instead, they provided discounted but above-cost prices, which any equally efficient competitor could match.[804] Furthermore, Meritor did not offer lower prices than Eaton and did not

795. *Ibid.*, para. 320.
796. *Ibid.*, para. 321.
797. *Ibid.*
798. *Ibid.*, para. 320.
799. *Ibid.*, para. 323.
800. *Ibid.*
801. *Ibid.*, Judge Greenberg, refer to Areeda and Hovenkamp, *Antitrust Law* (n. 339).
802. *Ibid.*, para. 327.
803. *Ibid.*, para. 333.
804. *Ibid.*

develop a full product line in order to compete effectively with Eaton.[805] Given this, Judge Greenberg concluded that Eaton's LTAs were not anticompetitive.[806]

[B] *Eisai Inc. v. Sanofi Aventis*

[1] Background

The facts of this case were as follows. Sanofi Aventis U.S., LLC, and Sanofi U.S. Services, Inc., (Sanofi) had monopoly power in the anticoagulant drugs market. It had a market share from 81.5% up to 92.3% on the relevant market, whereas the second largest competitor had a market share from 4.3% up to 8.2%.

From September 2005 until July 2010, Sanofi offered to US hospitals the 'Lovenox Acute Contract Value Program' (Program), which contained Sanofi's terms and conditions for the sale of Lovenox. Under the terms of the Program, hospitals received price discounts of 1% if the volume of Lovenox they purchased was below 75% of their total purchases of anticoagulant drugs and increasingly higher discounts, ranging from 9% to 30% (in 2008), if they increased their purchases above this threshold.[807] Discounts were calculated based on a combination of volume purchased and market share from the total requirements.

Hospitals were not contractually bound by these conditions: the only consequence of not reaching the 75% threshold was that the hospital would receive only the 1% discount.[808] Contracts could be terminated with thirty days' notice, after which future purchases would be for Lovenox's wholesale price.

Eisai, who was the main Sanofi's competitor, claimed that Sanofi harmed competition in the market for anticoagulant drugs by preventing hospitals from replacing Lovenox with competing drugs.

[2] Assessment

The Third Circuit had to determine whether Sanofi's programme constituted exclusive dealing arrangements or simply pricing practices.[809] In this regard, the Court declined to characterise the conduct as pricing practice and rejected the application of the price-cost test. It clarified that a price-cost test is applicable as a specific application of the rule of reason only when the price is the predominant mechanism of exclusion, and explained that the price itself did not function as the exclusionary tool in those cases.[810] In contrast, the District Court had found that the price was the predominant mechanism of exclusion under Sanofi's practices and decided that a price-cost test was

805. *Ibid.*, para. 334.
806. *Ibid.*
807. *Eisai*, para. 400.
808. *Ibid.*
809. *Ibid.*, para. 408.
810. *Ibid.*, para. 409.

applicable.[811] Since Sanofi's prices had never been below costs, summary judgment was granted in favour of Sanofi holding that the LTAs were not anticompetitive because they were above cost.

Eisai argued that Sanofi offered discounts that bundled incontestable and contestable demand and it was this bundling, and not the price, that served as an exclusionary tool.[812] The Court accepted the argument that the price was not the mechanism of exclusion but rejected the bundling claims stating that: 'Even if bundling of different types of demand for the same product could, in the abstract, foreclose competition, nothing in the record indicates that an equally efficient competitor was unable to compete with Sanofi.'[813] In this regard, the Court held that the facts showed that Eisai failed to prove the existence of non-contestable demand for Lovenox, which made it a must-stock product on the basis of its unique indication and customer preferences. For that reason, the Court found that Eisai was able to compete for the whole demand.

The Court rejected Eisai's argument that the Programme at issue substantially foreclosed the market for the following reasons. First, the coverage of the agreement was limited to a few dozen hospitals out of almost 6,000 in the US, which was considered not enough to demonstrate substantial foreclosure.[814] Second, customers were free to switch to a competitor's product without risk of penalty or of supply shortages.[815] For that reason, the Appeals Court affirmed the District Court's order, granting summary judgment in favour of Sanofi holding that the LTAs were not anticompetitive under the rule of reason analysis.

§6.03 THE DEBATE ABOUT THE APPROPRIATE TREATMENT OF FIDELITY REBATES IN US ACADEMIC SCHOLARSHIP

Following these decisions, the debate about the appropriate treatment of fidelity rebates in US academic scholarship is currently divided into two camps which broadly follow the opposing lines of reasoning similar to those already outlined in the description of the cases above.

[A] Fidelity Rebates Should Be Subject Solely to Price-Cost Test

The first camp holds that fidelity rebates are mainly pro-competitive discounting practices. Fidelity rebates will only be unlawful when a dominant company sets its prices below cost in order to exclude its competitors. Thus, the only mechanism of

811. *Eisai INC v. Sanofi Aventis LLC et al.*, No. 3:08-cv-04168, District Court of New Jersey, March 28, 2014.
812. *Eisai*, para. 409.
813. *Ibid.*, para. 406.
814. *Ibid.*, para. 404.
815. *Ibid.*, para. 408.

exclusion is predatory pricing, and fidelity rebates are to be subject to the law of predatory pricing where a price-cost test is applicable.[816]

Predatory pricing is a short-run conduct by a dominant company that lowers the price of its products below cost in order to exclude rivals from the market, after which it will be able to raise prices above the competitive level in order to recoup the losses from its predatory behaviour.[817] Under this framework, the relevant benchmark is whether the price charged by the dominant undertaking covers the costs that an equally efficient competitor would incur when producing the same goods/services. If the discounted price is above the discounter's own cost (e.g., an 'above-cost loyalty discount'), such price could theoretically be matched by any rival that is as efficient as the discounter. As a result, an equally efficient competitor will not be excluded from the market; instead, a fidelity rebates scheme would lead to intense competition that would benefit consumers. If the discounted price is below this measure of costs, however, the price could serve as a mechanism to exclude a competitor, who is at least as efficient as the dominant company – thereby allowing for the acquisition of market power, the charge of higher prices, and the reaping of monopoly profits by a dominant undertaking.

According to the proponents of this view, exclusive dealing and loyalty discounts require profit sacrifices to achieve exclusion in very similar circumstances to predatory pricing. Thus, a predatory pricing standard and the use of a price-cost test as a safe harbour is required as an appropriate measure to distinguish pro-competitive from anticompetitive rebates.[818] Aggressive but above-cost pricing should be legal; and less efficient rivals who lose sales due to the superiority of the dominant company should not be 'able to turn their defeat in the market into an antitrust claim'.[819] If prices are above cost, they will not amount to de facto exclusive dealing, and as such they should not be penalised.[820] In addition, the proponents of this view argue that the prohibition of above-cost pricing would amount to forcing firms to charge higher prices in order to

816. Lambert, 'Evaluating Bundled Discounts' (n. 784); Areeda and Hovenkamp, *Antitrust Law* (n. 339); Hovenkamp, 'Discounts and Exclusion' (n. 784); Thomas Lambert, 'Appropriate Liability Rules for Tying and Bundled Discounting' (2011) 72 Ohio St Law Journal 909, 980–81; Herbert Hovenkamp and Eric Hovenkamp, 'Complex Bundled Discounts and Antitrust Policy' (2009) 57 Buffalo Law Review 1227; Crane, 'Bargaining Over Loyalty' (n. 784); Brief for Eighteen Scholars as Amici Curiae in Support of Petitioner, Eaton Corp. v. ZF Meritor LLC, No 12-1045, 2013 WL 1309073.

817. For the intensive overview of predatory pricing theory *see* in general Patrick Bolton, Joseph Brodley and Michael Riordan, 'Predatory Pricing: Strategic Theory and Legal Policy' (1999) 88 Geo Law Journal 2239.

818. Crane, 'Bargaining Over Loyalty' (n. 784); Hovenkamp, 'Discounts and Exclusions' (n. 784); Lambert, 'Evaluating Bundled Discounts' (n. 784).

819. Brief for Eighteen Scholars as Amici Curiae in Support of Petitioner, *Eaton Corp. v. ZF Meritor LLC*, No. 12-1045, 2013 WL 1309073, 14.

820. *Ibid.*, (n. 819); Herbert Hovenkamp, 'Exclusion and the Sherman Act' (2005) 72(1) The University of Chicago Law Review 147, 154; Hovenkamp, 'Discounts and exclusions' (n. 784).

protect less efficient rivals, which would result in immediate consumer harm.[821] Consequently, above-cost discounts 'of any kind should be per se lawful'.[822]

It has also been argued that fidelity rebates may generate pro-competitive effects and consumer benefits in ways that simple volume discounts cannot,[823] and that the lack of a reliable safe harbour such as a price-cost test is likely to discourage companies from engaging in discounting that might be beneficial to consumers.[824] Such pro-competitive effects might occur in markets with high fixed costs and short product lifetimes, in which case the total costs of production are exceptionally sensitive to the volume sold. In such cases, it would be cheaper and more efficient if one firm can secure a certain share of the market demand – such efficiencies cannot be achieved through volume rebates.[825] As can be recalled from Chapter 3, there is substantial literature dealing with other pro-competitive effects of fidelity rebates, such as preventing dealers' free riding, stimulating retailers' effort or avoiding double marginalization, which provides further support to this position. The argument further holds that, without a price-cost test, it will be difficult to distinguish between pro-competitive and anticompetitive discounting practices, which might result in mistaken jury findings. Thus, the absence of a clear-cut test will deter companies from providing pro-competitive rebates, which may lead to a chilling effect on competition. In short, the price-cost test provides an administrable approach that creates legal certainty and can identify and condemn only practices that 'could injure consumers by excluding rivals that are, or are likely to become, as efficient as the discounter'.[826]

This position is reflected in Judge Greenberg's dissenting opinion in the *Meritor* judgment discussed in section 6.02[A] above and in the District Court position in *Sanofi* discussed in section 6.02[B] above. In both cases the price was considered to be the predominant mechanism of exclusion and as such, a price-cost test was applicable.

However, an important observation is that the proponents of this approach (as well as the US case law of rebates)[827] consider the application of a price-cost attributable to predatory pricing only for a single-product loyalty rebates and only if all sales are contestable, i.e., competitors are able to compete for the whole demand (not only for the non-contestable base of sales).[828] In both of the discussed cases above, the allegation was whether the rebate scheme can be tested under a standard predatory pricing price-cost test.

821. Herbert Hovenkamp, 'The Federal Trade Commission and the Sherman Act' (2010) 62 Fla Law Review 871, 887.
822. Daniel Crane, 'Multiproduct Discounting: A Myth of Non price Predation' (2005) 72(1) The University of Chicago Law Review 27, 29. The same approach was proposed by Brief for *Amici Curiae Morgan Stanley et al., 3M v. LePage's Inc.*, (2004) (No. 02-1865) 2003 WL 22428378.
823. Brief in Support of Petitioner (n. 819) 15.
824. Lambert, 'Evaluating Bundled Discounts' (n. 784) 1716.
825. Hovenkamp, 'The Federal Trade Commission and the Sherman Act' (n. 821) 889.
826. Lambert, 'Evaluating Bundled Discounts' (n. 784) 1757.
827. In referring to the settled case law of rebates the Third Circuit in *Eisai*, para. 409 held that the price-cost test applies in case when 'a firm uses a single-product loyalty discount or rebate to compete with similar products'.
828. Klein and Lerner, 'Price-Cost Tests in Antitrust Analysis of Single Product Loyalty Contracts' (n. 337) 633.

However, some of the proponents of this approach were aware that in some cases, customer preferences (or the unavoidable trading partner status of the discounter) might lead to the establishment of a non-contestable part of the demand, for which competitors would not be able to compete. Thus, the real competition is for part of sales, i.e., contestable part of demand. This in general, makes the applicability of predatory pricing price-cost test not relevant,[829] because the demand is separated into non-contestable and contestable parts and the real competition is only for the latter. They further considered that in such circumstances the test must be modified in order to compare the price with the loyalty discount applied only for the contestable sales with costs – if the discount attributed price of contestable sales is above costs, equally efficient rivals can compete for the contestable sales.[830] The rationale behind this argument is that if the attributed price is above the costs for the contestable part of sales, any as efficient as the discounter competitor will be able to compete for the contestable sales.[831]

This position is in line with the position adopted by the Commission's Guidance Paper of Article 102.[832] However, no US court has endorsed the application of this modified test to single-product fidelity rebates so far, and as the discussion of the position of the second camp will show, there are good reasons not to apply this modified test – for reasons which were already outlined in Chapter 3, and which is being discussed next.

[B] Fidelity Rebates Should Be Subject Solely to the Rule of Reason Approach Applicable to Exclusive Dealing

The second camp holds that when the effect of fidelity rebates might be similar to exclusive dealing, those rebates should be treated under the law of exclusive dealing – where a rule of reason standard applies – instead of under the law of predatory pricing – where a price-cost test applies.

Proponents of this view argue that fidelity rebates might lead to foreclosure by increasing the costs of the dominant company's competitors and, as such, they claim that the exclusionary conduct can be explained through the framework consistent with the economic theory of raising rivals' cost.[833] Although, the economic theories based on RRC are reviewed in Chapter 3, it is worthwhile to summarise the conclusions again.

First, the RRC theory explains that by adopting fidelity rebates a dominant company can exclude its competitors from sufficient access to markets/clients, which deprives them of the opportunity to compete and to achieve sufficient scope of sales. As described in Chapter 3, achieving a certain level of output is necessary for a competitor or an entrant to realise the economies of scale necessary to compete effectively with the dominant company. If a dominant company has a large non-contestable share of

829. *Ibid.*
830. *Ibid.*
831. Klein, 'The Economics of Alternative Legal Standards for Loyalty Discounts' (n. 347).
832. *See* Chapter 4 of this book.
833. Wright, 'Moving Beyond Naïve Foreclosure Analysis' (n. 313) 1164.

demand and ties some part of contestable share with fidelity rebates agreements, it might deprive a competitor from the ability of achieving MES.

Second, the RRC theory also explains that even if the modified discount attribution test proposed by the proponents of the first camp (and the Commission in its Guidance Paper) is met by the dominant company, there still might be an exclusionary effect if the contestable share of the sales is insufficient to allow the competitors to operate profitably given their fixed costs.[834] A body of literature regarding RRC models, already discussed in Chapter 3, shows that above-cost fidelity rebates can lead to anticompetitive foreclosure.[835] In this sense, whether the attributed price for the contestable part of sales is above or below the costs is not relevant, since any as efficient as the discounter competitor will not be able to achieve MES in order to be profitable and to compete effectively with the dominant company. The RRC literature demonstrates that fidelity rebates can exclude an equally efficient competitor without profit sacrifice and for that reason, 'the exclusion is possible even if the effective price is above the incremental cost of the dominant company',[836] which makes the price-cost test inappropriate.[837]

Another important consequence from RRC theory is that some discounting practices can be anticompetitive even if they do not completely exclude a rival from the market.[838] In these cases, a practice can be anticompetitive because by raising competitors' costs, their ability to compete effectively and to impose competitive constraints on the dominant company is reduced, which suggests that the degree of foreclosure might not be determinative.[839] In others, the degree of foreclosure might be significant but the lack of evidence that competitors' cost are raised leading to negative effect on price, output or other parameters of competition suggests no basis for liability.[840] Thus, the key issue is not the level of foreclosure, but whether rival's costs are raised, which suggests that although the level of foreclosure might be a proxy for a possible anticompetitive harm, it might be not enough basis for claim under the RRC theory.[841] The fact that rivals are not eliminated makes these strategies less detectable and less likely to invite prosecution than predatory pricing and, thus, they may even be preferable for a dominant company as a way of maintaining or enhancing its dominant position.[842]

The proponents of the RRC theory have recognised that raising rival's cost alone is not sufficient to establish that behaviour is anticompetitive and causes consumer harm. Anticompetitive effect will arise only if: (1) rivals' cost increases are significant, so that the rival has to increase its price to achieve the same level of profit; (2) the magnitude and duration are significant; and (3) the rivals cannot impose competitive

834. OECD Report (2016).
835. Text to (nn. 308–330) in Chapter 3.
836. Economides, 'Loyalty/Requirement Rebates and the Antitrust Modernization Commission' (n. 297) 259.
837. Moore and Wright (n. 280) 1218.
838. OECD Report (2016).
839. Jacobson, 'Exclusive dealing, Foreclosure and Consumer Harm' (n. 324) 349.
840. *Ibid.*, 362.
841. *Ibid. See also* OECD Report (2016) para. 57.
842. Hovenkamp, 'Exclusion and the Sherman Act' (n. 820) 158.

constraint on the dominant company which will be in a position to gain the power to raise prices.[843] In practice, the relevant benchmark for whether a strategy of RRC might result in competitive harm is whether that conduct forecloses a sufficient share of the market to deprive competitors of the possibility of achieving a MES so as to remain able to impose competitive constraint.[844] Apart from evidence of a significant degree of foreclosure, the analysis requires an assessment of the duration of the agreements, barriers to entry, the ability of a competitor to compete, and consideration of pro-competitive efficiencies.[845] Ultimately, the rationale behind this approach is that a dominant company can use fidelity rebates in order to induce their customers to purchase exclusively from it and to harm competition especially in cases when the dominant supplier's product is essential for the buyers and there are significant economies of scale.[846]

Supporters of the RRC theory go as far as to reject the view that foreclosure can lead to an anticompetitive effect only if an equally efficient competitor is excluded from the market. This is because in some cases, even entry of a less efficient competitor into the market can impose competitive constraints in monopoly markets, which will lead to price decreases, and, as such, consumer benefits.[847] For that reason, it was suggested that the 'liability for exclusionary conduct should not turn on the entrant's efficiency' but rather on 'how large a penalty the incumbent is placing on entrant'.[848] In these cases, focusing on whether the competitor is equally efficient competitor will lead to under-deterrence.[849] This position reflects one of the criticisms of the AEC test, which will be discussed in the next chapter.

A last argument in favour of RRC approaches to fidelity rebates is that this standard has administrative advantages over a complex price-cost test, because the assessment is over the terms and conditions under which rebates are granted rather than the price ultimately charged. In practical terms, it is easier to prohibit the condition rather than to regulate the price.[850] Underlying this argument is the insight that the price-cost test applied for fidelity rebates is not the traditional price-cost test, which compares the average price with average variable cost, and it is accepted that it is administratively efficient.[851] As already discussed in Chapter 3, the price-cost test applied to fidelity rebates is a 'modified' test that must compare the costs and prices for that part of demand that can realistically be switched to a competitor, the so-called contestable share. It was also outlined that the estimation of the contestable share of

843. Krattenmaker and Salop (n. 307) 255.
844. Wright, 'Simple but Wrong or Complex but More Accurate?' (n. 43) 24.
845. *Ibid.*, (n. 844).
846. Wright, 'Simple but Wrong or Complex but More Accurate?' (n. 43) 21; Moore and Wright (n. 280) 1215.
847. Salop, 'The Raising Rivals' Cost Foreclosure Paradigm' (n. 296) 28.
848. Fiona Scott Morton and Zachary Abrahamson, *A Unifying Analytical Framework for Loyalty Rebates* (2016) https://papers.ssrn.com/sol3/papers.cfm?abstract_id=2833563 accessed 1 December 2017.
849. Salop, 'The Raising Rivals' Cost Foreclosure Paradigm' (n. 296) 46.
850. *Ibid.*, 37.
851. *Ibid.*, 44.

demand is a complex task, subject to significant errors. Moreover, it is 'unlikely to shed much light on the ultimate question of competitive effect'.[852]

In short, this school of thought believes that RRC and predation are two completely different mechanisms of exclusion, and that each requires a different analytical framework.[853] Some fidelity rebates are similar to exclusive dealing and should be analysed under the same legal standard as exclusive dealing rather than predatory pricing[854] – with the presence or absence of profit sacrifice as the element that distinguishes the RRC and predatory pricing.[855] Some go as far as to argue that since such a conduct does not require a dominant company to suffer losses during the initial period that have to be recouped in the later stage – because the recoupment occurs simultaneously –non-predatory pricing may not only be a successful strategy but may even be more likely to harm consumers than predatory pricing.[856] From this perspective, most of the recent cases involving fidelity rebates, including the cases discussed in section 6.02, are 'based upon theories of economic harm grounded in the RRC framework'.[857]

§6.04 COMPARATIVE ANALYSIS

As described in the previous chapter, the recent EU case law on fidelity rebates in both the *Intel* and *Post Danmark II* judgments departed from the strict form-based approach and endorsed an approach based on an evaluation of the possible anticompetitive effects of fidelity rebates. This approach is close to the rule of reason standard applied in the recent US case law on fidelity rebates.

However, the legal assessment of fidelity rebates under EU competition law still lacks clarity in particular with regards to the relevance and circumstances in which a price-cost test should be pursued. In comparing the US and EU approaches in the treatment of fidelity rebates, this section aims to clarify under which circumstances a price-cost test might be a reliable tool to determine an anticompetitive effect of fidelity rebates.

852. OECD Report (2016).
853. Contrast Krattenmaker and Salop (n. 307) Moore and Wright (n. 280); Tom, Balto and Averitt (n. 298); Wright, 'Simple but Wrong or Complex but More Accurate?' (n. 43) with Ciara Fumagalli and Massimo Motta, *On the Use of Price-Cost Tests in Loyalty Discounts: Which Implications from Economic Theory?* (2015) https://papers.ssrn.com/sol3/papers.cfm?abstract_id=2596630 accessed 10 May 2017, arguing that exclusive dealing, including fidelity rebates and predation, could be interpreted through a common mechanism.
854. Tom, Balto and Averitt (n. 298); Wright, 'Simple but Wrong or Complex but More Accurate?' (n. 43); Brennan (n. 277) 335; Moore and Wright (n. 280).
855. Steven Salop and David Scheffman, 'Raising Rivals' Costs' (1983) 73 The American Economic Review 267, 268–270. They distinguish predatory pricing from raising rivals' costs using economic models; *see also* Krattenmaker and Salop (n. 307).
856. Salop, 'The Raising Rivals' Cost Foreclosure Paradigm' (n. 296).
857. Moore and Wright (n. 280) 1208.

[A] The Framework to Assess Fidelity Rebates

The position of the Third Circuit in the cases discussed above revealed that the assessment of fidelity rebates starts with the assessment of whether the contract was de facto exclusive dealing. A contract amounts to de facto exclusive dealing in two cases; when these conditions are in the contract, in which case if the customer does not meet the threshold, the dominant company would terminate the contract or in the case, when these conditions are not in the contract but the loss of rebates is large enough, making the contract economically exclusive.[858] In *Meritor*, the Court found exclusivity conditions in the contract. The evaluation of the facts in *Eisai* showed that, Sanofi's contracts did not contain exclusivity conditions and did not deprive Eisai of competing and for that reason the Court did not consider as relevant the need to evaluate whether the contract was economically exclusive. After the assessment as to whether the contract amounted to de facto exclusive dealing, an evaluation on whether the exclusivity provisions can deprive a competitor as efficient as the dominant company to compete was required. The relevant theory of harm is that a dominant company may be able to hinder a rival's ability to reach a large enough portion of the market to achieve the minimum economies of scale necessary to compete by locking up a sufficient part of demand – a theory consistent with the RRC literature. Thus, a de facto exclusive dealing can be anticompetitive only if the evaluation of the circumstances shows that a competitor as efficient as the dominant company can be foreclosed which would allow the dominant company to reduce output, increase prices, or reduce quality in goods or services to the detriment of consumers.

However, the Third Circuit also clarified that there is a general presumption of illegality in cases of exclusive dealing if the market is highly concentrated, the defendant possesses significant market power (and it is an unavoidable trading partner), and there is some element of coercion present. This presumption seems to resemble the EU's settled case law on fidelity rebates, described in Chapter 2, and the EU Court's position in creating an abbreviated test for the evaluation of fidelity rebates, according to which the strong dominant position and the 'unavoidable trading partners' status of the discounter makes customers dependent on the dominant company in which case competitors were not able to compete for the customers whole demand.

In *Meritor* and *Eisai*, the Third Circuit, held that in cases where there were not exclusivity requirements, the effect of the agreement in the real word needed to be assessed to find whether it constitutes de facto exclusive dealing. Next, an assessment on whether rebate schemes have an anticompetitive effect should follow. This includes evaluation of all the circumstances, including market conditions, coverage and duration of the contract. This assessment is different to the approach developed by the EU Courts for the evaluation of the 'other category' of rebates that are granted on the basis of certain non-exclusivity related conditions in terms of the resistance of the EU Courts

858. Klein, 'The Economics of Alternative Legal Standards for Loyalty Discounts' (n. 347).

to consider the coverage of the practice and the inconsistent position about the relevance of the relevant period, i.e., duration.

[B] The Relevance of the Price-Cost Test in the Case Law

As the discussion of the recent EU case law on fidelity rebates in Chapter 5 revealed, the application of a price-cost test for finding anticompetitive fidelity rebates under Article 102 is not clarified.

In *Intel*, the European Commission chose to apply the price-cost test for the evaluation of the anticompetitive effects of fidelity rebates without explaining why it considered Intel's rebates as a pricing conduct instead of exclusive dealing. On appeal, GC considered that, the test is irrelevant for the assessment of exclusivity rebates because the test cannot capture the rebates' anti-competitive nature'.[859] Moreover, the GC also held that: 'even in the case of rebates falling within the third ("other") category, for which an examination of the circumstances of the case is necessary, it is not essential to carry out an AEC test'.[860] This position was confirmed in *Post Danmark II*, where the CJEU held that charging a price below cost to the customers is not a prerequisite of a finding of abuse regarding a rebate scheme. The CJEU nonetheless observed that the test must be regarded as one tool amongst others when assessing whether there is an abuse.[861] Unfortunately, the Court did not go further in explaining under which circumstances the test might be appropriate.

In contrast, while the Third Circuit in *Meritor* rejected the test, it clarified that the existence of anticompetitive provisions (combined with discounts) made the rebates at issue 'de facto' exclusive dealing. For that reason, the price was not considered to be the mechanism of exclusion, which substantiates the classification of the conduct as non-price practices, and as such, a price-cost test was deemed irrelevant. The Third Circuit further clarified that a price-cost test might be useful in pricing practices in 'a case in which price is the clearly predominant mechanism of exclusion'.[862] The Court further explained that in those cases, the price-cost test might be applied as a specific application of the rule of reason. However, a clear indication as to when the price is the predominant mechanism of exclusion is put aside.[863]

In *Intel* the GC also observed that the rebates granted by Intel made it possible 'to use the non-contestable share of the demand of the customer as leverage to secure also the contestable share'.[864] In doing so, Intel made it more difficult for its competitors to compete for the contestable share of demand, because its competitors not only had to make an attractive offer for the contestable portion of the market, but also had to compensate the customer for the loss of the exclusivity rebate.[865] This position might be interpreted as saying that the GC considered Intel's rebates as de facto exclusive

859. GC Judgment, para. 78.
860. *Ibid.*, para. 144.
861. *Post Danmark II*, para. 56.
862. *Meritor*, para. 275.
863. Moore and Wright (n. 280) 1244.
864. GC judgment, para. 103.
865. *Ibid.*, para. 93.

dealing, which can substantiate the rejection of the price-cost test in line with what the Third Circuit held in *Meritor*. The similarity is even more apparent in *Eisai* where the Third Circuit discussed the bundling of non-contestable and contestable demand and clarified that such bundling might, in the abstract, foreclose competition if the review of the evidence shows that an equally efficient competitor was unable to compete for the contestable share of sales because of the bundling. This might be interpreted as saying that the retroactivity of rebates might be an indication of anticompetitive foreclosure if the facts of the case show that because of the bundling of non-contestable and contestable demand, a competitor cannot compete for the contestable part of demand. It also might be suggested that under different facts, 'the theory of bundling premised on non-contestability' may support a finding of liability, which nonetheless substantiates the irrelevance of the price-cost test in those circumstances.[866]

[C] Price-Cost Tests and Raising Rivals Costs

Another way through which the American experience can contribute to understanding developments in the EU is by reference to the US academic debate, and particularly the importance of the raising rivals' costs' theory. In Intel, the GC observed that an anticompetitive effect occurs 'not only where access to the market is made impossible for competitors, but also where that access is made more difficult'.[867] This statement might be interpreted as shifting the focus of analysis from the exclusion of rivals to their marginalization. In this regard, the relevant theory of harm seems to fit with the RRC framework explaining that when the rivals are not able to compete and to reach a large enough portion of the market to achieve MES, the dominant company would be in a position to successfully protect or enhance its market power. As discussed above, RRC theory foresees situations in which a dominant company restricts its competitors' access to crucial inputs (input foreclosure) or customers (customer foreclosure), causing them to raise their costs or reduce their output. As a result of that conduct, competitors might not be excluded from the market but they become less efficient, which ultimately decreases their ability to impose competitive constraint on the dominant company pricing.

In effect, Intel's rebate schemes fit very neatly with this theory. First, Intel produces central processing units (CPUs), which are a key component in the overall performance of a computer. Intel's customers are original equipment manufacturers (OEMs) such as Dell, HP, NEC and Lenovo, and one retailer, Media-Saturn Holding GmbH (MSH). Because of the strong dominant position of Intel, its customers obtained a substantial part of the demand (the so-called non-contestable share) from it. Intel's competitors could only compete for that portion of demand that exceeds Intel's non-contestable share, i.e., the 'contestable' share of demand.[868] The exclusivity agreements between Intel and the OEMs were condemned because they denied Intel's competitors access to the market, preventing them from competing for the contestable

866. Morton and Abrahamson (n. 883) 701.
867. GC judgment, para. 88.
868. *Ibid.*, para. 92.

share. Intel's exclusivity rebates could foreclose its competitors' access to a significant customer base, which might prevent them from reaching MVS and force them to exit the market. On the other hand, if a competitor of Intel was merely not able to achieve MES in order to compete effectively, that would ultimately raise its costs – in which case it might remain on the market but be marginalized as a competitor, thereby providing a lesser competitive constraint on the dominant firm's pricing. According to the RRC theory, a dominant company can marginalize or exclude competitors from the market depriving it of its ability to reach MES – which ultimately raises those competitors' costs. Thus, achieving MES is crucial for the successful performance of a company.

The industry in the Intel case was characterised by significant costs to enter the market and 'an enormous combination of ingenuity, time and capital to develop the required know how to design x86 CPUs or to obtain a license from Intel'.[869] In industries with these characteristics, achieving MES is a necessary prerequisite for a competitor or an entrant to become as efficient as the dominant company. The presence of a dominant company with unavoidable trading partner status means that a significant part of demand is secured for the dominant company and only a small part is open to competition. In those cases, even a small amount of foreclosure might deprive a competitor or an entrant to reach MES and as such, to create strategic barriers that might be enough to marginalise them. This interpretation seems to be in line with the GC's position that the coverage of the rebate schemes was irrelevant, and with the CJEU's refusal to consider the second ground of Intel's appeal, which dealt with the market coverage.

If rivals' costs are raised due to an inability to reach MES in the context of economies of scale, rivals would always be inefficient and as such, its 'higher costs would not be well accounted for by a price-cost test'.[870] Thus, because of its cost/efficiency advantage over its competitors, a dominant company might charge prices below which those competitors can charge without engaging in below-cost pricing (i.e., without profit sacrifice). This also means that anticompetitive behaviour may be pursued which is not caught by the price-cost test – making this test unsuitable as a legal standard. This may explain the GC's position regarding the irrelevance of the AEC test in the assessment of the legality of fidelity rebates in *Intel*.

A second way in which the condemnation of Intel's practices by the GC is in line with RRC theory is in the compounded impact of providing discounts to distributors. Intel's customers are OEMs, which manufacture computers and sell them to final consumers. In order to get its products to final consumers, Intel's competitor ADM needed access to the OEMs – because final consumers were only interested in purchasing computers, and not components such as CPUs. Access to OEMs may therefore be the only possible distribution channel for ADM, providing a crucial input for the ultimate marketing of CPUs. In providing OEMs with an incentive to purchase

869. *Ibid.*, para. 129.
870. Steven Salop, https://truthonthemarket.com/2013/06/07/wright-is-right-and-price-cost-safe-harbors-are-wrong-the-raising-rivals-cost-paradigm-loyalty-discounts-and-exclusive-dealing/, accessed 15 February 2015.

exclusively from it, Intel engaged not only in customer foreclosure of ADM (regarding direct purchasers), but also in input foreclosure (regarding final consumers). According to RRC theory, in cases of input foreclosure even if rivals achieve MES their costs will be higher. The fact that a competitor is still present in the market but its performance is made more difficult means that its competitiveness is reduced. Therefore, there is not actual foreclosure but the competitive process is nonetheless harmed because the competitor, even if he is still on the market, cannot impose competitive constraints on the dominant company. Input foreclosure may lead to reduced incentives to innovate and to an increase in prices charged to the customers. Thus, input foreclosure can reduce competition even if the competitor's performance is at MES. This might explain the GC's observation that the anticompetitive effect occurs 'not only where access to the market is made impossible for competitors, but also where that access is made more difficult'.[871]

From the above, it can be concluded that the EU Courts 'allegations appear consistent with an analytical approach based upon a raising rivals' cost theory of exclusion'.[872]

§6.05 CONCLUSION

The aim of this chapter was to compare the treatment of fidelity rebates in the recent federal courts judgments in *Meritor* and *Eisai,* and in the academic debate in the US, with the EU Courts' judgments in *Intel* and *Post Danmark II.* The goal was to obtain insights regarding the available tools to distinguish anticompetitive rebates from effective competition and the role of price-cost tests in the context of these tools.

The debate about the appropriate treatment of fidelity rebates under the US antitrust law is longstanding. The primary dispute has been whether fidelity rebates have to be treated under the predatory pricing law where the price-cost test is applicable, or whether they have to be treated under the law of exclusive dealing where the rule of reason is applicable. The recent split decisions by the Third Circuit in *ZF Meritor* and *Eisai* reflects this longstanding debate. In both cases, the Third Circuit declined to adopt the price-cost test while clarifying that the test might be applied as an element of the rule of reason only when the price is the predominant mechanism of exclusion, which according to the Court was not the case at issue.

Fidelity rebates in *Meritor* were characterized as 'de facto' exclusive dealing in which case the price was not the mechanism of exclusion and as such, a rule of reason assessment of their effect was required. Such a rule of reason analysis evaluates whether fidelity rebates are anticompetitive in a similar way to which the 'all the circumstances' test evaluates whether fidelity rebates have a fidelity-enhancing effect, which makes them anticompetitive. In both *Meritor* and *Eisai*, the Third Circuit rejected the application of the price-cost test because the price was not the predominant mechanism of exclusion in these cases – instead, the rebate schemes could exclude

871. GC judgment, para. 88.
872. Wright, 'Simple but Wrong or Complex but More Accurate?' (n. 43) 29.

equally efficient rivals irrespective of whether the pricing is below cost. In both judgments, the Third Circuit was clear that the evaluation of illegality of fidelity rebates can be based on their actual anticompetitive effect without performing a formal price-cost test, which confirms that the AEC framework is not reliant exclusively on a price-cost test. It seems that this is exactly the position of the CJEU in *Intel* by saying that the assessment of fidelity rebates requires evaluation of all the circumstances in order to assess the possible existence of a strategy aiming to exclude an as efficient competitor without mentioning the requirement for a price-cost test to be carried out.

Lastly, the discussion of the RRC theory explains how this approach holds that fidelity rebates can be assessed without a need to undertake a price-cost test. The RRC theory is based on the assumption that a fidelity rebate scheme can foreclose a competitor (or potential entrant) access to market/customers without pricing below cost. In addition, a successful RRC strategy does not necessarily require profit sacrifice, which means that a dominant company might set its prices above costs but still make competitors' access to input or access to customers more difficult and thereby marginalize them as a competitor. By raising rivals costs, a dominant company can make competitors' access to the market more difficult and hinder their possibility to compete effectively and to expand their market performance. Hence, the competitive process could be harmed due to competitors' inability to impose competitive constraint on the dominant company. The economic theory of RRC provides an alternative interpretation of why fidelity rebates can be anticompetitive even if the price is above costs, and provides a framework to understand the underlining rationale behind the rejection of the price-cost test in both the *Intel* and *Post Danmark II* judgments.

CHAPTER 7

Identifying the Standard for Evaluating Fidelity Rebates

§7.01 INTRODUCTION

Over the years, there has been a growing concern about how to distinguish between pro-competitive and anticompetitive conduct. Some commentators claimed that it is impossible to distinguish these practices with certainty because in some cases the practice may be considered as abusive when it is not, the so-called false convictions or type I errors; in others the practice may be considered pro-competitive when it is abusive, the so-called false acquittals or type II errors.[873] For them, the assessment of any practices should take into account the risk and cost of those mistakes. Thus, the appropriate legal test for exclusionary conduct requires a balance between the risk and cost of those mistakes.[874] In searching for the optimal standard to distinguish between exclusionary and pro-competitive behaviour, several different approaches have been developed.[875] These include the naked abuse test, the profit sacrifice test, the no economic sense test, the AEC test and the consumer welfare test. The courts and competition authorities have used each of the tests.[876]

The aim of this chapter is to describe each of the tests and to evaluate their suitability from a normative point of view regarding which one is best able to distinguish between pro-competitive and anticompetitive fidelity rebates. The optimal test should protect consumer welfare as the main objective of EU competition policy and create predictability and legal certainty for businesses, allowing them to self-assess their conduct in advance, while minimizing the risk of errors, and 'enforcement

873. Ahlborn and Padilla (n. 6) 77.
874. Susan Creighton and others, 'Cheap Exclusion' (2005) 72(3) Antitrust Law Journal 975, 979.
875. The overview of the main tests was made by Vickers, 'Abuse of Market Power' (n. 4); O'Donoghue and Padilla (n. 13); OECD Report, Competition on the Merits (2005) DAF/COMP(2005)27.
876. OECD Report (2005).

(agency) and compliance (firm) costs'.[877] In this context, this chapter also aims to understand why the European Commission chose the AEC test as a single unified test for all types of exclusionary abuses. Consequently, it aims to clarify whether the AEC test could be considered as a necessary condition for establishing an exclusionary abuse or a sufficient one.[878] Some authors suggested a single test applicable to all forms of abusive practices.[879] Others argue that each type of exclusionary conduct needs a different test.[880] Consequently, the final aim of the chapter is to clarify whether a single comprehensive test applicable for all types of conduct is needed for the sake of legitimacy and legal certainty.

§7.02 DIFFERENT STANDARDS FOR EVALUATING EXCLUSIONARY ABUSES

[A] The Naked Abuse Test

[1] Description

Naked exclusion has been defined as a conduct that 'has the sole or overwhelmingly predominant purpose of harming competition, has no conceivable redeeming virtue by way of economic efficiency ... and is reasonably capable of causing competitive harm as the most egregiously anti-competitive conduct'.[881] Creighton suggested a similar definition:

877. Petit, 'Intel, Leveraging Rebates and the Goals of Article 102 TFEU' (n. 705); *see also* Wils, 'The Judgment of the EU General Court in Intel and the So-Called "More Economic Approach" to Abuse of Dominance' (n. 399).
878. Frédéric Marty, 'As-Efficient Competitor Test in Exclusionary Prices Strategies: Does Post-Danmark Really Pave the Way towards a More Economic Approach? (2014) No. 2013-26 Groupe de REcherche en Droit, Economie, Gestion (GREDEG CNRS), University of Nice Sophia Antipolis.
879. Janusz Ordover and Robert Willig, 'An Economic Definition of Predation: Pricing and Product Innovation' 1981 91(1) The Yale Law Journal 8; Douglas Melamed, 'Exclusionary Conduct under the Antitrust Laws: Balancing, Sacrifice and Refusals to Deal' (2005) 20 Berkeley Tech Law Journal 1247 (support for the sacrifice test); Gregory Werden, 'Identifying Exclusionary Conduct under Section 2: The "No Economic Sense" Test' (2006) 73(2) Antitrust Law Journal 413 (support for the no economic sense test); Richard Posner, *Antitrust law* (n. 271) (support for the AEC test); Salop, 'Exclusionary conduct, Effect on Consumers, and the Flawed Profit-Sacrifice Standard' (n. 43) and O'Donoghue and Padilla (n. 13) (support for the consumer welfare test).
880. Gavil (n. 298) (support for the burden shifting); Mark Popofsky, 'Defining Exclusionary Conduct: Section 2, The Rule Of Reason, and the Unifying Principle Underlying Antitrust Rules (2006) 73 Antitrust Law Journal 435 (support for the rule of reason approach, which select distinct tests for different conduct); Lao (n. 742) (supporting different burden shifting on a rule of reason type of framework to achieve different effective standard for different types of conduct); Jorge Padilla and David Evans, 'Designing Antitrust Rules For Assessing Unilateral Practices: A Neo-Chicago Approach' (2005) 72 University of Chicago Law Review 73 (supporting the view that the appropriate approach to evaluate unilateral practices does not require that the same form of rule apply to every practice).
881. Nazzini, *The Foundation of European Union Competition Law* (n. 392) 59.

> [b]ehaviour that unambiguously fails to enhance any party's efficiency, provides no benefits (short or long-term) to consumers, and in its economic effect produces only costs for the victims and wealth transfers to the firm(s) engaging in the conduct (apart from its contribution to market power).[882]

From the definitions, three elements of the test can be extracted: the dominant company's conduct must impair the competitive process, the conduct must not prima facie create efficiencies, and the conduct must be capable of causing consumer harm.

This definition seems to align the concept of naked abuse of the 'by object' restriction of competition category.[883] It is useful to think about Article 101 in this context. Some collusive agreements such as price fixing, lack any cognisable efficiency justification and could be prohibited by object, whereas others can plausibly create efficiencies and, hence, require a further detailed analysis to determine whether the agreement is anticompetitive.[884] The idea behind the naked abuse test is that the same distinction can be drawn among different forms of exclusionary conduct.[885] In some cases, the negative effect of a conduct can be presumed, as for example in naked exclusionary conduct in standard-setting process,[886] some tortious conduct[887] and some abuses of governmental process.[888]

Some forms of fidelity rebates had been presumed anticompetitive by the EU Courts, without the need to undertake economic analysis of their actual effect. As outlined in Chapter 2, the rationale behind the Court's view is that some types of rebates are anticompetitive based on the presumption that there is a certain degree of probability that the practice will have an anticompetitive effect and as such there is no need for the effect to be shown. In those cases, the conduct is presumed to have a capability of restriction of competition in the absence of objective justifications. For that reason, the conduct should be condemned as abusive 'by object' without engaging in further analysis in a similar way as that applied under Article 101 TFEU. According to some prominent scholars, this test is appropriate where:

> [e]xperience and logic suggests that the benefit/harm resulting from a practice is so clear and unambiguous that there is no point in wasting court or regulatory

882. Creighton and others (n. 874) 982.
883. Jessen (n. 257) Ch. 4.
884. Creighton and others (n. 874) 977.
885. *Ibid.*
886. *Ibid.*, 987–989 (This could be an opportunistic behaviour in a private standard-setting process where the dominant company adopts a standard to confer its market power).
887. *Ibid.*, 989–990 (This could be the case when the dominant company is engaged in deception, as for example disparaging the quality of rival's products. The deceptive conduct can immediately damage a competitor ability to operate. An extreme example could be when a dominant company is engaged in destroying or damaging rival's property to hamper them from making or distributing their products); *see also* Einer Elhauge, 'Defining Better Monopolization Standards' (2003) 56 Stanford Law Review 253, 281.
888. Creighton and others (n. 874) 990–992 (It means that the dominant company is using the rules of government against its competitors, such as obtaining a patent by perpetrating fraud on the Patent Office. It could be the case of engaging in abusive litigation when the lawsuit could very costly for the rival than for the dominant company with the aim of exclusion).

resources in investigating its effects; and (2) the risk of false positives or false negatives is small.[889]

[2] Analysis

It seems, there are good reasons for the implementation of the naked abuse test, as it is easy to administer and saves enforcement costs. Moreover, the existence of such a standard creates legal certainty, so dominant companies are able to predict with reasonable certainty whether their conduct might violate competition law provisions.[890] However, the test is appropriate only if it is possible to identify a conduct that is harmful without engaging in a thorough economic analysis. Thus, this test has been criticised, because the prohibition of a conduct without evaluating its economic effect may give rise to a high risk of over enforcement (false positives).[891] As a consequence, companies may not engage in pro-competitive, efficiency-oriented activities for the benefit of consumers, 'for fear of becoming embroiled in costly, lengthy litigation'.[892]

Under the naked exclusion test, when the conduct is presumably abusive, the dominant company still can provide evidence that the conduct creates efficiency beneficial to consumers, thereby justifying its behaviour. This means that a naked abuse violation does not amount to a 'per se' violation of Article 102.[893] The same approach is adopted under Article 101, where an agreement falling within the scope of the provision might be exempted by the prohibition if the defendant provides supportive evidence that its conduct is not capable of restricting competition.[894] Arguably, the possibility for the dominant company to rebut the presumption of illegality if the defendant provides supportive evidence that its conduct is not capable of restricting competition was confirmed by the CJEU in *Intel*, as was indicated in Chapter 5.[895]

It should be noted that while US courts have adopted 'per se' liability rules as regards some conduct which cannot be justified, they also developed the so-called quick look approach applicable in cases, where a conduct may be considered as anticompetitive without applying a full rule of reason analysis.[896] The 'quick look' test was considered appropriate when a monopolist creates economic inducements, related to its monopoly/market position, making its customers buy the monopolist's products exclusively.[897]

889. O'Donoghue and Padilla (n. 13) 225.
890. Whish, 'Intel v Commission: Keep Calm and Carry on!' (n. 42) 2.
891. Nazzini, *The Foundation of European Union Competition Law* (n. 392) 61.
892. Pate (n. 49).
893. Nazzini, *The Foundation of European Union Competition Law* (n. 392) 110; Alison Jones and Brenda Sufrin, *EU Competition Law: Text, Cases and Materials* (6th edn, OUP 2016) 369–370.
894. Text to (n. 798) in Chapter 5.
895. GC judgment, para. 139.
896. Maurice Stucke, 'Does the Rule of Reason Violate the Rule of Law?' (2009) 42 University of California Davis Law Review 1375; Herbert Hovenkamp, *The Rule of Reason* (2017) https://papers.ssrn.com/sol3/papers.cfm?abstract_id=2885916 accessed 15 January 2018.
897. Jonathan Lave, 'The Law And Economics of de facto Exclusive Dealing' (2005) 50(1) The Antitrust Bulletin 143.

This approach seems to resemble the abbreviated test developed by the EU Court for fidelity rebates that could be viewed as abusive by object, as outlined in Chapter 2. Under this legal standard, rebates are presumably unlawful if the dominant company is an unavoidable trading partner for the significant part of demand and rebates are retroactive, which might be seen as a 'quick look' approach, appropriate for practices with a high probability of being capable of harming competition. This is because the dominant company can use the non-contestable part of demand as leverage to capture the contestable share, while competitors cannot offset the rebates and compensate the customers for the loss of rebate due to the limited scope of the contestable share.[898] Thus, when rebates granted to contestable share lead to a reduction of the price for the non-contestable share, it is reasonable these practices be presumed unlawful.[899]

[B] The Profit Sacrifice Test

[1] Description

The profit sacrifice test assumes that a dominant company is engaged in a conduct that sacrifices short-run profits in order to eliminate rival firms and to exercise its market power in the long run by raising prices. This test has been recognised as a general test in predatory pricing by some commentators.[900] In fact, the test was first advocated in predatory pricing cases where the profit sacrifice was due to pricing below a dominant company's costs (appropriate measure of cost) in which case the dominant company cannot cover its costs and loses money.[901]

Areeda and Turner developed a test that asks whether the dominant company actually loses money by pricing below costs, not just whether it makes less profits. In the leading predatory pricing case *AKZO*, the GC adopted this test and reasoned that pricing below average variable cost (AVC) is presumably predatory (the first AKZO rule), and as such anticompetitive.[902] This rule was reiterated by the CJEU in its *France Telecom* judgment, where the Court clarified that when the prices are below average variable cost, the conduct should be considered as prima facie abusive because it is presumed to pursue no other economic objective but elimination of competition.[903]

898. *See* Chapter 2, section 2.03.
899. Petit, 'Intel, Leveraging Rebates and the Goals of Article 102 TFEU' (n. 705) 41.
900. O'Donoghue and Padilla (n. 13) 227–228; Jones and Sufrin (n. 893) 364. It seem that the European Commission also did not make deferens between profit sacrifice and losses as it states in para. 63 of the Guidance Paper that: [t]he Commission will generally intervene where there is evidence showing that a dominant undertaking engages in predatory conduct by deliberately incurring losses or foregoing profits in the short term (referred to hereafter as 'sacrifice').
901. Phillip Areeda and Donald Turner, 'Predatory Pricing and Related Practices under Section 2 of the Sherman Act' (1975) 88 Harvard Law Review 697; *see also* Ordover and Willig (n. 879); William Baumol 'Predation and the Logic of the Average Variable Cost Test' (1996) 39(1) Journal of Law and Economics 49.
902. *AKZO*, para. 70.
903. Case C-202/07 P *France Telecom v. Commission* [2009] ECR I- 2369, para. 109 (hereinafter *France Telecom*); *see also Tetra Pak II*, para. 41.

However, the Areeda-Turner test focuses on one single factor, i.e., price below variable cost. This was criticised by many as over inclusive, leading to the development of a standard that includes not only a price-cost test but also consideration of the market structure and evidence of intent.[904] A good example is the second AKZO rule which applies when the dominant company's pricing is above average variable cost but below average total cost.[905] In this scenario, the test further asks whether the sacrifice is reasonable, and condemns the conduct as abusive if prices are low because they are a 'part of a plan for eliminating a competitor'.[906] As already discussed in Chapter 5, this principle was confirmed by the CJEU in price-cost abuses such as margin squeeze practices (*TeliaSonera* and *Deutsche Telekom*) or low price practices (*Post Danmark I*). In the *Post Danmark I* judgment, the Court clarified that prices below average total costs, but above average variable costs 'must be regarded as abusive if they are part of a plan for eliminating a competitor'.[907] In the same vein, in cases of margin squeeze, the Court clarified that the prices in themselves can be abusive only if they have an exclusionary effect.[908]

Thus, it is not the sacrifice of profits in itself but the existence of a strategy aiming to exclude an as efficient competitor that is the basis for finding an infringement. This explains the focus on intent and why the burden of proof is higher than those under the original price-cost test. However, unlike in the US, the EU Courts considered that evidence of recoupment is not necessary because the existence of dominant position was considered sufficient to determine that recoupment of losses is possible.[909] In contrast, in the US, a predatory pricing standard requires not only evidence of predatory prices but also evidence that the practice would be profitable after the exit of competitors, i.e., that the predator would be able to recoup the losses.[910] This difference came from the fact that under EU competition law, the existence of a dominant position (which nonetheless means that the company is able to influence the prices and other parameters of competition) is a prerequisite to trigger the application of Article 102 and to condemn predatory pricing without evidence of recoupment.[911] In contrast under the US antitrust law, predatory pricing is considered as an attempt to monopolise,[912] which means that predation might be considered as an intent to

904. Bolton, Brodley, and Riordan (n. 817) 2252.
905. *AKZO*, para. 70.
906. *Ibid.*, para. 7; *see also Tetra Pak II*, para. 41; *Wanadoo Interactive* (Case COMP/38.233) Commission Decision [2003] para. 256.
907. *Post Danmark I*, para. 27.
908. *Deutsche Telekom*, para. 183; *TeliaSonera*, para. 98.
909. *France Télécom*, para. 102; *Tetra Pak II*, para. 44.
910. Ordover and Willig (n. 879) 17; Douglas Melamed, 'Exclusive Dealing Agreements and Other Exclusionary Conduct – Are There Unifying Principles' (2006) 73 Antitrust Law Journal 389, 390.
911. *United Brands*, para. 65.
912. Section 2 of the Sherman Act makes it unlawful for any person to 'monopolize, or attempt to monopolize, or combine or conspire with any other person or persons, to monopolize any part of the trade or commerce among the several States, or with foreign nations' 15 U.S.C. § 2 (2007).

monopolise but only if there were a probability of recoupment to be achieved, that would make to attempt to monopolise successful.[913]

The test was elaborated in accordance with the definition of exclusionary abuse provided by Ordover and Willig, i.e., 'a response to a rival that sacrifices part of the profit that could be earned under competitive circumstances, were the rival to remain viable, in order to induce exit and gain consequent additional monopoly profit'.[914] Thus, under the test, a practice is anticompetitive if a monopolist earns additional profits resulting from the exit of competitors.[915] The strongest example is the recoupment test for predation first articulated by the Court in *Brooke Group*.[916]

The profit sacrifice test in predatory pricing covers only a situation of 'extreme sacrifice', where the dominant company not only sacrifices profits but also it actually incurs losses.[917] In this sense, the below-cost test used in predation cases is an extreme variation of the profit sacrifice test (negative-profit standard).[918] However, the essence of the profit sacrifice is connected with lower profits and not necessarily losses. A dominant company may make enormous sacrifices without making losses.[919]

For that reason, the traditional predatory pricing below-cost test proposed by Areeda and Turner was further developed to cover cases that entail profit sacrifice but not necessarily losing money. In technical terms, the test compares the short-run profit of a dominant company before the exclusionary conduct with the outcome after the exclusionary practice. Thus, the test consists of two phases: comparing the costs and revenues before and after the exclusion.[920] If the dominant company's outcome during the exclusionary conduct is lower than it was before, the dominant company sacrifices profit. In advocating the test, Patterson claimed that the profit sacrifice test is consistent with the standards applied in non-price cases, and, hence provides a desirable approach for litigation beyond price cases.[921] Finally, the sacrifice test provides simple guidance for the firms on how to evaluate their behaviour and to avoid antirust liability. Thus, the test creates legal certainty.

[2] Analysis

While there is agreement that the test is useful in some cases, such as the ones indicated above, it is often also noted that it fails to consider the efficiencies that could

913. William Adkinson and others, 'Enforcement of Section 2 of the Sherman Act: Theory and Practice' (2008) US FTC Working paper https://www.ftc.gov/system/files/documents/pub lic_events/section-2-sherman-act-hearings-single-firm-conduct-related-competition/section2 overview.pdf accessed 20 February 2017.
914. Ordover and Willig (n. 879) 9–10.
915. *Ibid.*, 15.
916. *Brooke Group Ltd v. Broun and Williamson Tobacco Corp.* 509 US 209 (1993).
917. Aaron Edlin, 'Academic Testimony on Unilateral Conduct Before the US Dept. of Justice and Federal Trade Commission Hearings' (2007) 29.
918. Salop, 'Exclusionary Conduct, Effect on Consumers, and the Flawed Profit-Sacrifice Standard' (n. 43) 326. *See also* Elhauge, 'Defining Better Monopolization Standards' (n. 887) 272.
919. Salop, *supra* 326.
920. Nazzini, *The Foundation of European Union Competition Law* (n. 392) 70.
921. Mark Patterson, 'The Sacrifice of Profits in Non-price Predation' (2003) 18 Antitrust 37.

be generated by the exclusionary conduct, especially in markets where investments or research and developments costs are high.[922] In those markets, the company may sacrifice profits in the short term, so as to implement investments or innovations, and thereby increase its revenues in the future.[923] In this case, the profit sacrifice has a legitimate explanation. However, without taking account of an economic explanation, the conduct may be condemned as abusive under the profit sacrifice test.[924] If the conduct is prohibited on that ground, the investment and innovations could be discouraged. Thus, the main weakness of the profit sacrifice test is that it ignores dynamic efficiencies.[925] Consequently, the test is prone to false negatives.[926] In addition, it has been argued that the test is prone to under enforcement in particular in sectors characterised with high fixed cost.[927]

Some further argue that the test could be a standard to assess intent but is not capable of providing 'a sufficient condition for a finding of exclusionary behaviour by firms with market power',[928] because in some circumstances it is possible for the exclusion of a competitor to occur without profit sacrifice.[929] Moreover, the short-run sacrifice of profit is neither necessary nor sufficient for conduct to be exclusionary.[930] The dominant company could exclude its rivals without profit sacrifice in two cases. First, an exclusionary abuse could occur in cases such as fraud, deception, sham litigation, and bad-faith administrative filings.[931] In those cases, the dominant company does not sacrifice profit to exclude its competitors, which means that the sacrifice test is unable to identify anticompetitive conduct.[932] Those cases should be evaluated under the naked abuse test. Second, a profit sacrifice test seems unreasonable in exclusive dealing because a competitor can be excluded without profit sacrifice under certain circumstances.[933] The same applies for tying, where the conduct might exclude a competitor without sacrifice and subsequently there will be an immediate recoupment, necessary to make the practice profitable for the dominant company.[934] This

922. OECD Report (2005).
923. Herbert Hovenkamp, 'The Antitrust Standard for Unlawful Exclusionary Conduct' (2008) 9 https://papers.ssrn.com/sol3/papers.cfm?abstract_id = 1140346 accessed 11 January 2017.
924. Werden, 'Identifying Exclusionary Conduct Under Section 2' (n. 879) 424.
925. Elhauge, 'Defining Better Monopolization Standards' (n. 887) 274.
926. Salop, 'Exclusionary Conduct, Effect on Consumers, and the Flawed Profit-Sacrifice Standard' (n. 43) 346, 357–363.
927. Herbert Hovenkamp, 'The Harvard and Chicago Schools and the Dominant Firm' in Robert Pitofsky (ed.) *How The Chicago School Overshot The Mark: The Effect of Conservative Economic Analysis on U.S. Antitrust* (OUP 2008) 109, 132.
928. Vickers, 'Abuse of Market Power' (n. 4) 16.
929. Brief for the United States and the FTC as Amici Curiae Supporting Petitioner in Verizon Communications Inc. v. Law Offices of Curtis V Trinko, S. Ct. Docket 02-682.
930. Werden, 'Identifying Exclusionary Conduct Under Section 2' (n. 879) 424; Elhauge, 'Defining Better Monopolization Standards' (n. 887) 255–260; Vickers, 'Abuse of Market Power' (n. 4); Gavil (n. 298) 72; Salop, 'Exclusionary Conduct, Effect on Consumers, and the Flawed Profit-Sacrifice Standard' (n. 43); Edlin (n. 917) 30.
931. Elhauge, 'Defining Better Monopolization Standards' (n. 887) 282; Gregory Werden, 'The No Economic Sense Test for Exclusionary Abuse' (2006) Journal of Corporation Law 293, 301.
932. Hovenkamp, 'Exclusion and the Sherman Act' (n 820) 158.
933. Salop, 'Exclusionary Conduct, Effect on Consumers, and the Flawed Profit-Sacrifice Standard' (n. 43); Elhauge, 'Defining Better Monopolization Standards' (n. 887) 283–293.
934. Hovenkamp 'The Antitrust Standard for Unlawful Exclusionary Conduct' (n. 923) 10.

reflects the empirical evidence found in the economic literature, and discussed in Chapter 3, that a dominant company can exclude a rival without profit sacrifice if it can deprive its rivals' access to crucial sales, causing them to raise their price and hindering their ability to compete.[935] Furthermore, the test was considered unreliable in evaluating the effect of mixed bundling.[936] In those cases, the dominant company does not sacrifice profit to exclude its competitors, which means that the sacrifice test is irrelevant.[937] Similarly, Salop limits the application of the profit-sacrifice test to refusal to deal, incompatible design change and predatory pricing as a way of illustrating how a company may achieve, maintain or enhance its monopoly power.[938]

Another set of criticisms concerns the difficult practical implementation of the test. The first one is related to the difficulty of identifying whether a profit was sacrificed and of determining how much sacrifice is enough for a conduct to be exclusionary.[939] The second difficulty occurs in markets where the dominant company is already pricing above the competitive level. In this case, the profit sacrifice test will show no sacrifice and thus, an absence of exclusionary conduct.[940] Thus, in that particular case the test is clearly unable to identify anticompetitive conduct. Moreover, the focus of the test is on the dominant company's conduct and it fails to recognize that this conduct could have different effects on consumer welfare depending on the circumstances.[941] The third difficulty is associated with the need to compare the profits earned in the absence of an exclusionary effect with the profits earned following the exclusion.[942] A last difficulty concerns the collection of proper information and how to choose the correct price and quantity benchmark.[943]

In conclusion, it could be suggested that the sacrifice test, 'appropriately specified, appears useful in a number of contexts – especially predation – but not in providing a general foundation for distinguishing competition on the merits from conduct that is exclusionary'.[944] These criticisms of the profit sacrifice test have led to the development of a related, but broader test, that looks at the economic logic of the conduct – the so-called no economic test.

935. Chapter 3, section 3.03.
936. Daniel Crane, 'Mixed Bundling, Profit Sacrifice, and Consumer Welfare' (2006) 55 Emory Law Journal 423. For the evaluation of mixed bundling, a discount attribution test was developed; *see* text to (nn. 340–343) in Chapter 3.
937. Hovenkamp, 'Exclusion and the Sherman Act' (n. 820) 158.
938. Salop, 'Exclusionary Conduct, Effect on Consumers, and the Flawed Profit-Sacrifice Standard' (n. 43) 322.
939. Lang and O'Donoghue, 'The Concept of an Exclusionary Abuse under Article 82 EC' (n. 14) 44.
940. Robert O'Donoghue, 'Verbalizing a General Test for Exclusionary Conduct under art. 82 EC' in Claus-Dieter Ehlermann and Isabela Atanasiu (eds) *European Competition Law Annual 2003: What is Abuse of Dominant Position* (Bloomsbury Publishing 2006) 327, 336.
941. Gavil (n. 298) 52.
942. Nazzini, *The Foundation of European Union Competition Law* (n. 392) 70.
943. Salop, 'Exclusionary Conduct, Effect on Consumers, and the Flawed Profit-Sacrifice Standard' (n. 43) 358–371.
944. Vickers, 'Abuse of Market Power' (n. 4) 18. The US DoJ also believes that the test: 'raises serious concerns of enforcement error and administrability and should not be the test for Section 2 liability'. *See* DoJ Single-firm conduct under Section 2 of the Sherman Act Report, 2008 (withdrawn).

[C] The No Economic Sense Test

[1] Description

The 'no economic sense' test was developed to avoid basic flaws in the application of the profit sacrifice test stemming from the fact that a short-run sacrifice of profit is neither necessary nor sufficient for conduct to be exclusionary.[945] Under the no economic sense test 'the conduct is exclusionary only if it would not make business or economic sense apart from its tendency to reduce or eliminate competition'.[946] It means that the anticompetitive conduct depends not on whether the dominant company sacrifices profit, 'but rather on the nature of the conduct … and its likelihood of harming competition'.[947] Under the test, the conduct of a dominant company is exclusionary only if the company gains additional economic benefit because it eliminates competition and is able to exploit its market power to the detriment of consumers.[948]

[2] Analysis

It has been suggested that the test is very useful in cases of low-cost exclusion.[949] Short-run profit sacrifice may occur in many circumstances, for example in high technology markets in which investment in research and development is crucial for the competitiveness of the companies, or when a company needs to achieve optimal scale (e.g., network effects) or to gain the learning experience needed to reduce costs over time.[950] In all those cases, short-term profit sacrifice may be necessary in order for the company to be competitive and profitable in the future – it is normally not exclusionary conduct because it makes economic sense and the short-term profit sacrifice can be explained as not being an attempt to eliminate competition.[951] While the dominant company sacrifices profits, the no economic sense test further asks whether the sacrifice is reasonable. Thus, under the test, a monopolist will not be punished (in contrast to the sacrifice test) because the profit sacrifice seeks to create efficiencies (e.g., reduced costs or improved products) and make it more successful than its competitors.[952] These examples show that the no economic sense test is appropriate in cases of pricing conduct, in which, the profit sacrifice has a rational explanation.

The test is also applicable in cases where a dominant company is involved in exclusionary strategy which does not entail profit sacrifice, the so-called above-cost

945. Werden, 'The No Economic Sense Test for Exclusionary Conduct' (n. 931).
946. Brief for the United States and the FTC as amici curiae supporting petitioner in *Verizon v. Trinko* (n. 929) 7.
947. Melamed, 'Exclusive Dealing Agreements and Other Exclusionary Conduct – Are There Unifying Principles' (n. 910) 391.
948. Werden, 'Identifying Exclusionary Conduct Under Section 2' (n. 879) 426.
949. Werden, 'The No Economic Sense Test for Exclusionary Conduct' (n. 931) 305.
950. O'Donoghue and Padilla (n. 13) 344.
951. Werden, 'The No Economic Sense Test for Exclusionary Conduct' (n. 931) 300.
952. Melamed, 'Exclusive Dealing Agreements and Other Exclusionary Conduct – Are There Unifying Principles' (n. 910) 392–393.

price cuts abuses. Exclusionary above-cost abuses under Article 102 TFEU have been identified in several cases.[953] A possible explanation of the decisional practice of the European Commission and EU Courts in those cases is that pricing above cost 'is only unlawful when it is coupled with a range of other exclusionary measures, i.e., there is cumulative evidence of abuse as part of a plan to eliminate a rival'.[954] It seems that this explanation resembles the context of the no economic sense test.

The no economic sense test was considered appropriate for non-price abuses and has been endorsed in the US courts in refusal to deal cases such as *Trinko*[955] and *Aspen Skiing.*[956] In the *Trinko* case, the US Supreme Court stated that the conduct is anticompetitive if it would not make economic sense except as an effort to eliminate or soften the competition. Similarly, in the *Aspen* case, the Court held that a conduct is exclusionary if it excludes rivals on some basis other than efficiency. Some authors have suggested that the no economic sense test is not only 'particularly efficient for analysing non-price strategies such as predatory innovation' but it is the only test that can guarantee avoiding implementation errors and, as such, would encourage companies to innovate.[957]

Some have gone as far as to hold that the no economic sense test: 'can provide a sound unifying antitrust principle for analyzing all exclusionary conduct that has efficiency benefits'.[958] At the same time, the test has been subject to numerous criticisms. According to Werden, who is one of the most prominent defenders of the test, its implementation in practice may be difficult.[959] These difficulties are related as to how to distinguish between conduct that creates profits due to price discrimination and conduct that creates profits because of the elimination of competition, as for example in the context of fidelity rebates (because the dominant company discriminate between the loyal and disloyal customers).[960] Another difficulty might be related as to how to distinguish between conduct that create efficiencies and conduct that creates profits because of the elimination of competition, in the case in markets involving a network effect where the investments would only make economic sense if rivals are eliminated.[961] In those cases, the no economic sense test cannot distinguish pro-competitive from anticompetitive conduct. Another objection to the no economic sense test is that it does not capture all anticompetitive single-firm conduct.[962] For example, Jacobson claims that its application to exclusive dealing is not appropriate because it

953. *Hilti;* Joined Cases C-395/96 P and C-396/96 P *Compagnie Maritime Belge Transports SA and Others v. Commission* [2000] ECR I-1365.
954. O'Donoghue and Padilla (n. 13) 335.
955. *Verizon Communication Inc v. Law Offices of Curtis Trinko LLP*, 305 F.3d 89 (2d Cir. 2002).
956. *Aspen Skiing Co. v. Aspen Highlands Skiing Corp.*, 472 U.S. 585 (1985).
957. Thibault.Schrepel, *The 'Enhanced No Economic Sense Test': Experimenting with Predatory Innovation* (2018) https://papers.ssrn.com/sol3/Papers.cfm?abstract_id=3115949 accessed 16 July 2018.
958. Melamed, 'Exclusionary Conduct under the Antitrust Laws' (n. 879) 1267; *see also* Gregory Werden, 'Competition Policy on Exclusionary Conduct: Toward an Effects-Based Analysis?' (2006) 2 European Competition Journal 53.
959. Werden, 'Identifying Exclusionary Conduct Under Section 2' (n. 879) 414.
960. Werden, 'The No Economic Sense Test for Exclusionary Conduct' (n. 931) 421.
961. O'Donoghue and Padilla (n. 13) 230.
962. Pate (n. 49), Werden, 'The No Economic Sense Test' (n. 931) 303.

fails to separate the economic efficiency from exclusionary effect that the exclusive dealing might have.[963] According to him, an exclusive dealing might make economic sense but the question as to whether the effect of this agreement is likely to raise prices/reduce output or affect other parameters of competition that might harm consumers is not taken into account. From this perspective, the no economic sense test fails to balance the positive and the negative effects on competition, or otherwise it fails to consider the effect of the conduct on consumer welfare.[964] For these reasons some suggested that, the test 'appears to operate more as a screen than a comprehensive standard'.[965]

[D] The AEC Test

[1] Description

The origin of the AEC test can be traced to the Chicago School.[966] Chicago School theorists argued that competition could be harmed only if the exclusion of a competitor is not based on efficiency or competition on the merits, and if it creates or protects market power.[967] Put differently, the fundamental idea behind the AEC test is that competition can be harmed only if the observed conduct excludes from the market an equally or more efficient competitor. The rationale behind this idea is that the overall effect of competition between efficient companies will result in an increase of efficiency and consumer welfare. Thus, an exclusion of an equally or more efficient competitor will harm effective competition and would allow the dominant company to exercise its market power to the detriment of consumers. It also means that a conduct that excludes less efficient rivals is a consequence of effective competition, the so-called competition on the merits; in these circumstances, even if some competitors are excluded from the market, effective competition is not eliminated. If a dominant company had to set prices not at the level of their costs (marginal costs) but at the level of the less efficient competitor's cost, this would protect competitors who are less efficient and would artificially raise prices. For that reason, Posner claimed that 'it would be absurd to require the firm to hold a price umbrella over less efficient entrants'.[968] It was this effect that Robert Bork described as the paradox of antitrust enforcement.[969]

---

963. Jonathan Jacobson and Scott Sher, 'No Economic Sense' Makes no Sense for Exclusive Dealing' (2006) 73(3) Antitrust Law Journal 779.
964. Jonathan Jacobson, Scott Sher and Edward Holman, 'Predatory Innovation: An Analysis of Allied Orthopedic v. Tyco in the Context of Section 2 Jurisprudence' (2010) 23 Loy. Consumer Law Review 1, 30; Gavil (n. 298) 52; Salop 'Exclusionary Conduct, Effect on Consumers, and the Flawed Profit- Sacrifice Standard' (n. 43) 314.
965. Barry Hawk, 'Article 82 and Section 2: Abuse and Monopolizing Conduct' in *Issues in Competition Law And Policy* (Vol. 2, Ch. 36, ABA Section of Antitrust Law 2008) 871, 882.
966. *See* in general Richard Posner, 'The Chicago School of Antitrust Analysis' (1979) 127(4) University of Pennsylvania Law Review 925.
967. Jacobson, 'Exclusive Dealing, Foreclosure and Consumer Harm' (n. 324) 346.
968. Posner, *Antitrust Law* (n. 271) 196.
969. Bork, *The Antitrust Paradox* (n. 271).

Posner originally proposed the AEC test for the evaluation of predatory pricing.[970] According to him, a conduct should be prohibited as a predation if the dominant firm's pricing is below its short-run marginal cost or 'below long-run marginal cost with the intent to exclude a competitor'.[971] Later on, he refined this approach into a two-step test for evaluating exclusionary abuse under the US antitrust law:[972]

> [T]he plaintiff must first prove that the defendant has monopoly power and second that the challenged practice is likely in the circumstances to exclude from the defendant's market an equally or more efficient competitor .... [P]ractices that will only exclude less efficient firms, such as monopolist's dropping his price nearer to (but not below) its costs, are not actionable, because we want to encourage efficiency. Only when monopoly is used to discourage equally or more efficient firm and thus perpetuate a monopoly not supported by superior efficiency should the law step in. Even then, it should be alert to the possibility that the exclusionary effect of the monopolist's practice is offset by efficiency gains.[973]

[2] Analysis

Posner's proposal could be seen as 'the basis of the rule of reason approach, for which a business practice is not "per se" illegal, but can be justified if it does not harm consumers or if it creates efficiency'.[974] In a similar vein, when elaborating the standard for the evaluation of predatory pricing, Areeda and Turner focused on pricing below average variable cost, because this 'has the effect of destroying an equally efficient rival'.[975] The general presumption behind the test is that pricing above average variable cost should be presumed lawful because 'the low price at or above average cost is competition on the merits and excludes only less efficient rivals'.[976] As indicated in section 7.02[B] above, Areeda and Turner considered the evidence of profit sacrifice as a sufficient condition for liability. This conclusion assumes that firms that are equally or more efficient than the dominant firm can compete on the merits on the basis of pricing above average variable cost and that there is no reason why antitrust law should offer them a safe haven against price competition in that circumstance. This perspective of the AEC test resembles the substance of the profit sacrifice test, developed for price-based abuses, as discussed above.

The general idea of the AEC test is that competition law should only protect competitors who are at least no less efficient than the dominant company and that will guarantee an effective competitive process to the benefit of the final consumers. Consequently, the test is consistent with the main objective of the EU competition law – maximising consumer welfare. This may explain why, as outlined in Chapter 4, the AEC test was adopted by the European Commission in its Guidance Paper, where it was

970. Posner, 'Exclusionary Practices and the Antitrust Laws' (n. 273) 506.
971. *Ibid.*, 519.
972. Posner, *Antitrust law* (n. 271).
973. *Ibid.*, 194–196.
974. Etro and Kokkoris (n. 654).
975. Areeda and Turner (n. 940) 710.
976. *Ibid.*, 707.

considered that a conduct should be considered anticompetitive only if it has hampered or is capable of hampering competition from competitors which are considered to be as efficient as the dominant undertaking.[977] The Commission considered that price-based exclusion should be evaluated through comparing actual costs and prices of a dominant company in order to assess whether the dominant company is sacrificing profits by its conduct. Thus, the presumption is that if a dominant company's pricing is below an appropriate measure of cost, an as efficient competitor with the same cost structure would not be able to match its prices and, thus, to compete without incurring a loss. As already indicated in Chapter 4, the Commission considered the price-cost test (requiring profit sacrifice as a key element) as a specific instrument to verify whether an as efficient competitor will be foreclosed. Hence, the object of the test suggests that profit sacrifice is a key element in finding a violation of Article 102. From this perspective, the AEC test is a price-cost test, similar to the profit sacrifice test as discussed above. The EU Courts made clear that in price-cost abuses there is an obligation for a price-cost test to be carried out because 'it is impossible to assess whether a price is abusive without comparing it with other prices and costs'.[978] Thus, the anticompetitive effect cannot be presumed without conducting an economic analysis and the AEC test has been recognised as a *sine qua non* of the assessment of price-based abuses. In this sense, the AEC test has strong roots in the established EU case law as regard price-based exclusionary conduct. As far as the test prescribes as a benchmark the dominant company's own cost structure it suggests that the test could be used as an *ex ante* self-assessment by the dominant company. Thus, the test creates legal certainty and this is one of the reasons why the EU Courts adopted the test in *TeliaSonera*, *Deutsche Telekom* and *Post Danmark I*. In this sense, the AEC test in terms of price-cost test is the appropriate standard for the evaluation of price-based exclusionary conduct.

Despite its advantages, and the recognition of the AEC test as a necessary part of the assessment of price-based abuses, this approach has been the subject of sustained criticism – particularly as regards its practical implementation and usefulness in evaluating different forms of abusive behaviour. Below, the main lines of critique of the AEC test are reviewed in terms of its recognition as a price-cost test.

[3] Criticism of the AEC Test

[a] Implementation of the AEC Test in Naked Abuse Cases

The first problem with the AEC test is its under-inclusiveness.[979] For example, if the AEC test was the sole abuse test it would allow naked exclusionary practices. In a case of naked abuse, for example when a dominant company provides misleading information to the patent office, the practice will not be prohibited unless it excludes an as

977. The Guidance Paper, para. 23.
978. GC judgment, para. 152.
979. Nazzini, *The Foundation of European Union Competition Law* (n. 392) 74–76.

efficient competitor.[980] An illustrative example of this point is the *AstraZeneca* case.[981] In this case, the Commission found that providing misleading representation to the patent office could delay new entry and as such, constitute an exclusionary abuse. Thus, the exclusionary conduct would arise regardless of whether the entrant is efficient or not. As explained above, in those cases the AEC test is not applicable.

[b] Implementation of the AEC Test in Non-price Abuses

Similarly to the profit sacrifice test, the AEC test requires a profit sacrifice to be found in order for a dominant company's practice to have an anticompetitive exclusionary effect. Some forms of conduct might have an anticompetitive effect without the dominant company's pricing having to be set below costs, as discussed in the section criticising the profit sacrifice test above. As outlined in Chapter 3, in the case of exclusive agreements, the potential for anticompetitive exclusion is very strong and can arise even if the dominant company's price is above the appropriate measure of cost. In that case, the dominant company has to offer exclusive agreements only to a minimum number of buyers so as to deter the entrant from reaching MES and to cover its fixed costs, in which case a competitor can be excluded/marginalised from the market. In those cases, the conduct would not be condemned as abusive under the AEC test because the rival's costs are higher than the dominant company's which benefits from economies of scale.

As mentioned above, the effect of fidelity rebates could be anticompetitive even if the discount is above cost.[982] The same can be observed in unconditional price cuts cases where prices that remain above the dominant company's costs can be abusive under certain circumstances.[983] Thus, even if the price is not below cost, the practice could still have an exclusionary effect. In those cases, under the AEC test, the practice should not be prohibited because the prices of the dominant company are above cost. In this case, the AEC test cannot capture the anticompetitive effect of rebates.

[c] Over-Inclusiveness of the AEC Test and Lack of Contextual Awareness

A second type of problem with the AEC test is its potential for over-inclusiveness.[984] In some cases, the exclusion of an equally efficient competitor may not reduce but may instead increase consumer welfare. For example, the elimination of an as efficient

980. Hovenkamp, 'The Harvard and Chicago Schools and the Dominant Firm' (n. 927) 117.
981. *AstraZeneca* (Case COMP/A.37.507/F3) Commission Decision [2005] 1757 [2006] OJ L 332/24, upheld in case T-321/05 *AstraZeneca AB v. Commission* [2010] ECR II-2805, upheld in case C-457/10 P *AstraZeneca AB v. Commission* [2012] ECR I-770.
982. Elhauge, 'How Loyalty Discounts Can Perversely Discourage Discounting' (n. 277); Elhauge and Wickelgren, 'Anticompetitive Market Division Through Loyalty Discount Without Buyer Commitment' (n. 277); Elhauge and Wickelgren, 'Robust Exclusion and Market Division Through Loyalty Discounts with Buyer Commitment' (n. 277); George Bulkley, 'The Role of Loyalty Discounts when Consumers are Uncertain of the Value of Repeat Purchases' (1992) 10 International Journal of Industrial Economics, 91.
983. Lang and O'Donoghue, 'Defining legitimate competition' (n. 4) 46.
984. Nazzini, *The Foundation of European Union Competition Law* (n. 392) 76–77.

competitor could result in elimination of double marginalisation. In the case of fidelity rebates, the client (downstream firm) has to reach the target threshold, which is the condition of obtaining the rebates from the upstream supplier. The downstream firm would have the incentive to sell more products to final consumers by lowering the prices through cutting the second mark-up. As a consequence of the fidelity rebates scheme, the double marginalisation problem will be solved in favour of final consumers, even though an as efficient competitor was excluded as a result of a fidelity rebate scheme.

Another set of criticisms is related to the implementation of the test in markets characterised by sector-specific issues, such as network effect, economies of scale and scope, first-mover advantages or high technologies and in markets where competition is based on differentiation of the products.[985] In some industries with high fixed costs in the form of investment in research and development and very low variable costs, a price-cost test fails to provide valuable evidence of anticompetitive conduct and might lead to over enforcement.[986] Similarly, in markets characterised by economies of scale and scope, the dominant company's average cost decreases with increase of output (economies of scale) or because two or more products are produced jointly (economies of scope).[987] Some commentators suggest that in those markets, the dominant company will always have a different cost structure than their rivals because of its economies of scale and scope.[988] In these cases, when a new competitor enters the market, at the beginning their costs will be higher than the dominant company's because the rival has not yet reached its MES.[989] At this stage, the new entrant will be less efficient than the incumbent. However, this situation could change if the entrant were able to establish itself in the market and reach economies of scale and scope comparable to those of the dominant company.[990]

In such circumstances, the dominant company's prices could be set at levels above cost but a competitor would still not be able to match this price because of the economies of scope and scale, which does not necessarily mean that less efficient entrant cannot exercise competitive constraint.[991] On the contrary, even the entry of a less efficient rival can stimulate competition and can decrease prices if an incumbent was charging at monopoly prices before the entry.[992] The dominant company's reaction to the new entry could be to reduce its price in order to deter the entry, which

985. O'Donoghue and Padilla (n. 13) 232.
986. Gates (n. 326).
987. Massimo Motta, *Competition Policy: Theory and Practice* (Cambridge University Press 2004).
988. Brian Sher, 'Leveraging Non-contestability: Exclusive Dealing and Rebates under the Commission's Article 82 Guidance' (2009) 2(1) Antitrust Chronicle 1, 9.
989. O'Donoghue, 'Verbalizing a General Test for Exclusionary Conduct under Art. 82 EC' (n. 940) 339.
990. Renda and Lang (n. 14) 31.
991. Economides, 'Tying, Bundling and Loyalty/Requirement Rebates (n. 276) 33; Patrick Rey, 'Abuses of Dominant Position and Monopolization: An Economic Perspective' in Abel Moreira Mateus and Teresa Coelho Moreira (eds) *Competition Law and Economics: Advances in Competition Policy Enforcement in the EU and North America* (Edward Elgar 2010) 189, 191.
992. Gavil (n. 298) 59; Ioannis Lianos, *The Price/Non Price Exclusionary Abuses Dichotomy: A Critical Appraisal* (2009) https://papers.ssrn.com/sol3/papers.cfm?abstract_id=1398943 accessed 22 December 2017.

means that consumers will benefit from the low prices. In this sense, the entrance of a less efficient competitor can enhance consumer welfare.[993] Hence, the entry of a less efficient competitor may impose a competitive constraint on the dominant company and improve consumer welfare.[994] The same observations may apply to markets where the dominant company has first-mover advantages, benefits from a statutory monopoly, or are state-owned or privileged enterprises.[995] In those markets, the only competition that dominant firms are likely to face is the competition from less efficient rivals.[996] As indicated in Chapter 4, the European Commission in its Guidance Paper described some circumstances in which a less efficient rival can stimulate competition, and explained that this should be taken into account.[997] The CJEU shared a similar approach in *Post Danmark II*.[998]

The AEC test has also been criticised for having a limited practical use in cases of competition with differentiated products, which was indicated in Chapter 3.[999] If a less efficient rival offers differentiated competing products, it will impose competitive constraint on the dominant company's pricing because some of the consumers would prefer the entrant's product. In this case, a less efficient competitor 'can constrain a dominant firm's pricing and thereby increase consumer surplus, because it offers differentiated products'.[1000] In those cases, the AEC test will be focused on competitors rather than competition, which could generate many false negatives and some anticompetitive conducts could not be recognized.[1001]

[4] The European Commission's Modified AEC Test

As can be recalled from Chapter 4, the European Commission indicated in its Guidance Paper that the AEC test applicable to conditional rebates is not the same as that applied in predatory pricing but it is 'a modified' AEC test. The modified test required the identification of the effective price calculated over the relevant range of sales for the relevant period of time, which for retroactive rebates depends on the contestable share of demand (how much of a customer's purchase requirements can realistically be switched to a competitor). Thus, defining the contestable portion of demand is outcome determinative.[1002]

993. Salop, 'Avoiding Error in the Antitrust Analysis of Unilateral Refusals to Deal (n. 556); Salop, 'Exclusionary Conduct, Effect on Consumers, and the Flawed Profit – Sacrifice Standard' (n. 43) 328–329.
994. Lang and O'Donoghue, 'Defining Legitimate Competition' (n. 4); Hovenkamp 'The Antitrust Standard for Unlawful Exclusionary Conduct' (n. 923) 14; Petit, 'The Judgment of the EU Court of Justice in Intel and the Rule of Reason in Abuse of Dominance Cases' (n. 792).
995. Lang, CEPS Special Report (n. 6) 28.
996. Lao (n. 742) 446.
997. The Guidance Paper, para. 24.
998. *Post Danmark II* Judgment, paras 59–60.
999. *See* Chapter 3, section 3.03[C].
1000. Economides, 'Loyalty/Requirement Rebates and the Antitrust Modernization Commission' (n. 297) 259; *see also* Bishop (n. 4).
1001. Salop, 'Exclusionary Conduct, Effect on Consumers, and the Flawed Profit-Sacrifice Standard' (n. 43).
1002. Moore and Wright (n. 280) 1242.

This has been reviewed in Chapter 3, but it is worthwhile to summarise the conclusions again.[1003] First, contestable share is different for each of the customers and it is likely to vary depending on the industry and product characteristics, which makes its determination difficult to implement in practice.[1004] Second, the dominant company will not be able to obtain information about this contestable share in order to estimate the effective price in advance and to decide whether their conduct is likely to be illegal.[1005] This could be very difficult if not an impossible task, which creates legal uncertainty.[1006]

In addition, except for the difficulties in the practical implementation of the modified test, there is little theoretical basis to conclude that it can be used as a tool to capture anticompetitive fidelity rebates in cases when the product is differentiated, when rebates are not real price reduction and when rebates limit a competitor's ability to reach MES, resulting in raising their cost, as indicated in Chapter 3. Moreover, in some cases competition from a less efficient competitor may increase consumer welfare, which suggests that focusing on competitor's efficiency might lead to enforcement errors. In all of the cases, the application of the test is also subject to implementation errors. This additional qualification makes the approach more uncertain and unpredictable. As a result of the uncertainty of the approach and difficulties for the dominant company to make those calculations, their willingness to provide rebates will be discouraged. These arguments invite the conclusion that the modified AEC test creates legal uncertainty and its practical implementation as regard fidelity rebates is questionable. Moreover, it is 'unlikely to shed much light on the ultimate question of competitive effect.'[1007] Another shortcoming of the modified AEC test is the uncertainty around an investigation of 'other factors' where the effective price is between AAC and LRAIC. This additional qualification makes the approach even more uncertain and unpredictable. As a result of the uncertainty of the approach and difficulties for the dominant company to make those calculations, their willingness to provide rebates will be discouraged.

From this perspective, it seems the modified price-cost test although economically rational, does not 'meet the requirements of "administrability" and "certainty" that should always apply to the tests used by competition authorities and courts for

1003. *See* Chapter 3, section 3.03[D].

1004. In its submission to the OECD 2008 Report, the OFT recognised that the estimation of the contestable part of demand is the most difficult aspect of the test. *See also* OECD Report (2016) para. 64.

1005. Renda and Lang (n. 14) 12. Similar comments was made by Ariel Ezrachi, *The European Commission Guidance on Article 82 EC – The Way in Which Institutional Realities Limit the Potential for Reform* (2009) http://papers.ssrn.com/sol3/papers.cfm?abstract_id = 1463854 accessed 9 October 2015, 13; Faella (n. 4); Geradin and others, 'The Concept of Dominance in EC Competition Law' (n. 503).

1006. Petit, 'The Judgment of the EU Court of Justice in Intel and The Rule of Reason in Abuse of Dominance Cases' (n. 792); Geradin, 'A Proposed Test for Separating Procompetitive Conditional Rebates from Anticompetitive Ones' (n. 4) 41; Damian Geradin, *Is the Guidance Paper on the Commission's Enforcement Priorities in Applying Article 102 TFEU to Abusive Exclusionary Conduct Useful?* (2010) https://papers.ssrn.com/sol3/papers.cfm?abstract_id = 1569502 accessed 14 December 2017; Crayencour and Lang (n. 14) 52.

1007. OECD Report (2016).

assessing the legality of dominant firms' practices'.[1008] The lack of legal certainty might lead to discouraging a dominant company's incentive to innovate and to provide better services due to inability to self-assess in advance whether their practices would be illegal.[1009]

[E] The Consumer Welfare Test

[1] Description

Consumer welfare became the goal of antitrust law in the US following the development of a new line of thinking advocated by the Chicago School of thought. According to Bork, who is one of the most prominent protagonists of this Chicago School, the only goal of antitrust law is the protection of competition by promoting productive efficiencies to the benefit of consumers, rather than protecting inefficient competitors.[1010] To achieve this goal, it is not appropriate for practices that could create efficiency to be banned without proper evaluation of their effect.[1011] Thus, many practices that had been considered anticompetitive could in reality be efficient and pro-competitive.[1012] For the Chicago School economists, the protection of economic efficiency, which would lead to maximization of consumer welfare, is the main goal of antitrust law.[1013]

From the above, it could be suggested that a consumer welfare standard requires a rule of reason analysis to be applied to all practices in order to distinguish harm to competition from conduct that could plausibly be justified by efficiency considerations (static and dynamic). However, over the years, the meaning of consumer welfare has remained a controversial topic, particularly regarding whether it requires the maximisation of consumer or total surplus (welfare).[1014] It seems that there is an agreement

1008. Geradin, 'A Proposed Test for Separating Pro-Competitive Loyalty Rebates from Anticompetitive Ones' (n. 4) 25.
1009. Text to (n. 6) in Chapter 1.
1010. Bork (n. 271). Bork's interpretation of consumer welfare was challenged by many, arguing that he aligned consumer welfare with economic efficiency. *See* in general Barak Orbach, 'The Antitrust Consumer Welfare Paradox' (2010) 7(1) Journal of Competition Law and Economics 133; ICN, Competition Enforcement and Consumer Welfare – Setting the Agenda 14 (2011) http://www.internationalcompetitionnetwork.org/uploads/library/doc857.pdf accessed 17 December 2017.
1011. Bork (n. 271) 406.
1012. Joshua Wright, 'Overshot the Mark? A Simple Explanation of the Chicago School's Influence on Antitrust' (2009) 09(23) Competition Policy International, George Mason University Law and Economics Research Paper Series 6.
1013. Posner, *Economic Analysis of Law* (n. 51) 5–7.
1014. John Kirkwood and Robert Lande, 'The Fundamental Goal of Antitrust: Protecting Consumers, Not Increasing Efficiency' (2008) 84 Notre Dame Law Review 191; Russell Pittman, *Consumer Surplus as the Appropriate Standard for Antitrust Enforcement* (2007) https://papers.ssrn.com/sol3/papers.cfm?abstract_id=996643 accessed 17 December 2016; Dennis Carlton, 'Does Antitrust Need to be Modernized?' (2007) 21(3) The Journal of Economic Perspectives 155. Similar debates can be found in the European scholarship, *see* e.g., Pinar Akman, 'Searching for the Long-Lost Soul of Article 82EC' (2009) 29(2) Oxford Journal of Legal Studies, 267; Akman, 'Consumer Welfare' and Article 82 EC (n. 393) 71; Pinar Akman, '"Consumer versus Customer": The Devil in the Detail' (2010) 37(2) Journal of Law and Society 315; Gormsen, 'The Conflict Between Economic Freedom and Consumer Welfare in

that the standard should be maximisation of total surplus (i.e., consumers and producers welfare),[1015] seen as long-term social welfare being the ultimate objective of competition law.[1016] Achieving this objective requires a standard that evaluates circumstances in which consumers might be harmed due to reduced total welfare.[1017]

In any event, a consumer welfare test is focused directly on the effects of exclusionary conduct, and in particular on whether the practice might reduce consumer welfare.[1018] Under the consumer welfare test: 'exclusionary conduct violates the antitrust laws if it reduces competition without creating a sufficient improvement in performance to fully offset these potential adverse effects on prices and thereby prevent consumer harm'.[1019] According to Salop, the consumer welfare test focuses on the assessment of a dominant company's conduct 'to predict the likely overall impact on consumers'.[1020] Similarly, Hovenkamp argues that unlawful exclusionary conduct, is 'one that reduces welfare, which should be the same as making the market less competitive'.[1021]

An interesting question that these definitions raise is whether this test requires the measurement of consumer harm, or whether what really matters is that a negative effect on effective competition be identified from where consumer harm can be presumed.[1022] The presumption underpinning this second option is that, once effective competition is harmed, the dominant company will be in a position to exercise its market power, which is the power to increase prices/reduce output, diminish quality, or significantly restrict consumer choice.[1023] Thus, the source of consumer harm is the creation, enhancement, or protection of market power.[1024] In the same vein, Areeda and Hovenkamp offer a frequently cited definition of 'exclusionary conduct' connected with consumer welfare, which an exclusionary conduct is an actions that:

---

the Modernisation of Article 82 EC' (n. 391) 329; Christian Ahlborn and Carsten Grave, 'Walter Eucken and Ordoliberalism: An Introduction from a Consumer Welfare Perspective' (2006) 2(2) Competition Policy International 197.

1015. Orbach (n. 1010); *see also* Jorge Padilla, Panel I – the Objectives of Competition Policy in Claus-Dieter Ehlermann and Mel Marquis (eds) *European Competition Law Annual 2007: A Reformed Approach to Article 82 EC* (Hart Publishing 2008) 7, stating that the 'Brussels consensus' is that the goal of Art. 102 TFEU should be aggregate consumer welfare.

1016. Nazzini, *The Foundation of European Union Competition Law* (n. 392) Ch. 2; Motta (n. 985) 17–22.

1017. Orbach (n. 1010) 18.

1018. Salop, 'Exclusionary Conduct, Effect on Consumers, and the Flawed Profit-Sacrifice Standard' (n. 43) 313.

1019. *Ibid.*, 330; *see also* Lao (n. 742).

1020. Salop, 'Exclusionary Conduct, Effect on Consumers, and the Flawed Profit-Sacrifice Standard' (n. 43) 331.

1021. Hovenkamp 'The Antitrust Standard for Unlawful Exclusionary Conduct' (n. 923) 4.

1022. The debate on whether there is requirement harm to consumers to be shown is still alive in the US. Contrast Salop, 'Exclusionary Conduct, Effect on Consumers, and the Flawed Profit-Sacrifice Standard' (n. 43) with Howard Chang, David Evans and Richard Schmalensee, 'Has the Consumer Harm Standard Lost Its Teeth?' AEI-Brookings Joint Center Working Paper (2002) https://papers.ssrn.com/sol3/papers.cfm?abstract_id=332021 accessed 13 January 2017.

1023. Jacobson, 'Exclusive Dealing, Foreclosure and Consumer Harm' (n. 324) 348.

1024. *Ibid.*

> [a]re reasonably capable of creating, enlarging, or prolonging monopoly power by impairing the opportunities of rivals; and that either do not benefit consumers at all, or are unnecessary for the particular consumer benefits claimed for them, or produce harms disproportionate to any resulting benefits.[1025]

According to this approach, a conduct is anticompetitive if it harms competition in a way which allows the dominant company to increase prices/decrease output or to influence other parameters of competition, such as innovation, quality and consumer choice to the detriment of consumers. This interpretation of the consumer welfare test seems to resemble the European Commission's understanding of the effects-based approach, outlined in Chapter 4. Under this approach, a conduct would be unlawful only if its 'probable effect' is likely to substantially lessen competition in the relevant market, which requires an evaluation of a possible anticompetitive effect considered in the light of any pro-competitive effect.

The consumer welfare test – like the effects-based approach – should be based on an analysis which 'involve a variety of evidence relevant to evaluating competitive effect, including both structural and behavioural evidence'.[1026] These tools may include price-cost tests. A conduct leading to consumer harm may include different tests, including profit-sacrifice evidence which might be relevant in some cases, but not in all because 'proof of profit sacrifice would be neither necessary nor sufficient for a liability finding'.[1027] However, in some cases, the profit-sacrifice test might be enough to condemn the conduct of a dominant company for its likely negative effect on consumer welfare. In these cases – such as predatory pricing – the 'profit-sacrifice and consumer welfare effect standards will reach the same outcome'.[1028] A good tool for evaluating other types of exclusionary abuses relies on the RRC theory outlined in Chapter 3.[1029] The RRC theory shifted the focus from an exclusion of rivals to their marginalisation. As a result of practices that raise rivals costs, competitors might be not excluded from the market but become less efficient, exert less competitive pressure on the incumbent and may exit the market in the long term. In this sense, conduct that infringes the consumer welfare standard can on some occasions be evaluated effectively through the RRC theory, which evaluates 'whether the conduct harms competitors by raising their costs and whether those higher costs harm consumers and competition by allowing the defendant to achieve, maintain, or enhance monopoly power'.[1030]

In short, the assessment of a conduct that may have a material adverse effect on consumers can involve different tests depending on the case. In the light of this, it seems appropriate for the focus of the assessment to be on establishing likely harm to

1025. Areeda and Hovenkamp, *Antitrust Law* (n. 339) 651.
1026. Salop, 'Exclusionary Conduct, Effect on Consumers, and the Flawed Profit-Sacrifice Standard (n. 43) 330.
1027. *Ibid.*
1028. *Ibid.*, 334.
1029. For a general analysis, *see* Salop and Scheffman, 'Raising Rivals' Costs' (n. 855) 268–270 and Krattenmaker and Salop (n. 307); *see also* Herbert Hovenkamp, 'Post-Chicago Antitrust: A Review and Critique' (2001) Columbia Business Law Review 257, 318–323.
1030. Salop, 'Exclusionary Conduct, Effect on Consumers, and the Flawed Profit-Sacrifice Standard' (n. 43) 318.

the competitive process, which may ultimately harm consumers.[1031] Moreover, it is reasonable not to require harm to consumers to be realised; it suffices that there is a sufficient risk of it occurring.[1032] Ideally, a regulatory intervention should occur at the stage at which there is a threat to effective competition in order to avoid consumer harm from occurring. If the intervention is at the next stage when competitors are excluded from the market and the dominant company is in position to raise prices/reduce output, it will be too late.[1033] From this perspective, it has been suggested that an 'effects-based analysis after the event is of little use to competition if, in the meantime, a competitor has been irreversibly pushed out of the market'.[1034] Thus, the intervention should take place before the actual effect of the conduct on competition has become visible and consumer harm has occurred.[1035] Thus, 'it is imperative for the enforcement action to take place at the time when the dominant firm is excluding rivals'.[1036] At this stage, a measurement of consumer harm in terms of output and prices is not possible because the anticompetitive effect has not occurred yet.[1037] Additionally, at this stage any efficiency consideration cannot be taken into account as far as they would also occur *ex post*.[1038]

In short, it is submitted that even under the consumer welfare standard evidence of direct consumer harm is not a necessary component for anticompetitive abuses, because consumer harm may be likely enough to follow if the competitive process is harmed.[1039] For that reason, the prohibition of practices that distort the competitive process without proof of actual consumer harm is reasonable under the consumer welfare standard.[1040] In this sense, the consumer welfare standard provides a framework to predict whether the anticompetitive outcome that might harm consumers is

1031. Steven Salop, 'Question: What is the Real and Proper Antitrust Welfare Standard-Answer: The True Consumer Welfare Standard' (2010) 22(3) Loy. Consumer Law Review 336, 343.
1032. Phillip Areeda and Herbert Hovenkamp, *Fundamentals of Antitrust Law* (Aspen Publishers Online 2011) 6–36. They explain that the threat of consumer harm is enough in the same way as 'to condemn a drunken driver who has not caused harm to anyone. The point is that drunken driving is highly likely to cause social harm and it is less socially costly to arrest such before rather than after harm occurs.'
1033. Monti, *EC Competition Law* (n. 443) 175.
1034. John Ratliff, 'Abuse of Dominant Position and Pricing Practices: A Practitioner's Viewpoint' in Claus-Dieter Ehlermann and Isabela Atanasiu (eds) *What is an Abuse of a Dominant Position? European Competition Law Annual 2003* (Hart Publishing 2006) 427, 438.
1035. Hovenkamp, 'The Antitrust Standard for Unlawful Exclusionary Conduct' (n. 923) 6.
1036. Monti, *EC Competition Law* (n. 443) 175.
1037. Odudu (n. 461) Ch. 5, 125; *see also* Maurice Stucke, 'Reconsidering Antitrust's Goals' (2012) 53 Boston College Law Review 551, 574.
1038. Brodley, 'The Economic Goals of Antitrust: Efficiency, Consumer Welfare and Technological Progress' (n. 453) 1030–1031. He defined economic efficiency as productive, allocative and innovative efficiency and concludes that: 'considered ex post, production efficiencies are the most measurable of the three types of efficiencies, while innovation and allocative efficiencies present severe measurement problems. Considered ex ante, none of the efficiencies appears measurable.'
1039. Dunkan Sinclair, 'Abuse of Dominance at a Crossroads: Potential Effect, Object and Appreciability under Article 82 EC' (2004) 25 European Competition Law Review 491, 494.
1040. Eleanor Fox, 'Abuse of Dominance and Monopolization: How to Protect Competition Without Protecting Competitors' in Claus-Dieter Ehlermann and Isabela Atanasiu (eds) *European Competition Law Annual 2003: What is Abuse of Dominant Position* (Bloomsbury Publishing 2006) 69; Sinclair (n. 1039) 494.

more likely to occur. Predicting likely consumer harm 'minimises the social cost of any harmful practice when the practice is apprehended before it occurs or in an early stage'.[1041] For that reason it has been argued that harm to the effective competition and harm to consumers 'in fact amount to the same thing: there is no harm to the "structure of competition" that, ultimately, does not also lead to direct consumer harm'.[1042] Therefore, consumer interest can be protected only by preserving the competitive process over the long run. As Akman put it: 'if the standard of harm is "consumer welfare" then harm to competition resulting in harm to consumers should be the test of abuse'.[1043]

[2] Analysis

The consumer welfare test differs from the other tests, discussed above in that it asks directly whether the conduct is likely to harm consumer welfare, whereas the sacrifice test, non-economic sense test and the AEC test ask the same question but in a less direct manner.[1044] None of the tests seek to assess directly consumer harm, it relies on presumptions.[1045] This insight could suggest that the consumer welfare test is a comprehensive test covering all kinds of exclusionary conduct.[1046]

However, the consumer welfare test has been subject to criticisms because of the difficult practical implementation, which can lead to both over- and under-inclusiveness.[1047] One criticism concerns the difficulty in measuring the effects of business practices. For example, it is extremely difficult to measure the effects of conduct that increases market power but at the same time creates efficiencies which could be condemned as abusive unless the dominant company proves that the efficiencies are being passed to consumers or that the benefits for consumers outweigh the price increase.[1048]

The difficulty in practical implementation of the test balancing pro- and anticompetitive effects is noted by Geradin, who claimed that 'balancing ex ante v. ex post efficiencies is obviously a very difficult process, which even the most sophisticated economists may find daunting. The risk of mistaken decisions is therefore high'.[1049] This problem is even more pressing in innovative markets where technology evolves rapidly and the entrance of a new competitor could change the expected market

1041. Areeda and Hovenkamp, *Fundamentals of Antitrust Law* (n. 1032) 37.
1042. Lang and O'Donoghue, 'Defining Legitimate Competition' (n. 4) 47.
1043. Akman, '"Consumer Welfare" and Article 82 EC' (n. 393).
1044. Monti, *EC Competition Law* (n. 443) 214.
1045. Gavil (n. 298).
1046. Lang, CEPS Special Report (n. 6) 27.
1047. Melamed, 'Exclusionary Conduct Under the Antitrust Laws' (n. 879) 1252–1255; Werden, 'Identifying Exclusionary Conduct under Section 2' (n. 879) 431–432; Nazzini, *The Foundation of European Union Competition Law* (n. 392) 94.
1048. Nazzini, *The Foundation of European Union Competition Law* (n. 392) 94.
1049. Damian Geradin, 'Limiting the Scope of Article 82 of the EC Treaty: What Can the EU Learn from the US Supreme Court's Judgment in Trinko in The Wake of Microsoft, IMS, and Deutsche Telekom' (2004) 41 Common Market Law Review 1519.

outcome.[1050] These measurement difficulties would put into question the application of the test by the courts because, as Easterbrook argues, the courts are of limited utility in examining difficult economic issues.[1051] Thus, the difficulties in the practical implementation of the test could create legal uncertainty.

On the other hand, the balance between anticompetitive and pro-competitive effects *ex ante* may be further complicated because of the uncertainty as to whether these effects would materialise *ex-post*.[1052] This is the simpler version of a wider problem with the consumer welfare approach: it is extremely difficult, even from a conceptual standpoint, to compare the short-term consumer welfare effects of a practice with the potential dynamic efficiency effects that that same practice may create for the benefits of consumers. This is particularly important because it has been recognised as the main factor for economic growth.[1053] As such, a test that focuses on short-term consumer welfare may lead to the dominant company choosing not to engage in conduct that would generate efficiency in the long run because of the risks of infringement of competition rules (false positive error). Such a test would limit innovation because it cannot accurately measure the long-run harmful effects of reduced innovation caused by antitrust intervention.[1054]

A related criticism is that a pure consumer welfare approach is not suitable for the assessment of conduct that does not harm consumers in the short run, as for example in predatory pricing cases.[1055] When a dominant company is engaged in predatory pricing it sets the prices below some measure of cost in an attempt to eliminate competition in the long run. The effect of predation in short-run terms does not harm consumers because the prices are lower than before. Under a (static) consumer welfare test conducted at the time of the predation the conduct would be lawful. For that reason Carlton noted that 'the most significant practical problem with a consumer surplus standard is that, as commonly applied, it tends to favour short-run price reductions over long-run efficiency gains'.[1056] In those cases, the test should be conducted by balancing the negative effect of exclusion of a rival against benefits for the consumers in the long run, which make the test 'beyond the ability of jury, but also beyond the competence of the competition authority and courts'.[1057] Similar arguments have been

1050. O'Donoghue, 'Verbalizing a General Test for Exclusionary Conduct under Art. 82 EC' (n. 940) 342.
1051. Easterbrook, 'The Limits of Antitrust' (n. 6) 28; *see also* Melamed, 'Exclusionary Conduct under the Antitrust Laws' (n. 879) 1247 and Pate (n. 49).
1052. O'Donoghue and Padilla (n. 13) 236; Nazzini, *The Foundation of European Union Competition Law* (n. 392) 95; OECD Report (2005).
1053. OECD Report, Innovation and Growth: Rationale for an Innovation Strategy (2007); OECD Report, Policy Roundtables: Dynamic Efficiencies in Merger Analysis 10 (2007) DAF/COMP(2007)41; Bishop and Walker (n. 246) 31–32. The authors argued that: 'If regulators treat the pursuit of consumer welfare in an entirely static framework, then this can lead to significantly sub-optimal outcomes. ... Such an attitude might be reasonable in a static framework such as that outlined above, but s not reasonable in a dynamic framework in which firms invest and innovate to the ultimate benefit of consumers.'
1054. Lao (n. 742) 450.
1055. Melamed, 'Exclusionary Conduct under the Antitrust Laws' (n. 879); Werden, 'Identifying Exclusionary Conduct Under Section 2' (n. 879) 428–432.
1056. Carlton, 'Does Antitrust Need to be Modernized?' (n. 1014) 155–157.
1057. Nazzini, *The Foundation of European Union Competition Law* (n. 395) 96.

outlined by Werden, who criticises the consumer welfare test arguing that demonstration of the effect of the conduct on consumer welfare in each particular case is not desirable and 'should not be used as a legal test because the focus should be on competitive process itself'.[1058] In other words, a conduct is anticompetitive if 'it is apt to produce effects associated with elimination of competition'.[1059] However, as outlined above, these criticisms reflect the (mis)understanding that the consumer welfare test requires (a static) demonstration of negative effect on consumers, instead of considering total welfare in the long run.

In this sense, the only reasonable criticism of the test is related to the flexibility of the tools that can be used in the analysis.[1060] As outlined in section 7.02[E][2] above, under the consumer welfare test, the demonstration of a possible anticompetitive effect can be established by using different tools depending on the circumstances in each particular case. For that reason, some suggested that the existence of many different tests would result in a lack of clear guidelines, which creates legal uncertainty.[1061]

§7.03 DISCUSSION: WHICH OF THE TESTS COULD BE APPLICABLE IN FIDELITY REBATES? – STRENGTHS AND WEAKNESSES OF EACH TEST

Several different tests that purport to be able to distinguish between anticompetitive conduct and competition on the merits have been analysed in the second part of the chapter (section 7.02). The analysis shows that all these tests – the naked abuse test, the profit sacrifice test, the no economic sense test, the AEC test and the consumer harm test – are able to identify at least some anticompetitive conduct, and that all have particular advantages and shortcomings. In effect, while each test has significant advantages and is perfectly capable of determining whether the conduct by a dominant company is abusive in some cases, the same test seems unavoidably inappropriate in other cases.

Some of the tests ask whether the conduct could eliminate competition with a certain degree of probability without engaging in analysis of the possible effect. Others, ask whether a competitor who is as efficient as the dominant company is foreclosed, which will lead to harming effective competition; or whether the conduct makes no economic sense but to eliminate effective competition. The starting point is that the elimination of effective competition will reduce consumer welfare. One asks the same question but in a direct way, namely whether the conduct will lead to consumer harm. In any event, the difference between all these tests should not be overstated because they were all elaborated to identify a conduct that is inefficient and creates harm to consumer welfare.[1062] The starting point of all these tests is that the elimination of

1058. Gregory Werden, *Essays on Consumer Welfare and Competition Policy* (2009) 20 https://papers.ssrn.com/sol3/papers.cfm?abstract_id=1352032 accessed 9 June 2017.
1059. Werden, 'Essays on Consumer Welfare and Competition Policy' (n. 1056).
1060. Gates (n. 325).
1061. Stucke, 'Does the Rule of Reason Violate the Rule of Law?' (n. 896).
1062. O'Donoughue and Padilla (n. 13) 227; Monti, *EC Competition Law* (n. 443) 213.

effective competition will reduce consumer welfare. Each test asks the same question in a different way.

The discussion of the naked abuse test revealed that the test seems appropriate and reasonable in terms of saving enforcement costs in cases where it is possible to identify a conduct that is manifestly harmful without engaging in a thorough economic analysis. The fact that the conduct is capable of strengthening and maintaining the dominant position means that the consumer harm is presumed. Thus, the naked abuse test implies an element of consumer harm. However, even in these cases the presumption of illegality can be rebutted if the dominant company is able to provide sufficient evidence that its conduct is not anticompetitive and creates efficiencies. In this sense, the rebuttable presumption of illegality minimises type I errors of enforcement.

The same rationale seems to underpin the harsh treatment of exclusive dealing and fidelity rebates under EU case law. The Commission and the EU Courts seem to take the view that the potential for an anticompetitive effect is extremely high in those cases. Hence, they seem to adopt a form-based approach to these conducts according to which there is no need to prove an actual or potential effect on competition, unless the dominant company provides evidence of objective justifications.[1063] As indicated in Chapter 3, the economic theories provide a theoretical foundation that providing fidelity rebates by a dominant company is capable under a set of circumstances (identified in the facts pattern of the case law discussed in Chapter 2) to result in an anticompetitive exclusion. In those cases, it seems appropriate and reasonable in terms of saving enforcement costs, the conduct to be considered as illegal in the absence of objective justifications under the naked exclusion test.[1064]

The discussion of the profit sacrifice test and the AEC test (in terms of price-cost test) revealed that these tests are focused on whether the dominant company sacrifices short-run profit in order to achieve long-run monopoly profit, leading to consumer harm, when the competitors are excluded from the market. Thus, these two tests have in common the requirement of short-run profit sacrifice, which is used to identify anticompetitive conduct. The analysis above shows that the adoption of these tests is appropriate in some cases, such as pricing conduct – with advantages not only in terms of minimising enforcement errors and cost, but also in creating legal certainty and reducing compliances costs. In the context of rebates, the application of a price-cost test is economically appropriate when rebates are incremental or when the dominant company is not an unavoidable trading partner, in which case, a competitor can compete for the whole demand and competition is based on prices.[1065]

However, price-cost test is not appropriate in pricing conduct, in cases in which the profit sacrifice has a legitimate explanation or where the exclusion can be anticompetitive without profit sacrifice due to other evidences of a plan of the dominant company to eliminate a competitor. In those cases, the no economic sense test can be used. This might be the case in markets characterised by economies of scale and scope, in which case a dominant company has cost advantage over its competitors.

1063. *See* Chapter 2 of this book.
1064. Nazzini, *The Foundation of European Union Competition Law* (n. 392) 101.
1065. *See* Chapter 3, section 3.02[C].

In those cases, the dominant company's prices could be set at levels above cost but a competitor would not be able to match this price due to an inability to reach the same scope of production in order to benefit from similar cost savings. The price-cost test is also not appropriate in non-price conduct because the mechanism of exclusion does not require pricing below cost, in which case the test cannot capture the anticompetitive effects of a conduct. This situation is particularly relevant in the context of retroactive rebates as already discussed in Chapter 3.[1066]

As can be recalled from Chapter 4, the AEC test should be interpreted as a concept, rather than a formal price-cost test, in which case the exclusion is anticompetitive only if a competitor as efficient as the dominant company is excluded, leading to consumer harm. The general idea behind the AEC concept is to focus on identification of exclusion of a competitor that will lead to harm to competition; in some cases an exclusion of a less efficient competitor may lead to a negative effect. Thus, it is not important whether the competitor is less or more efficient; it is important whether the exclusion of a competitor will lead to competitive harm. From this perspective the concept of the test is to distinguish that the protection of competition is distinct from protecting competitors.[1067] In this sense, the concept of the AEC test (which as indicated in Chapter 4 can be equated with the effects-based approach) resembles the concept of the consumer welfare test. From this perspective, identifying a strategy aiming to exclude an as efficient competitor can adopt different tools depending on the case. In some cases, a price-cost test might be sufficient evidence for liability, as for example in predatory pricing (profit sacrifice test). In others, the price-cost test might be used in combination with the other circumstances of the case (no economic sense test). In the third, as in the case of fidelity rebates, an evaluation of a set of circumstances might be enough to consider a real risk of anticompetitive foreclosure. Consequently, the different practices require an application of different standards depending on the circumstances, which nonetheless minimise the cost and risk of errors – both false positives and false negatives.

§7.04 CONCLUSION

The case law of Article 102 seems confused because the EU Commission and EU Courts have applied various different standards applicable to exclusionary conduct. For some practices, such as predatory pricing and margin squeeze there is an obligation for a price-cost test to be carried out and they are prohibited only if the exclusionary conduct can be established. For others, such as fidelity rebates, a number of categories have been distinguished with different standards applied to each.[1068] In other words, the law of exclusionary abuses seems to remain controversial and unsettled because Article 102 is not implemented through a single legal test but rather, through different liability tests for different conduct.

1066. *See* Chapter 3, section 3.03.
1067. Vickers, 'Abuse of market power' (n. 4).
1068. *See* the discussion in Chapter 5 of this book.

A single test may seem desirable first for the sake of legitimacy and legal certainty and, second, because the same concern with anticompetitive effects underpins the case law despite the fact that such an effect could be achieved by different practices, such as exclusive dealing, predatory pricing, fidelity rebates, etc. However, while any of these practices could create competitive harm, 'in reality they are more or less likely to have an anti-competitive purpose and more or less likely to be competition on the merits'.[1069] Thus, different business practices create different risks of competitive harm.[1070] In some cases, the conduct of a dominant company is prima facie abusive and should be prohibited under the naked abuse test. In others, the conduct may be less likely to cause harm, which requires an assessment of the real/potential effect of the practice. In some cases, for example, an anticompetitive effect requires profit sacrifice, which means a price-test may be the most effective way of identifying an anticompetitive effect.

Thus, depending on the circumstances and the degree of likely competitive harm caused by each business practice, a different standard should apply. The application of a single standard to all practices ignoring the different concerns that they may create could lead to false positives and false negatives.[1071] Some practices, such as exclusive dealing, tying, loyalty and bundled rebates create greater risks for anticompetitive harm and deserve great concern.[1072] These practices can cause immediate consumer harm if they raise rival's costs, making them become less efficient and leading them to exit the market.[1073] As a result, it seems inappropriate to subject different practices to the same legal test.

In its evaluation of the different possible tests for identifying anticompetitive conduct, this chapter contends that there is a logic for the different exclusionary practices to be treated under a different standard. For that reason, the different practices should be evaluated under a case-by-case basis, 'based on actual facts, rather than stylized models'.[1074] In this regard, no single test should be suitable for the assessment of all abusive practices by a dominant company.[1075]

The AEC test as a concept (not as a price-cost test) is in line with the consumer welfare standard and it seems perfectly suitable in terms of consistency with the main objective of EU competition law, focused on protection of competition for the benefits of consumers. Thus, the concept of the AEC test is appropriate as a general normative standard for all types of exclusionary abuses.

1069. Nazzini, *The Foundation of European Union Competition Law* (n. 392) 53.
1070. Gavil (n. 298) 75.
1071. Lao (n. 742) 434.
1072. Gavil (n. 298) 75.
1073. Krattenmaker and Salop (n. 307) 214.
1074. Gates (n. 325).
1075. Nazzini, *The Foundation of European Union Competition Law* (n. 392) 52; Lao (n. 742); Popofsky (n. 917); Lang, CEPS Special Reports (n. 6).

CHAPTER 8
Conclusions

§8.01 OVERVIEW

The aim of this book has been to clarify the controversy over the application of the AEC test as a tool to distinguish pro-competitive from anticompetitive fidelity rebates and to answer the research questions namely: (1) whether the AEC test is an important part of the assessment of fidelity rebates and in which circumstances it could be used as one tool amongst others; and (2) whether the treatment of fidelity rebates could be effects-based, without necessarily carrying out the AEC test.

The analysis in this book was conducted in an attempt to offer an appropriate comprehensive, systematic and administrable legal standard for the assessment of the legality of fidelity rebates in accordance with the EU law principles. The research has been motivated by the lack of a clear and coherent standard to evaluate the legality of fidelity rebates under Article 102 TFEU, which creates legal uncertainty.

In order to reach that aim, the research applied a combination of a legal approach and law and economics methodology. While some of the chapters applied positive law theory in order to understand how the assessment of fidelity rebates is conducted so as to deduce the rationale behind the EU Court's approach, the others go further in clarifying how the law can be improved by relying on law and economics methodology. An economic approach was applied in order to provide supporting evidence and arguments on how the anticompetitive effect of fidelity rebates can be demonstrated in the most efficient way, i.e., a way that will not only minimise enforcement costs, but also making administration easy in terms of the limited resources of the enforcement agencies (both the Commission and the National Competition Authority) and the courts.

§8.02 MAIN CONCLUSIONS

The analysis conducted in this book reached several conclusions which should help clarify the controversy over the application of the AEC test for the assessment of the legality of fidelity rebates and to answer research questions.

This book first pursued an analysis of the case law on fidelity rebates before the modernisation of Article 102 TFEU, in order to understand what motivated the EU Courts to develop a legal test that leads to a very strict test, akin to per se prohibition for certain types of fidelity rebates. The analysis demonstrated that the EU Courts identified two categories of abusive rebates under Article 102 – rebates linked to exclusivity obligations, which were condemned as abusive 'by object', and rebates that have a fidelity-enhancing effect, for which an assessment of all the circumstances in order to evaluate their effect is required. The analysis concluded that the EU Courts set a very low threshold, above which every form of fidelity rebates was equated to exclusive dealing and condemned as abusive with no further evaluation of their effect. The rationale behind this strict standard is a presumption that there is a certain degree of probability that the practice will have an anticompetitive effect and as such, there is no need for the effects to be shown.

This strict approach had led to criticism from academics and other commentators. The main criticisms stem from the fact that fidelity rebates might have a pro-competitive or anticompetitive effect depending on the case; and that therefore, their prohibition without an assessment of their effect is not justified. To assess the validity of these criticisms one must understand under which circumstance fidelity rebates can have an anticompetitive effect and when they can be justified by efficiencies. Thus, Chapter 3 of this book was focused on the economic theory of fidelity rebates in order to understand under which circumstance fidelity rebates can have an anticompetitive effect. Having mapped the effect of the different types of rebates, this chapter argued that whether rebates might have anticompetitive effects always depends on the circumstances in each particular case. For that reason, a clear-cut categorisation of rebates depending on their form is not plausible. However, some rebates do seem to have a greater risk of anticompetitive effects than others. As such, form-based approaches may makes sense as a starting point of the analysis, identifying those categories of rebates that are more likely to have anticompetitive effects.

The analysis further revealed that a price-cost test is an important part of the assessment and can be accepted as a decisive factor in determining whether a rebate scheme is anticompetitive in two cases. First, when a dominant company applies incremental rebates and the price for the incremental units is lower than the average incremental cost per unit. Because the lower price for the additional units is the feature that urges the customers to purchase more units from the discounter, this means that the price is the feature that is driving customer's behaviour. In those cases a rebate scheme is a pricing conduct and the assessment should be the same as in normal predation. If the price for the additional units is predatory, it will fall under the law of predatory pricing where the price-cost test is applicable. Second, a price-cost test may be appropriate if the dominant company is dominant but not necessarily an unavoidable trading partner. In this case, the dominant company and its competitors compete for the whole demand (not only for the non-assured base of sales), which means that competition is based on prices. In those cases, if a dominant company's pricing is predatory, an anticompetitive exclusion of competitors is more likely. From the above, it can be concluded that the application of a price-cost test is an important tool in the assessment of the legality of rebates when rebates constitute price-based conduct and the price is the mechanism of exclusion.

On the other hand, the analysis revealed that in other cases the conditions of granting rebates might be anticompetitive by themselves, and as such sufficient to foreclose a competitor who is as efficient as the dominant company, regardless of whether the price is predatory or not. When the dominant company is an unavoidable trading partner, customers normally buy certain amounts of their requirements from the dominant company, the so-called assured base of sales (or non-contestable part of demand). Thus, competitors are able to compete only for the contestable part of sales. For that reason, some economists suggested the application of a modified price-cost test, which aims to compare the price with the fidelity discount applied only for the contestable sales with the costs of providing these incremental units. The analysis suggested that there is no evidence that the modified price-cost test can help to distinguish pro-competitive from anticompetitive rebates in the case of single-product fidelity rebates when applied retroactively and the dominant company is an unavoidable trading partner in the following situations. First, when the product is differentiated, it makes no economic sense to compare a dominant firm's costs with the price to evaluate the survival of the rival's products that differ in quality and variety from those of the dominant firm. Second, when rebates are not real price reduction, the discounter's prices will always remain above cost, which makes the application of a price-cost test irrelevant. Next, a price-cost test will not be able to identify all anticompetitive effects when rebates limit a competitor's ability to reach minimum efficient scale, which results in raising their cost. If a competitor is not able to achieve MES, its cost will rise, being higher than the dominant company. In these circumstances, it makes no economic sense to compare a dominant firm's cost with the price in order to assess whether a competitor can offset the effect of rebates. In this sense, whether the attributed price for the contestable part of sales is above or below the costs is not relevant, in so far as any as efficient as the discounter competitor will not be able to achieve MES in order to be profitable and to compete effectively with the dominant company. Lastly, in some cases the entry of a less efficient competitor can impose competitive constraints on a dominant company's conduct. In others, a competitor might be less efficient until it reaches economies of scale and scope compatible to the dominant company. In both cases, focusing on competitors' efficiency and using as a benchmark a dominant company's own cost structure will fail to provide evidence of anticompetitive foreclosure, which means that the application of a price-cost test cannot capture the anticompetitive effect of rebates.

This analysis further demonstrated that under certain circumstances – such as significant market power of the discounter, inelastic demand for the assured base of sales which makes the discounter an unavoidable trading partner, retroactivity of rebates, existence of barriers to entry, economies of scale, a long duration of the reference period (or inability for a customer to breach the contract without penalty)

– rebates can have a fidelity-enhancing effect which makes them similar to exclusive dealing. In those cases, an anticompetitive foreclosure might arise without profit sacrifice, which again makes the price-cost test irrelevant.

Having outlined the circumstances under which fidelity rebates can be price or non-price conduct which require different treatment, the next part of the analysis aimed to understand whether the modernisation of Article 102 by the European Commission satisfied those who criticised the treatment of fidelity rebates and whether the analytical framework proposed in its Guidance Paper is in line with the economic theories of fidelity rebates analysed in Chapter 3.

The analysis of the reform of Article 102 TFEU revealed that the protection of competition is the main objective of the provision. Protecting effective competition guarantees consumer welfare and ensures an efficient allocation of resources. It was concluded that the introduction of an effects-based approach to Article 102 aimed to ensure an assessment of the effect of practices on competition that might harm consumers by reference to the concept of anticompetitive foreclosure. The analysis revealed that the meaning of the term anticompetitive foreclosure can be found in the settled case law of the EU Courts as a conduct that is capable of having a market-distorting foreclosure. Further, the analysis revealed how the modernisation of Article 102 presumed that a conduct is likely to result in anticompetitive foreclosure if a competitor that is at least as efficient as the dominant company is foreclosed. This view is reflected in the adoption of the AEC test. The analysis revealed that, the concept of the AEC test could be interpreted more broadly, beyond the understanding that the AEC test is limited to a price-cost test. It was concluded that the AEC test can be a standard aiming to evaluate whether a competitor as efficient as the dominant company is excluded, which can be done without necessarily carrying out a formal price-cost test. From this perspective, the AEC test is rather a concept than a price-cost test, which means that it is not limited to price-based abuses only.[1076] Ultimately, it was concluded that the concept of the AEC test could be equated with the effects-based approach.

The analysis demonstrated that an anticompetitive foreclosure could be assessed through different tools, depending on the circumstances, including a price-cost test as a specific instrument that could be deployed in cases of price-based exclusionary conduct. However, the analysis demonstrated that the Commission's Guidance Paper fails to clarify under which circumstances rebate schemes are price-based conduct in which case a price-cost test is crucial for the proper assessment of a possible anticompetitive foreclosure, and when rebates are similar to exclusive dealing, in which case, the price-cost test is unable to capture a possible harmful effect.

This lack of clarity became a central issue when the application of a price-cost test in fidelity rebates was subject to judicial scrutiny. Thus, the analysis continued with the evaluation of recent case law on fidelity rebates, where the applicability of the AEC test (in terms of price-cost test) in relation to the anticompetitive effects of fidelity rebates was raised as a central issue. The analysis of this recent case revealed that the

1076. Mandorff and Sahl (n. 543) 13.

treatment of fidelity rebates is still an outstanding issue due to the controversy mainly related as to whether the price-cost test is relevant when assessing rebate schemes. In *Post Danmark II*, the CJEU made it explicit that the treatment of fidelity rebates should be based on the evaluation of all the circumstance, which represents a clear effects-based approach, although the application of the price-cost test was considered irrelevant. Similarly, the CJEU in *Intel* held that if a defendant disputes the Commission's assessment, the Commission is required to evaluate all the circumstances in order to assess the possible existence of a strategy aiming to exclude an as efficient competitor without mentioning the outcome of a price-cost test. It was concluded that this position of the CJEU confirms that the treatment of fidelity rebates can be effects-based without necessarily carrying out a price-cost test.

The next step in clarifying when the price-cost test can be used as a tool for the evaluation of fidelity rebates was the analysis of the recent case law of fidelity rebates in the US where the relevance of the test was raised as a central issue. This revealed that the possible anticompetitive effect of fidelity rebates could be evaluated under the law of exclusive dealing or predatory pricing depending on whether the price is the predominant mechanism of exclusion. This position reflects the conclusions reached in the analysis of the economic theory of fidelity rebates in Chapter 3. The analysis also showed that the assessment of fidelity rebates starts with an evaluation of all the circumstances in order to evaluate whether the conduct is price-based in which case a price-cost test is relevant, or constitutes a de facto exclusive dealing, in which case a rule of reason approach applies. When rebates include exclusivity clauses or a combination of rebates with other clauses conditioned on exclusivity, a rebate scheme constitutes de facto exclusive dealing. In those cases, the assessment is focused on whether the anticompetitive provisions are the mechanism able to exclude equally efficient rivals and to harm competition irrespective of whether pricing was below cost or not. In addition, the question on whether the retroactivity of rebates might be an indication of anticompetitive foreclosure because of the bundling of non-contestable and contestable demand, in which case a competitor cannot compete for the contestable part of demand was analysed. It was concluded that, when the product is 'must stock', customers are not willing to switch to rivals products, which leads to the existence of a non-contestable part of demand for which competitors are not able to compete. In those cases, the bundling of non-contestable and contestable demand may be an indication of finding the existence of a strategy aiming to exclude an as efficient competitor.

By comparing the case law with academic debates in the US, it was revealed that the relevant theory of harm in these cases was based on the RRC concept, according to which a dominant company may be able to hinder a rival's ability to reach a large enough portion of the market to achieve MES necessary to compete by locking up a sufficient part of demand, which would allow the discounter to successfully protect or enhance its market power. Based on this, the analysis concluded that fidelity rebates can be evaluated under the rule of reason approach in accordance with their actual anticompetitive effect and this can be done without carrying out a price-cost test.

The last part of the analysis focused on identifying the appropriate standard for the evaluation of the legality of fidelity rebates. This standard should be in line with the protection of consumer welfare as the main objective of EU competition policy, create predictability and legal certainty and minimise the risk of enforcement errors and costs, in terms of the conclusions so far.

First, it was concluded that although a single test may be desirable for the sake of legitimacy and legal certainty, the different business practices create different risk of competitive harm. Thus, depending on the degree of harm, different tests should apply. Second, in evaluating the possible tests for evaluation of an anticompetitive conduct, it was concluded that exclusionary conduct could be evaluated under the naked abuse test, the profit sacrifice test, the no economic sense test, the AEC test and the consumer harm test. It was concluded that all of the tests were developed to identify certain conducts that are inefficient and create harm for consumer welfare. While most of them ask whether a conduct eliminates certain facets of effective competition, which reduces consumer welfare, there is a test – namely the consumer welfare test – which asks the ultimate question encompassing the whole of competition law (including those other tests) – namely whether the conduct will lead to consumer harm. However, it was concluded that none of the tests contain screening devices appropriate to identify all instances of consumer harm. The consumer welfare test contains no such screens at all; and the other tests rely on presumptions that harm to effective competition will allow the dominant company to increase prices/decrease output or to influence other parameters of competition, such as innovation, quality and consumer choice to the detriment of consumers, but these screens do not operate in all circumstances. Third, it was concluded that the concept of the consumer welfare test resembles the concept of the AEC test, which as indicated above can be equated with an effects-based approach. Under the AEC standard, only a conduct that is likely to foreclose as efficient as the dominant company competitor, will result in an anticompetitive foreclosure, leading to consumer harm. Fourth, it was concluded that an existence of a strategy to exclude an as efficient competitor could be assessed using different tools, depending on the circumstances in each particular case, as for example, a price-cost test for the assessment of some forms of price-based conduct, a combination of a price-cost test with the evaluation of the other evidence in others, qualitative evaluation of all the circumstances for the third and even, in some cases, where the conduct is likely to result in consumer harm, a detailed assessment is not required to be carried out. From this perspective, the anticompetitive effect of a conduct aiming to exclude a competitor as efficient as the dominant company can be established by using different tools depending on the case, which means that using more or less economic tools or more qualitative than quantitative evidence is not decisive.[1077] It was concluded that this approach minimises the risk of errors – both false positives and false negatives but also the cost of administrability.

This leads to the conclusion that, although the case law of fidelity rebates has been criticised by many for being 'form-based', focusing on the form of the practice rather than its actual/probable effect of competition, this approach is appropriate and reasonable in terms of administrability, saving enforcement cost and improving legal

1077. Peeperkorn, 'Coherence in the Application of Articles 101 and 102: A Realistic Prospect or an Elusive Goal?' (n. 392) 394.

certainty, where it is possible to identify a conduct that is harmful without engaging in a thorough economic analysis. The analysis showed that this approach is reasonable in cases when a company is possessing significant market power; offering rebates on condition of exclusivity; rebates are retroactive; the product is 'must have', which puts the dominant company in a position of an unavoidable trading partner and separates the market into a contestable and non-contestable part, which means that competitors are not able to compete for the customers whole demand; there are economies of scale and barriers to entry. When all these conditions are met, the anticompetitive effect can be presumed with high probability, which means that the conduct is capable of strengthening and maintaining the dominant position from where consumer harm is presumed. Thus, the standard implies an element of consumer harm.

The criticism that this approach ignores the possible pro-competitive effect leading to type I errors is diminished by the possibility for the dominant company to rebut the presumption of illegality if it is able to provide sufficient evidence that the conduct is not anticompetitive and creates efficiencies. The discussion of the *Intel* judgment showed that the CJEU made it clear that the presumption of illegality of fidelity rebates stands, but also clarified that now it can be rebutted if the defendant provides supportive evidence that its conduct is not capable of restricting competition. In those cases, the Commission is required to evaluate all the circumstances in order to assess the possible existence of a strategy aiming to exclude an as efficient competitor, including a price-cost test as an element of the assessment, if the Commission or the defendant can substantiate that the rebates at issue are price-based conduct.

The analysis conducted in this book shows that the treatment of fidelity rebates has been subject to uncertainty related to the unclear position of the EU Courts on whether or when a price-cost test should be a part of the legal standard. It was concluded that the uncertainty is due to the wrong decision of the European Commission to apply the test in the case of fidelity rebates, which contain exclusivity clauses, without mentioning supportive arguments in economic terms in order to explain what differentiates Intel's rebates from an exclusive dealing (or single branding obligation).

The conclusions throughout this book showed that a price-cost test can be a useful tool for the evaluation of a possible anticompetitive foreclosure if the price is the mechanism of exclusion in price-based conduct. If fidelity rebates contain a combination of discount and other provisions leading to exclusivity, they should be evaluated under the law of exclusive dealing, in which case the existence of a strategy aiming to exclude an efficient competitor does not require a price-cost test. In those cases the treatment of fidelity rebates is clearly effects-based without necessarily conducting a price-cost test.

Table of Cases

Judgements of the Court of Justice of the European Union

Judgements of the General Court

Opinions by Advocate Generals

US Case Law

Eisai INC v. Sanofi-Aventis LLC et al., No. 08-04168 (2014) District Court of New Jersey, **142**
Eisai Inc v. Sanofi-Aventis U.S., LLC, 821 F.3d 394 (3d Cir. 2016), **9, 141–142**

European Commission Decisions

Airtours/First Choice (Case IV/M.1524) Commission Decision [1999] OJ L 93/1, **82**
Tetra Laval (Case COMP/M. 2416) Commission Decision [2001] OJ 2004 L 38/1, **82**
Schneider (COMP/M.2283) Commission Decision [2002] OJ L 101/134, **82**
Wanadoo Interactive (Case COMP/38.233) Commission Decision [2003] not published in the OJ, **160**
AstraZeneca (Case COMP/A.37.507/F3) Commission Decision [2005] OJ L 332/24, **169**
Velux (Case COMP/39.451) [2007] Closed investigation (not published), **60**
Intel (Case T-286/09) Commission Decision 2009/C 220/86 [2014] OJ C 220/41, **2, 8, 120, 121, 132**

Table of Legislation

EU Materials

EC Regulations, Directives, Guidelines, Notices and Proposals

US

Index

INTERNATIONAL COMPETITION LAW SERIES

1. Ignacio De Leon, *Latin American Competition Law and Policy: A Policy in Search of Identity*, 2001 (ISBN 90-411-1542-0).
2. Wim Dejonghe & Wouter Van de Voorde (eds), *M & A in Belgium*, 2001 (ISBN 90-411-1594-3).
3. Yang-Ching Chao, Gee San, Changfa Lo & Jiming Ho (eds), *International and Comparative Competition Law and Policies*, 2001 (ISBN 90-411-1643-5).
4. Martin Mendelsohn & Stephen Rose, *Guide to the EC Block Exemption for Vertical Agreements*, 2002 (ISBN 90-411-9813-X).
5. Clifford A. Jones & Mitsuo Matsushita (eds), *Competition Policy in the Global Trading System: Perspectives from the EU, Japan and the USA*, 2002 (ISBN 90-411-1758-X).
6. Christian Koenig, Andreas Bartosch, Jens-Daniel Braun & Marion Romes (eds), *EC Competition and Telecommunications Law*. Second Edition, 2009 (ISBN 978-90-411-2564-4).
7. Jürgen Basedow (ed.), *Limits and Control of Competition with a View to International Harmonization*, 2002 (ISBN 90-411-1967-1).
8. Maureen Brunt, Economic Essays on Australian and New Zealand Competition Law, 2003 (ISBN 90-411-1991-4).
9. Ky P. Ewing, Jr., *Competition Rules for the 21st Century: Principles from America's Experience*, Second Edition, 2006 (ISBN 90-411-2477-2).
10. Joseph Wilson, *Globalization and the Limits of National Merger Control Laws*, 2003 (ISBN 90-411-1996-5).
11. Peter Verloop & Valérie Landes (eds), *Merger Control in Europe: EU, Member States and Accession States*, Fourth Edition, 2003 (ISBN 90-411-2056-4).
12. Themistoklis K. Giannakopoulos, *Safeguarding Companies' Rights in Competition and Anti-dumping/Anti-subsidies Proceedings*, Second Edition, 2011 (ISBN 978-90-411-3404-2).
13. Marjorie Holmes & Lesley Davey (eds), *A Practical Guide to National Competition Rules across Europe*, Second Edition, 2007 (ISBN 978-90- 411-2607-8).
14. Sigrid Stroux, *US and EU Oligopoly Control*, 2004 (ISBN 90-411-2296-6).
15. Tzong-Leh Hwang and Chiyuan Chen (eds), *The Future Development of Competition Framework*, 2004 (ISBN 90-411-2305-9).

16. Phedon Nicolaides, Mihalis Kekelekis and Maria Kleis, *State Aid Policy in the European Community: Principles and Practice,* Second Edition, 2008 (ISBN 978-90-411-2754-9).
17. Doris Hildebrand, *Economic Analyses of Vertical Agreements: A Self- Assessment,* 2005 (ISBN 90-411-2328-8).
18. Frauke Henning-Bodewig, *Unfair Competition Law: European Union and Member States,* 2005 (ISBN 90-411-2329-6).
19. Duarte Brito & Margarida Catalão-Lopes, *Mergers and Acquisitions: The Industrial Organization Perspective,* 2006 (ISBN 90-411-2451-9).
20. Nikos Th. Nikolinakos, *EU Competition Law and Regulation in the Converging Telecommunications, Media and IT Sectors,* 2006 (ISBN 90-411- 2469-1).
21. Mihalis Kekelekis, *The EC Merger Control Regulation: Rights of Defence. A Critical Analysis of DG COMP Practice and Community Courts' Jurisprudence,* 2006 (ISBN 90-411-2553-1).
22. Mark R. Joelson, *An International Antitrust Primer: A Guide to the Operation of United States, European Union and Other Key Competition Laws in the Global Economy,* Third Edition, 2006 (ISBN 90-411-2468-3).
23. Themistoklis K. Giannakopoulos, *A Concise Guide to the EU Anti-dumping/Anti-subsidies Procedures,* 2006 (ISBN 90-411-2464-0).
24. George Cumming, Brad Spitz & Ruth Janal, *Civil Procedure Used for Enforcement of EC Competition Law by the English, French and German Civil Courts,* 2007 (ISBN 978-90-411-2471-5).
25. Jürgen Basedow (ed.), *Private Enforcement of EC Competition Law,* 2007 (ISBN 978-90-411-2613-9).
26. Jung Wook Cho, *Innovation and Competition in the Digital Network Economy: A Legal and Economic Assessment on Multi-tying Practices and Network Effects,* 2007 (ISBN 978-90-411-2574-3).
27. Akira Inoue, *Japanese Antitrust Law Manual: Law, Cases and Interpretation of the Japanese Antimonopoly Act,* 2007 (ISBN 978-90-411-2627-6).
28. René Barents, *Directory of EC Case Law on Competition,* 2007 (ISBN 978-90-411-2656-6).
29. Paul F. Nemitz (ed.), *The Effective Application of EU State Aid Procedures: The Role of National Law and Practice,* 2007 (ISBN 978-90-411-2657-3).
30. Jurian Langer, *Tying and Bundling as a Leveraging Concern under EC Competition Law,* 2007 (ISBN 978-90-411-2575-0).
31. Abel M. Mateus & Teresa Moreira (eds), *Competition Law and Economics – Advances in Competition Policy and Antitrust Enforcement,* 2007 (ISBN 978-90-411-2632-0).
32. Alberto Santa Maria, *Competition and State Aid: An Analysis of the EC Practice,* 2007 (ISBN 978-90-411-2617-7).
33. Barry J. Rodger (ed.), *Article 234 and Competition Law: An Analysis,* 2007 (ISBN 978-90-411-2605-4).

34. Alla Pozdnakova, *Liner Shipping and EU Competition Law,* 2008 (ISBN 978-90-411-2717-4).
35. Milena Stoyanova, *Competition Problems in Liberalized Telecommunications: Regulatory Solutions to Promote Effective Competition,* 2008 (ISBN 978-90-411-2736-5).
36. *EC State Aid Law/Le Droit des Aides d'Etat dans la CE. Liber Amicorum Francisco Santaolalla Gadea*, 2008 (ISBN 978-90-411-2774-7).
37. René Barents, *Directory of EC Case Law on State Aids,* 2008 (ISBN 978- 90-411-2732-7).
38. Ignacio De Leon, *An Institutional Assessment of Antitrust Policy: The Latin American Experience*, 2009 (ISBN 978-90-411-2478-4).
39. Doris Hildebrand, *The Role of Economic Analysis in EU Competition Law: TheEuropean School,* Fourth Edition, 2016 (ISBN 978-90-411-6245-8).
40. Eugène Buttigieg, *Competition Law: Safeguarding the Consumer Interest. A Comparative Analysis of US Antitrust Law and EC Competition Law,* 2009 (ISBN 978-90-411-3119-5).
41. Ioannis Lianos & Ioannis Kokkoris (eds), *The Reform of EC Competition Law: New Challenges,* 2010 (ISBN 978-90-411-2692-4).
42. George Cumming & Mirjam Freudenthal, *Civil Procedure in EU Competition Cases before the English and Dutch Courts*, 2010 (ISBN 978-90-411-3192-8).
43. A.E. Rodriguez & Ashok Menon, *The Limits of Competition Policy: The Shortcomings of Antitrust in Developing and Reforming Economies*, 2010 (ISBN 978-90-411-3177-5).
44. Mika Oinonen, *Does EU Merger Control Discriminate against Small Market Companies? Diagnosing the Argument with Conclusions*, 2010 (ISBN 978-90-411-3261-1).
45. Eirik Østerud, *Identifying Exclusionary Abuses by Dominant Undertakings under EU Competition Law: The Spectrum of Tests*, 2010 (ISBN 978-90-411-3271-0).
46. Marco Botta, *Merger Control Regimes in Emerging Economies: A Case Study on Brazil and Argentina*, 2011 (ISBN 978-90-411-3402-8).
47. Jürgen Basedow & Wolfgang Wurmnest (eds), *Structure and Effects in EU Competition Law: Studies on Exclusionary Conduct and State Aid*, 2011 (ISBN 978-90-411-3174-4).
48. George Cumming (ed.), *Merger Decisions and the Rules of Procedure of the European Community Courts*, 2012 (ISBN 978-90-411-3671-8).
49. Eduardo Molan Gaban & Juliana Oliveira Domingues (eds), *Antitrust Law in Brazil: Fighting Cartels,* 2012 (ISBN 978-90-411-3670-1).
50. Giandonato Caggiano, Gabriella Muscolo & Marina Tavassi (eds), *Competition Law and Intellectual Property: A European Perspective,* 2012 (ISBN 978-90-411-3447-9).
51. Ben Van Rompuy, *Economic Efficiency: The Sole Concern of Modern Antitrust Policy? Non-efficiency Considerations under Article 101 TFEU*, 2012 (ISBN 978-90-411-3870-5).

52. Liyang Hou, *Competition Law and Regulation of the EU Electronic Communications Sector: A Comparative Legal Approach*, 2012 (ISBN 978-90-411-4047-0).
53. Barry Rodger, *Landmark Cases in Competition Law: Around the World in Fourteen Stories*, 2012 (ISBN 978-90-411-3843-9).
54. Andreas Scordamaglia-Tousis, *EU Cartel Enforcement: Reconciling Effective Public Enforcement with Fundamental Rights*, 2013 (ISBN 978-90-411-4758-5).
55. Bernardo Cortese (ed.), *EU Competition Law: Between Public and Private Enforcement*, 2014 (ISBN 978-90-411-4677-9).
56. Barry Rodger (ed.), *Competition Law: Comparative Private Enforcement and Collective Redress across the EU*, 2014 (ISBN 978-90-411-4559-8).
57. Nada Ina Pauer, *The Single Economic Entity Doctrine and Corporate Group Responsibility in European Antitrust Law*, 2014 (ISBN 978-90-411-5262-6).
58. Urška Petrovčič, *Competition Law and Standard Essential Patents: A Transatlantic Perspective*, 2014 (ISBN 978-90-411-4960-2).
59. David Telyas, *The Interface between Competition Law, Patents and Technical Standards*, 2014 (ISBN 978-90-411-5418-7).
60. Katerina Maniadaki, *EU Competition Law, Regulation and the Internet: The Case of Net Neutrality*, 2014 (ISBN 978-90-411-4140-8).
61. Horacio Vedia Jerez, *Competition Law Enforcement and Compliance across the World: A Comparative Review*, 2015 (ISBN 978-90-411-5815-4).
62. Kadir Ba, *The Substantive Appraisal of Joint Ventures under the EU Merger Control Regime*, 2015 (ISBN 978-90-411-5816-1).
63. Alberto Santa Maria, *Competition and State Aid: An Analysis of the EU Practice*, Second Edition, 2015 (ISBN 978-90-411-5818-5).
64. Lúcio Tomé Feteira, *The Interplay between European and National Competition Law after Regulation 1/2003: "United (Should) We Stand?"*, 2016 (ISBN 978-90-411-5663-1).
65. Giovanni Pitruzzella & Gabriella Muscolo(eds), *Competition and Patent Law in the Pharmaceutical Sector: An International Perspective*, 2016 (ISBN 978-90-411-5927-4).
66. Małgorzata Cyndecka, *The Market Economy Investor Test in EU State Aid Law: Applicability and Application*, 2016 (ISBN 978-90-411-6102-4).
67. Damiano Canapa, *Trademarks and Brands in Merger Control: An Analysis of the European and Swiss Legal Orders*, 2016 (ISBN 978-90-411-6717-0).
68. Inge Graef, *EU Competition Law, Data Protection and Online Platforms: Data as Essential Facility*, 2016 (ISBN 978-90-411-8324-8).
69. Anders Jessen, *Exclusionary Abuse after the* Post Danmark I *Case: The Role of the Effects-Based Approach under Article 102 TFEU*, 2017 (ISBN 978-90-411-8996-7).
70. Baskaran Balasingham, *The EU Leniency Policy: Reconciling Effectiveness and Fairness*, 2017 (ISBN 978-90-411-8479-5).
71. Eugene Stuart & Iana Roginska-Green, *Sixty Years of EU State Aid Law and Policy: Analysis and Assessment*, 2018 (ISBN 978-90-411-8869-4).

72. Anna Renata Pisarkiewicz, *Margin Squeeze in the Electronic Communications Sector: Critical Analysis of the Decisional Practice and Case Law*, 2018 (ISBN 978-90-411-6246-5).
73. Ploykaew Porananond, *Competition Law in the ASEAN Countries: Regional Law and National Systems*, 2018 (ISBN 978-90-411-9102-1).
74. Corinne Ruechardt, *EU State Aid Control of Infrastructure Funding*, 2018 (ISBN 978-90-411-9099-4).
75. Amalia Athanasiadou, *Patent Settlements in the Pharmaceutical Industry under US Antitrust and EU Competition Law*, 2018 (ISBN 978-94-035-0113-0).
76. Miroslava Marinova, *Fidelity Rebates in Competition Law: Application of the 'As Efficient Competitor' Test*, 2018 (ISBN 978-94-035-0570-1).